Local government in liberal democracies

Local government in Britain is often viewed as being bureaucratic and impersonal. In America or France local government can be genuinely local, and permit small communities to determine their future and their standards of basic public services. The quality and nature of local government varies widely between different countries.

A full understanding of different systems of local government can only be understood by comparing one with another. J.A. Chandler has drawn together a range of contributors who have outlined the structures and workings of local government in England and Wales, the Republic of Ireland, France, Italy, Germany, Sweden, the United States of America and Canada . This introduction to local government has been designed to provide the student with chapters that have a similar format in order to offer a framework for systematic comparisons of the different case studies. This book also includes a conclusion summarising major differences and relationships between the structures studied.

Local Government in Liberal Democracies has been written to meet the needs of undergraduate and 'A' level students who require an easily accessible analysis of local government.

J.A. Chandler is Senior Lecturer and Research Leader in public sector management in the Business School of Sheffield City Polytechnic. He has published several books and articles on central–local relations and comparative local government studies.

Local government in liberal democracies

An introductory survey

Edited by J.A. Chandler

Routledge
London and New York

First published 1993
by Routledge
11 New Fetter Lane, London EC4P 4EE

Simultaneously published in the USA and Canada
by Routledge
a division of Routledge, Chapman and Hall, Inc.
29 West 35th Street, New York, NY 10001

Typeset in Bembo by
NWL Editorial Services, Langport, Somerset

Printed and bound in Great Britain by
Biddles Ltd, Guildford and King's Lynn

British Library Cataloguing in Publication Data

A catalogue record for this book is available from the British Library.

ISBN 0–415–02233–9
ISBN 0–415–08875–5 (pbk)

Library of Congress Cataloging in Publication Data
Local government in liberal democracies: an introductory
    survey/edited by J.A. Chandler.
        ISBN 0–415–02233–9   ISBN 0–415–08875–5 (pbk)
        1. Local government.   2. Comparative government.
        3. Democracy.
        I. Chandler, J.A.   1002106 61 X
    JS78.L653   1992   92–13197
    320.80 – dc20   CIP

                        61 24 78

Contents

Figures and tables

Preface

In the absence of a comparative context it is impossible to understand fully any social system. No one should believe that the political and social structures of their own country necessarily harbour the only, let alone the best, possible administrative arrangements. The study of government and administration is of little value unless it can lead to the development of better practice through understanding of alternative structures and methods.

In the arena of local government, for example, an ethnocentric Briton may be excused for believing that all local authorities are necessarily large impersonal bureaucracies that, despite a locally elected council, are largely concerned with administering functions on behalf of central government. The student would certainly not realise that, in other democracies, systems of local government may have more communally based structures and, nevertheless, be governed by politicians who have national standing. In the United States or France local government can be genuinely local and permit small communities of only a few hundred souls to be major actors in determining their future and their standards of basic public services. In France local politicians are respected representatives of their localities and may even hold ministerial political office within the state. The abject condition of local government in Britain is not a universal phenomenon.

There are several excellent studies that give a valuable insight into the basic political structures and processes of larger liberal democracies. These studies, however, cover too large a range of political institutions and processes to give much more than a cursory analysis of the administrative structures of most states. Students must frequently obtain more detailed information on particular aspects of political systems by collating studies dealing with one specific country. These will frequently emphasise differing aspects of each system and thus make effective comparison a problematic exercise.

This book emerged from the experience of a number of academics teaching public administration courses in Sheffield City Polytechnic, that students found it difficult to obtain material that would enable them to begin placing administrative structures and processes in a comparative context. The authors, therefore, decided to produce a series of books that would systematically introduce particular administrative structures in a comparative context. This is a companion volume to *Civil Services in Liberal Democracies*, edited by John Kingdom and published by Routledge, which was written largely by the same team of authors who produced this book. It is hoped these studies will enable students to obtain an outline of political structures and processes in a number of countries, which can serve as a basis for obtaining a much greater understanding of the administrative process in liberal democracies.

Chapter 1

Introduction

J.A. Chandler

In recent years local government has ceased to be one of the 'also rans' of comparative politics, confined to a lecture at the end of a year's study that could cheerfuly be abandoned by teachers who failed to keep up with their lecture schedule. This change reflects both the concerns of practising politicians and new theoretical developments in the fields of urban political analysis.

In several liberal democracies ideological differences between conservatives and socialists are reflected in struggles between central and local governments. For many years conflict between communist controlled industrial cities and Christian Democrat dominated governments has been an important feature of Italian politics. In Britain new right-wing Governments have been opposed as effectively by radical left-wing city governments as by the national opposition parties. In many countries the growth of interest in local politics reflects a concern and an impatience with policies affecting the quality of life in metropolitan areas. The plight of the inner cities, with attendant problems of urban crime, poverty and industrial decline, has become a major item on the political agendas of Britain and the United States, while modernisation of societies, particularly in the Mediterranean countries, has created pressures leading to restructuring of systems of local government that have remained little changed since the beginning of the nineteenth century.

In addition to the more obvious political debates concerning local politics, recent research has shown that in some states local politics has considerable importance in shaping the national political system and should not be percieved as simply a subordinate localised interest. In some supposedly highly centralised nations local interests play a major role in national policy making. This is most clearly observed in France, where mayors of larger cities are frequently elected members of the Assembly and Senate and, although holding national office, still retain their local posts in order to gain resources from the centre for their communities (Ashford 1982). Similarly many Congressmen in the United States bring local interests into their deliberations on national issues.

Several important theories on the nature of democracy and the state have been developed in the last two decades from studies of local political systems. Community power theories, for example, helped generate a highly influential pluralist model of democracy through the analysis of decision making in city government. Several neo-Marxist writers such as Manuel Castells (1977) and Peter Saunders (1981) have developed important and challenging theories on the nature of the state, based largely on analyses of urban politics. They argue that local government plays an important role within the capitalist state by helping to provide the conditions necessary for the maintenance of a workforce sufficiently healthy and well educated to keep the wheels of industry in motion. In contrast, public choice theorists such as Paul Peterson (1981) have constructed models of urban development and decision making that depict the process as a product of economic self interest. It is not possible in this introductory work to detail these theories of urban politics. They cannot, however, be fully appreciated without some knowledge of the basic structures and functions of the local government systems that gave rise to these theories.

Despite the growing importance of local government in both the practice and theory of politics it remains for many students of comparative government a somewhat inaccessible subject on account of the paucity of literature in this field. Although there are detailed studies of the local government systems of Britain and the United States available to the serious student, the subject is often glossed over in textbooks on the politics of these countries. Full-scale studies of the local government systems of other major liberal democracies are rare in the English language, and students of comparative politics must glean information about these local systems from either detailed journal articles or rather sketchy accounts in textbooks.

This book is aimed at providing an introduction to the structure and processes of local government in eight Western liberal democracies. The countries have been chosen partly to reflect the specialisms of the authors but also to present studies of systems of local government that demonstrate differences between political systems. Spain has, therefore, been omitted because its system of local government has considerable similarities to those of France and Italy, while Sweden stands as a representative of the broadly similar structures of local government within the Scandinavian states. The number of regimes has also been limited to provide sufficiently detailed studies of the systems we have surveyed rather than a greater number of brief and insufficiently complete sketches.

Before the study is further advanced it is necessary to define what is meant in this book by 'local government'. The term as used here refers to political institutions that are subject to directly elected policy makers. The studies, therefore, exclude government agencies such as the British National Health Service which, although operating at a local level, are commanded by political appointees of central government. Local government is also distinguished from federal government. In a federal system the constitution of the state divides power so as to prevent either the federal or state governments eroding each other's powers. Local governments, whether they be a small commune or large populous regions, are established by national or federal polities that retain the right to regulate through legislation the power and functions of their subordinate local units. The West German *Länder*, the Canadian Provinces or the states of the USA are not, therefore, to be considered in this study except in so far as they affect local governments within these nations.

THE STRUCTURE OF THE BOOK

This book is not intended as a comparative study in the sense that it attempts to establish theories and models that identify common characteristics of all local government systems in liberal democracies. Such a task would involve theoretical complexities that are out of keeping with the introductory intentions of this work. It is, moreover, highly tendentious to construct generalisations based on studies of eight different countries. The chapters are, nevertheless, structured in accord with a common format of sections. This framework has been devised to allow readers easily to perceive similarities and differences between particular aspects of the eight local government systems that are the subject of this book.

Each chapter begins with an outline of the structure and functions of the local government system under review, which is divided into the following sections.

The structure of central government

If sense is to be made of the local government system within any nation it is essential that the reader has a basic understanding of the structure and political processes of central government. Local governments are largely creations of the state and are sustained by it, although they may also, in turn, have a major influence on central decision making. The interrelationships that exist between local and central authorities frame the local system of government, which cannot be considered as an isolated political structure. Since some readers may not be fully aware of the basic political structure of the regimes considered in this book, this section provides a succinct outline of the central and federal institutions most relevant to the local government systems.

The development of the system

It is impossible to appreciate fully the nature of any political system unless it is seen as a developing organisation that has been created as a consequence of political change. This section outlines the antecedents to the structures and functions of local government systems and identifies important aspects of political culture and tradition that underlie the present local governments structures.

The structure and functions of the system

This section discusses the legal relationship of local government within the constitutions of each state, describes the formal organisation of the system in terms of the hierarchy of local government units, their spheres of jurisdiction and the powers and duties with which they are entrusted.

Finance

Complex political organisations entrusted with a wide range of duties cannot function without economic resources. Adequate finance and the ability to control their budgets are crucial factors determining the role and independence of local authorities.

Internal structures

This section describes the internal organisation of local governments in terms of the role and method of election of their policy makers and the structures through which they appoint and organise the permanent bureaucracy of the system.

Personnel, recruitment and training

The effectiveness of local authorities is to an extent a function of their political masters and the personnel whom they appoint. This section describes the backgrounds and consequent attitudes of local government personnel.

The preceding sections on structure and function are followed by sections that consider the policy making role of local government systems, in terms of both the extent to which the centre can determine local policy and, within the confines of influence allowed to local governments, who makes policy within the local authorities. These sections are concerned with the following issues.

Intergovernmental relations

Local authorities may, at one extreme, be agents of central government with little facility for devising policies that oppose the interest of national government and, at the other extreme, not only be free from central control but also be able to influence national policies. This section analyses for each regime the extent to which central and local interests are interrelated with respect to policy making.

Parties and pressure groups

This element considers the realities of policy making within local government by analysing the extent to which parties and interest groups, whether organised at national or local levels, can influence the local decision making process.

The electorate

The local authorities discussed in this study are all organised, at least in theory, on liberal democratic lines. Ideally, their policies should, therefore, be determined by either local or national electors. This section evaluates the extent to which electors in reality have any influence over the governments responsible for their communities.

The final section of each chapter assesses the major issues and problems that may currently be facing the local government systems within each country and also, when present, the pressures for reforms of the systems.

Although the structure of each chapter follows a broadly similar structure, no two countries that have been studied are similar, so that certain elements of the pattern of variables may require greater emphasis in certain regimes than in others. In the final analysis each system is unique, but in the concluding chapter it is possible to argue that there are certain characteristics common to most systems.

BIBLIOGRAPHY

Ashford, D.E. (1982) *British Dogmatism and French Pragmatism*, London, Allen and Unwin.

Castells, M. (1977) *The Urban Question*, London, Edward Arnold.

Peterson, P. (1981) *City Limits*, Chicago, Chicago University Press.

Saunders, P. (1981) *Social Theory and the Urban Question*, London, Hutchinson.

Chapter 2

England and Wales

John Kingdom

The United Kingdom consists of four countries, England, Wales, Scotland and Northern Ireland. Local government in Scotland and Northern Ireland exhibits certain differences from that in England and Wales, which, though not great, would render some of the generalisations made in this chapter invalid. For this reason the study is confined to England and Wales.

Britain, as a constitutional monarchy, formally consolidates the authority of the state at the centre through a doctrine of Parliamentary sovereignty. The British Parliament is a bicameral assembly, though effective power is restricted to the House of Commons, the popularly elected chamber. The electoral system provides for territorial representation of the country through some 650 constituencies, each returning a single member on the basis of a simple plurality. Thus, members of the House can be said to articulate the interests of the localities at the capital though it remains questionable how far, in practice, this amounts to an effective form of areal representation. There are, in fact, several theories suggesting what representation in Parliament actually means in the context of the British constitution, and the idea that members represent their constituencies as geographically defined entities is but one model among several.

Though formed on a basis of spatial representation, the constitutionally sovereign assembly, for a number of reasons, effectively subscribes to a unitary power structure, which has its legal origins in the highly centralised institution of the monarchy and is buttressed by the modern party system. As a result it can do little to represent the interests of the localities as such, presenting an environment which is legally and politically inhospitable to local government per se.

The Cabinet with the Prime Minister is the Head of Government and nominally the chief agent of policy making. However, the Cabinet does not decide all policy issues and it plays only a small part in the process of implementation. The anatomy of the public sector in Britain is complex, having evolved throughout history organically, rather than being the product of a rationally conceived plan. At its heart is the Civil Service, centred in London with a network of outposts, or field agencies, throughout the country.

The principle of parliamentary sovereignty demands that all actions of civil servants in policy making or implementation can be examined by Parliament through the convention of ministerial responsibility, which, broadly speaking, means that there is always a Minister who will be answerable to the House of Commons. In theory this gives MPs a high degree of control over the administrative machine.

In addition to the field agencies of the Civil Service and the regional organisations of the nationalised industries there are some major ad hoc public authorities operating on a geographically dispersed basis. The ad hoc authority was particularly in evidence in the nineteenth century, before the modern system of local government was created. The device is still used widely today, for example in the form of the National Health Service.

Beyond the agencies of public administration outlined above there remains a further, diverse range of ad hoc bodies, each created by the state for some particular purpose. This category is really a residual one with few defining characteristics, but it includes advisory bodies such as Royal Commissions, consultative bodies such as the Consultative Council for Local Government Finance, promotional bodies such as the agricultural marketing boards and bodies with responsibility for the distribution of Government money such as the Arts Council. The feature that all these have in common is that at some time government has considered it expedient for political, moral, ethical, technical or financial reasons to entrust the performance of some public function to an agency not formally subject to the immediate scrutiny of Parliament.

The structure outlined above provides machinery for the administration of a wide range of functions, many of which are services received directly by citizens. All manifest some degree of territoriality; civil service departments often operate through field agencies, most of the public corporations are regional in their organisation, as are the National Health Service and many organisations among the range of quasi-autonomous bodies. A number of these geographically dispersed organisations, such as the public utilities and the National Health Service, include in their constitution provision for representation of local interests. Thus, although it can be said without equivocation that Britain is a unitary state, there is, through political representation in Parliament and through the complex system of dispersal of the agencies of public administration, a substantial recognition of heterogeneity.

It is within this framework that we must examine the system of local government: the remaining component of the public sector in Britain. This system may be considered singular in that it, unlike any other part of the public sector, enjoys a source of direct popular legitimacy beyond Parliament. In other respects the local authorities have much in common with the other agencies of public administration. Their powers are devolved rather than original, they are bound by the doctrine of *ultra vires*, and they rely heavily on central government for finance. Furthermore, they are not entirely beyond the ambit of Parliament. The doctrine of ministerial responsibility can operate through the involvement of a number of central government departments in the administration of various local government functions including, for example, education, social services and police. In fact, the precise degree of responsibility through Parliament for local government functions, particularly in sensitive areas like policing, is a subject of considerable debate.

STRUCTURE AND POWERS

Historical

The traditions of local government in Britain can be traced back as far as the history of the state itself. However, it is possible to speak of a 'modern' system, which has certain characteristics distinguishing it from the earlier forms. The emergence of this modern system is, to a great extent, contingent on the complex of events comprising the industrial revolution and can be said to have been, no less than the scientific, engineering and commercial innovations, an invention of that period: a product of the same kind of thought and imagination which dramatically altered the nature of British society across a wide front.

The industrial revolution created a new kind of demand for local government administration. Paradoxically, in an age of laissez-faire, the emergence of the huge urban industrial centres created an unprecedented need for public services, including the roads required to provide an infrastructure for the increased commercial activity and, as they gradually became technologically feasible, a range of public facilities such as water treatment plants and electricity supply. In addition, many new functions were necessary as a result of the social upheaval to combat consequences such as ill health, poverty, illiteracy and lawlessness.

The forms of local government existing prior to these traumatic events continued the medieval traditions. Some local authorities had evolved under the guidance of public-spirited individuals and well organised trade guilds, but many were inefficient and corrupt, even on their own primitive terms, and quite ill-fitted to the demands of the newly emerging urban society. However, within the industrial centres were the entrepreneurs, industrial leaders, lawyers and bankers who were themselves principal agents of the change, and it was in their interests to attend to the society that supported their enterprises. They met this functional requirement in two ways: by compensating for the outmoded local government structures through the creation of ad hoc bodies charged with the responsibility for providing particular services, and by a reform of the existing municipal institutions and practices.

The areas

The origins and development of the local government areas reflect a general dichotomy between centre and locality which continues to colour most contemporary debate. On the one hand, there is the organic development resulting from the quest for self-government by communities and manifested mainly in the form of parish government and later in the emergence of the substantially autonomous boroughs; on the other, there is ubiquitous pressure from the centre seeking to establish a unitary rule through a convenient system of administrative spatial units, which is seen mainly in the development of the counties.

The origins of the parish as a unit of local government in England and Wales are not usually recorded in works on the Constitution. It has no statutory basis, having evolved from the old manorial system and the ecclesiastical districts. Probably more than any other spatial unit, the parish represents the organic growth of a form of genuinely local democracy, as opposed to locally based state administration. For the great majority of ordinary citizens it was the parish, rather than the county, which perceptibly impinged upon their lives.

However, in practice many parish governments tended to reflect not these democratic ideals but the economic and social order of the local community, with domination by a local élite transforming the 'open' vestry into one which was effectively 'closed', with a self-perpetuating group representing landed interests ruling largely for its own ends. One effect of the industrial revolution was to precipitate a number of official and unofficial enquiries into the state of parish government, and these tended to be highly critical. These led to the reform of the poor law administration and the establishment of larger, rationally planned areas.

Superimposed upon the development of parish government was that of the county. In this case the motive force came not from the intrinsic demand for self-government arising spontaneously from the community but from the will of central government, originally through the institution of the monarchy. The shires could provide the monarch with three things essential to central rule: finance, with the reeve collecting taxes; military support (regiments of the British army still carry the names of the shires); and law and order, with each shire having its own court.

In fact, the courts did more than dispense justice. They would meet as an assembly of citizens to select and appoint certain officials, they would receive the king's orders, and would select a member to represent them at the centre in Parliament. The courts themselves began to pose a threat to the royal authority, which was averted by the twelfth century through the expedient of creating a rival system with the king sending his own justices around the country on circuits. These justices of the peace (JPs) became, through the implications of their judicial role, important figures in local administration, extending their influence down to the level of the parish, and a series of statutes in the Tudor period greatly enlarged their jusrisdiction, giving them direct supervisory responsibilities for important functions such as bridges, roads, and relief of poverty.

The central role of the justices in local administration remained even after the constitutional upheavals of the eighteeenth century which transferred supreme state power from the monarchy to parliament, but it did not survive the traumas of the industrial revolution. It was in essence part of the old order and declined in a similar way, and for similar reasons, as did the parish. In 1835 the Municipal Corporations Act confined the role of the JPs in largest boroughs to judicial matters. However, the system that had evolved under the justices had welded the county and the parish into a complex tiered system, and, in so doing, brought together the centralist and local traditions of local government in an inherently contradictory relationship which remains, to the present day, a practical and theoretical paradox.

Between the levels of the parish and the county has been the development of the borough. Anglo-Saxon England was not an urban society but one of village settlements serving an essentially agrarian order. However, from the tenth century, towns began to emerge as bases for trading activities, and to offer safety through fortification. Gradually, certain of these evolved as fiscal and judicial centres and sought independence from their parent counties and central government. This they were able to obtain formally by securing a charter of incorporation from the monarch, permitting them to tax themselves though paying a fixed amount to the Crown.

The peak in the movement towards autonomy through incorporation was reached in the fifteenth century, so that by the end of the Middle Ages the boroughs of England stood side by side with the counties as centres of local administration and indeed some boroughs had actually been elevated to county status. It is in the boroughs that we see the first signs of what may be termed modern local government, incorporating such features as the election of officials, efficiency in administration, and financial probity. They provided a model for the reform of local government, which would enable it to meet the challenge of the industrial revolution. The creation of this modern system took place between 1834 and 1894, when first the urban and then the rural areas were reformed on a statutory basis.

The inadequacies of the traditional system in the face of the demands placed upon it by the process of industrialisation resulted in a further development, which took place outside the formal structure of local government through the creation, mainly by means of Private Acts of Parliament, of a wide range of local statutory bodies charged with the responsibility to administer particular functions including the poor law, education, highways, public health, various public utilities, and general civic improvement. The bodies were often able to levy a local rate and provision was made for members to be elected. In addition to these ad hoc authorities there were private undertakings, also acting with statutory authority, providing public utilities on a commercial basis. The pattern of development permitted wide-ranging experimental initiative, which led to a variety of technical and administrative improvements in the provision of local services. As the borough authorities became more efficient and self-confident they sought to take over the private undertakings in manoeuvres which were often acrimonious and intensely political. In the long term they were largely successful in this, though much expense was involved in the purchase of capital equipment and the payment of legal fees.

In spite of the functional and organisational changes the reformed system retained much of the traditional terminology and nomenclature. The most important newly styled local authority was the county borough, the term denoting the status of the largest of the urban areas which, having developed largely autonomously, jealously wished to preserve their independence. Outside these major urban centres the local government system which emerged out of the nineteenth century consisted essentially of counties: large areas divided into boroughs, urban and rural districts, each undertaking some of the local authority functions shared according to the importance of the unit.

The system had remarkable powers of endurance and survived, in spite of a number of reviews, until the 1970s. Throughout the post-war period it was criticised as anachronistic, having failed to respond to economic, social and democratic changes which had led to a build up of population in the regions surrounding the major cities, reflecting changed patterns of industrial location and improvements in communications. The conurbations around London became particularly densely populated and created intensified pressure for reform, as a result of which the government set up a Royal Commission (the Herbert Commission) to conduct an enquiry and make recommendations. This led to the creation in 1963 of a new, enlarged, administrative area of 'Greater London', to be governed by a directly elected Greater London Council which replaced the older London County Council created in 1888. The area of Greater London was subdivided into thirty-two second-tier authorities to be known as London Boroughs. Though reasonably successful this reform left the rest of the country untouched and another Royal Commission was set up to remedy this, which reported in 1969.

The Redcliffe-Maud Commission actually recommended replacing the complex multi-tier pattern with a single-tier system for most of the country, the exception being the three largest conurbations where a two-tier system resembling the London model was proposed. However, the Conservative Government, to which fell the task of implementing the proposals, rejected this radical conception and implemented a reorganisation which retained the two-tiered system, although a distinction was made between the densely populated conurbations and the shires. In the former, it was the lower tiers which had the most important functions, while in the latter these were administered by the top tier. However, in 1985 the Government decided to abolish the top-tier authorities in the metropolitan areas and the Greater London Council, and to distribute their functions between ad hoc bodies, which were not directly elected, and the constituent lower-tier authorities. This was seen as a largely political move by the Conservative Government, which had experienced difficulties with these Labour-controlled metropolitan councils, arising from its desire to reduce public expenditure.

FINANCING

Local government spending in Britain accounts for over a quarter of all public spending in Britain and in 1989/90 it amounted to 56,153 million. There are three principal sources of finance, including fees and charges paid directly by the users of certain local government services, grants from central government, and local taxation.

Fees and charges paid at the point of delivery by consumers represent a diminishing source of revenue for local authorities. Many Labour-controlled councils see their role as primarily in welfare state terms so that services such as housing, social care and recreation are provided, with only a nominal cost falling upon the user and the main costs of provision coming from the other sources of revenue. Not suprisingly policies of this kind are the subject of fervent political debate between the political parties, between central and local government, and between local associations of ratepayers and their councils. In the nineteenth century charging for services was much more acceptable, so certain public utilities were actually able to subsidise other services and in a number of cases allowed authorities to experiment, innovate, or reduce levels of local taxation.

Since the nineteenth century, grants from central government have grown considerably in absolute and relative terms. Initially, they gave central government a means to stimulate the development of new, or under-provided, services and to improve provision in the poorer areas of the country. Increasingly, however, the system has become an instrument whereby central government can exert political control over the activities of local government through the principle of paying the piper.

In 1976 the Layfield Report on local government finance stressed the link between finance and local self-determination. It argued that any reform of local government finance must reflect either a centralist or localist bias. If one were to choose a centralist solution then the size of the central grant would have to be less reflective of local needs, resources, and political decisions. In fact, in 1980 the Local Government Planning and Land Act moved clearly in the latter direction through the reform of the block grant system. Under the new system the Secretary of State for the Environment assesses what is termed Grant Related Expenditure for each authority and apportions the grant accordingly. Later legislation further refined the system, which allowed the Secretary of State for the Environment to withhold grant if a local authority was considered to be spending too much. During the 1980s a number of authorities faced quite severe financial deprivation resulting from central government's withholding a part of their grant in response to their refusal to comply with central directives.

The total size of the central government grant to local authorities in 1988/89 was £19,079 million, which represented 37 per cent of all local government spending. Over half this sum was in the form of a block grant permitting the authorities some discretion in allocation between services, and the remainder was given as specific grants to be used in designated areas such as housing, policing and public transport.

Local taxation in Britain was based on the occupation of property in what is known as the rates system. Each household, shop, office or factory paid a tax to the local authority, which tended to be larger for bigger and more expensive properties. It was a matter of some debate that a system created in the early seventeenth century for the relief of poverty should be central to the system of public finance. Certainly the system contained a number of anomalies and apparent inequities. However, it was felt that a complete abolition of local tax would remove a time-honoured basis of local autonomy and would undermine the *raison d'être* of local government in a drastic way.

The post-1979 Consevative Government did, however, remove the freedom of local governments to raise as much in local taxes as they thought necessary and electorally prudent. After attempts to curb high-spending authorities by withholding grant failed, the 1984 Local Government Finance Act introduced 'rate capping' to permit the Government to set a maximum limit to the rate set by a local authority. When this also failed to reduce local expenditure the Government took the astonishing step of abolishing the rating system for domestic property and replacing it with a poll tax, extracting the same flat rate from most adults in a community regardless of their financial circumstances. There were set reductions in payments from the poorest citizens, but even the destitute had to pay something. The Government retained the right to set the maximum level of tax that could be raised by a local authority. They also further restricted local government's capacity to raise income by modifying the rating system for commercial and industrial property, setting the rate at a uniform level nationally and distributing it to local authorities on a formula of its own devising.

The poll tax proved to be highly unpopular, expensive and difficult to collect. After the Prime Minister, Mrs Thatcher, a principal advocate of the tax, fell from power, the Conservative Government began legislation designed to replace the system by a modified form of the rates to be known as the council tax. Under the new system, a government would still retain the power to determine how much a local authority may raise in local taxes.

While income to pay for the revenue costs of a local authority has only recently been curbed by central government, there have been restrictions on capital spending by local governments since the nineteenth century. Local authorities raise most of their capital by borrowing from the government, private banks or the public through interest paying bonds. However, the amount that may be raised each year is limited by the government, which announces each year how much can be borrowed for particular categories of work such as house building or the police.

INTERNAL STRUCTURE

Local authorities are organisations that administer and deliver services to clients and, if we ignore the democratic structures, we find that they exhibit many features that are shared with other organisations. In the first place there is a broadly familiar line–staff dichotomy, which distinguishes between those employees who provide the services, such as police officers, teachers and street cleaners, and those who perform functions that facilitate their activities, who may broadly be termed administrators. This second group, though important, is essentially parasitic upon the first. Both groups tend to be organised hierarchically, with individual members receiving orders or instructions from those above and information from those below. The administrative group is the one that characteristically receives the greatest amount of attention from students of public administration, and plays the major role in policy formation.

The size and diversity of the task facing the local administration within each authority necessitates a further subdivision into departments. The allocation of responsibilities in this respect tends to follow the functional principle, with certain departments providing specific services to the public, and carrying appropriate names such as the education department or social services department. Others provide services to the authority itself, such as the finance department, or personnel and training.

The functional division of the local bureaucracies is mirrored by the organisation of the body of elected representatives, the council. In addition to the general assembly of the full council there are specialist committees, which tend to parallel specialist departments so that, for example, an education department is under the political control of an education committee.

Recent decades have seen a widespread movement to achieve better co-ordination in policy making through a reduction in the number of departments. At the same time there have been moves to improve leadership through the establishment of senior committees of councillors, resembling boards of directors or cabinets, and the appointment of chief administrators as managers to replace the traditional, legalistic town clerks. This has been termed the corporate movement, and two relevant major reports have been those of the Maud (1967) and Bains (1972) Committees. The structure presented as a model in the Bains Report is shown in Figure 2.1.

Following local government reorganisation in 1974 many authorities instigated some variant of the Bains model. However, more recently an element of disillusionment has set in and some have returned to older

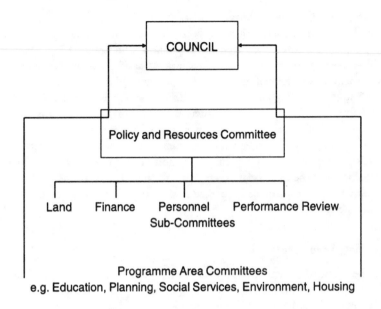

Figure 2.1 The Bains model for local government organisation.

forms of management structure. Generally, it is probably true to say that councillors are jealous of their roles, both in the determination of broad policy and in matters of more detail, and are unwilling to relinquish these to chief executives or cabinets. In 1991 the new Secretary of State for the Environment began to speak of a move towards elected chief executives, though this remained highly speculative.

PERSONNEL, RECRUITMENT AND TRAINING

Local democracy in Britain is secured through the popular election of representatives who work through a permanent bureaucracy consisting of full-time salaried employees of the corporation. Thus there are, broadly speaking, two main categories to consider, councillors and officers, the recruitment and training processes of whom are quite different.

In terms of democratic theory it might be expected that the councillors within any particular authority would be largely charged with the policy making function while that of implementation would fall to the officers. Indeed, the Bains Report reiterated such a classical division in its recommendation for management structures. However, in practice the policy–administration dichotomy breaks down in local government much as it does in most other agencies of public administration. The precise division of labour varies from one authority to another; in some cases there is a tradition of councillor domination, in others officers have established a firm hold, leaving councillors to concern themselves with the minutiae of administration, and in yet others there is something of a mix. The resolution of this allocation of power is to some extent the result of the operation of local bureaucratic politics, with an infinite variety of relationships possible. Councillors are most likely to be a force in policy making in those authorities where there is a safe majority for the dominant party and this is particularly marked in the Labour-controlled councils of the metropolitan districts.

Elected representatives

The electoral system employed in local government is based on single-member constituencies, the winner requiring only a simple plurality of the votes cast in order to be returned for a four-year term. The counties have elections every four years to which the whole of the council is exposed, while the districts usually hold them three times in every four-year period, with one-third of the council seeking re-election each time. Thus, many voters directly elect members to two authorities. Before 1974 there was also a system of indirect elections when members of councils themselves elected certain of their number to serve as aldermen; by the time of its abolition this system was considered undemocratic and anachronistic.

A frequent observation, often intended as a criticism, made of the people who become councillors in Britain is that they as a group do not represent, in a microcosmic sense, their constituents. Research reveals the group on average to be better educated, to be older, and to contain more males than would a randomly chosen group from the population at large (Widdecome Report 1986).

Because of the fairly firm party allegiances of voters today there is little chance of electoral success for independent candidates. Parties are thus important agents of political recruitment. This has been particularly so in the case of Labour, where candidates from working-class backgrounds have lacked access to the traditional routes to local political leadership through wealth or professional position. In a similar way the Labour Party has been able, through its various forms of political activity, to offer a training to those whose education would not automatically furnish them with the more sophisticated skills for political life. However, developments in the political system since the Second World War have resulted in the emergence of a number of highly educated, relatively young Labour councillors, the offspring of working-class parents, who have retained their class allegiance. These people have begun to play a significant role in local government, particularly in the cities.

There is no formal training for councillors and, although some universities and polytechnics offer various short courses on aspects of the work, the ethos remains essentially amateur in what might be termed the British tradition. It is part of this tradition that one learns 'on the job', a process which is made easier by the hierarchical nature of political organisation on the council. New councillors will usually have junior status, quietly sitting on relatively unimportant committees while they undergo a process of education and socialisation.

However, in spite of the amateur ethos characteristic of the training acquired by councillors, a period of uninterrupted service with a concentration on a limited number of areas can result in the development of a high level of expertise, so that the chairs of committees can become influential figures in particular areas, often making national pronouncements on policy.

Officers

The general characteristics of local government officers may be contrasted with their central government counterparts in the civil service. With respect to the senior positions, civil servants inherit a tradition from the nineteenth century, which places the generalist administrator in a position of dominance vis-à-vis the expert. However, the relative status of specialists and generalists in local government is reversed, so that the senior positions, the chief officers who head the departments and their deputies and assistants, tend to be occupied by individuals who hold professional qualifications in a relevant area; and it is this group that is largely involved in the functions of management and policy making. Hence, the generalists occupy the more lowly levels in the bureaucratic pyramid with promotional prospects strictly circumscribed, regardless of any flair they may demonstrate.

This state of affairs is subject to academic and professional criticism, with the allegation being made that the professions and specialists are ill-equipped to fulfil effectively the management function, being unable to perceive the wider horizons against which policy for the local authorities, as a whole, should be made. This is one of the factors inhibiting the corporate approach in management.

As in the case of central government, the reasons for the relative status of specialists and generalists in local government are historical rather than rational. Local government has, until recently, not effectively attracted graduates from a wider range of disciplines in the way that the civil service has done; neither has it sought to recruit entrants to a special administrative cadre comparable to the administrative grade of the central bureaucracy. Recruitment to senior positions has been largely on the basis of promotion from within the local service, where technical skills are at a premium, and professional and other bodies representing practitioners in a variety of areas have jealously guarded the rights of those with the specialist qualifications, even though this means the specialist is being taken out of the job for which s/he has been trained and placed in one for which s/he has not.

The absence of a generalist element in the upper reaches of the local government service was the subject of an official enquiry in 1967, the report of which argued that there should be a development towards the employment of generalist administrators. To some extent there has been some action on the Mallaby Report (1967), with the establishment of what has now evolved into the Local Government Management Board, and the growth within a number of polytechnics and universities of undergraduate and postgraduate courses that might be considered suitable for the training of a new breed of local government administrator. However, the traditional patterns of recruitment and training die hard, as they tend to do in all British public sector institutions, and one cannot say that there has been a dramatic movement in the direction indicated by Mallaby.

Thus, it may be said that the principal method of training for local government officers lies in the form of a specialist education in, say, accountancy, law, education, or any of the many professions employed, followed by employment in a local authority in a junior capacity and steady promotion in reward for dependable service. During a career of this kind the officer will be invited to attend various short courses at universities, or on an in-house basis, intended to impart managerial and policy making skills which may be grafted on to a fundamental body of essentially professional, technical knowlege.

POLICY MAKING

The relationship between central and local government

At the heart of any discussion on British local government are questions relating to autonomy in administration and policy making, and the twin traditions, localist and centralist, can be traced through history. As observed above, at a very early stage in the growth of local government the parish was the organic unit for the expression of self-determination by the local community, while the larger county represented a division of the state for the king's purpose. With the emergence of the modern system in the nineteenth century the localist tradition was manifested in the Municipal Corporations Act (1835), giving a high level of independence to the boroughs; the centralist tradition was preserved in the creation of the Poor Law Authorities, which represented, through the Poor Law Reform Act (1834), a highly centralised system of administration reflecting a 'rational' view inspired by utilitarian thought.

Throughout the present century the centralist–localist debate has continued, though in practical terms central government has increased its capacity to control local administration. This it has accomplished by a number of means. Certain functions have been removed from the local government portfolio altogether, and of those remaining a substantial number are defined by the statute in terms of partnership with central government, so that there is at the centre a Department for Education, a Department of Health and the Home Office with a wide range of interests in the affairs of local authorities. In addition there is the Department of the Environment, concerned with areas such as roads and housing and being, in effect, a virtual department of municipal affairs. The central departments conduct a continuous series of bilateral dialogues with the authorities through a stream of communications giving directions on administrative minutiae and policy.

Because local government has no legal basis other than that defined in Acts of Parliament, it is possible for central government, through its control of the legislature, to make any changes it wishes to its structure and functions. Thus, virtually the whole system was reformed by the Local Government Act of 1972. In 1985 the Metropolitan County Authorities and the Greater London Council were wiped out by means of an Act of Parliament, after a protracted battle with central government.

Perhaps most important of all facets of the central–local relationship is finance. The central government has a number of ways of either paying the piper, or exercising a considerable degree of control over his income, through regulation of the central grants system, influence over local authority pricing policies, the loan sanction process and, most recently, attempts to restrict the money that can be raised from the hitherto sacrosanct source of local taxation. Where such methods have been unable to secure compliance, central government has sometimes been able to have recourse to the courts.

However, following the local government reorganisation of 1974, many of the councils of the large conurbations have sought to re-establish a degree of autonomy through a persistence with policies frowned upon by central government. For example, they continued to operate public transport services substantially below cost, dragged their feet over the central policy of selling off their housing stock, and the Council of Liverpool, with Beatle-like insouciance, seriously threatened to bring in an illegal (unbalanced) budget by refusing to increase the local tax demand and challenging the central government to provide more assistance from central funds. During the 1960s some academics sought to show that the diversity in the level of provision made in certain services by different local authorities demonstrated a significant degree of local autonomy. Such conclusions were debatable at the time, and today few doubt the extent to which the centre has been able to dominate the 'partnership'.

Rhodes (1986) has argued that the relationship between local and central governments should be seen neither as a partnership nor as a system in which local authorities are agents of the centre. He argues that, while central government is more powerful, both organisations have the ability to challenge one another depending on their resources of power and influence on any particular issues. It has, however, been suggested by Chandler (1991) that the relationship is best described as stewardship, in which central government allows local authorities some autonomy to manage efficiently tasks on behalf of the centre provided they stick to principles laid down by the government. The central–local issue remains a critical aspect of local government in Britain today.

THE ROLE OF POLITICAL PARTIES AND PRESSURE GROUPS

Political parties

Political parties are a well established feature of the local political systems in Britain. There is some dispute about the date when they originated, but it appears that organisations seeking to mobilise the popular vote in their favour in order to gain control of agencies of local government predate the establishment of the modern, all-purpose local authority. Thus, elections to the various ad hoc boards administering functions such as the relief of poverty were fought on party lines, though these 'parties' were not representative of the ideological differences characteristic of their modern counterparts, being more concerned with matters of religion and levels of spending.

Political life of the major towns and cities is dominated by the two main protagonists, Labour and Conservative, with a number of lesser forces including the Liberal-Democrats. In addition there are various fringe parties such as the Communists, Greens and the National Front who do not make a serious electoral challenge. In some areas there are citizens' parties with a purely local orientation but these are usually short-lived.

Often the stimulus for the central–local conflict is party–ideological, relating to the amount of public spending and the level and nature of service provision. The cities, with acute problems of unemployment and other manifestations of urban decay, tend to be under Labour control and, since 1979, this has resulted in prolonged conflict, with the national Conservative Government seeking to pursue a policy of tight monetary control with curbs on public spending.

Once a party gains control of a council, which it does by winning a majority of seats, it is in a position to dominate the policy making processes by ensuring a majority for itself on all committees, and awarding all chairs to its own members. This control is sometimes enhanced by the presumption of longevity since, in many areas, voters are irrevocably committed to one or other of the parties. Generally speaking, rural areas tend to be Conservative while solid Labour support is characteristic of the urban areas. Critics allege that this security of tenure affords the parties unreasonable power without proper accountabilty, and leads to extreme policies.

The arguments advanced in favour of parties at the local level are that they vitalise local political life by educating people in political issues, acting as agents of communication, mobilising the electorate at voting times and generally providing a sound basis for a local democracy at state as well as local level. Without them local government might well become merely local administration. The Conservative Government set up the Widdecombe Committee (1986) to question the 'politicisation' of local government, but British political culture seems to accept the legitimacy of parties in local politics.

Interest groups

There are a great number and wide variety of local interest groups in Britain; one study estimated that there were over four thousand operating in the city of Birmingham alone (Newton 1976). Some of these are local branches of national organisations while others are purely local in character. The group configuration tends to reflect the socio-economic profile of the area; where, for example, there are substantial stocks of public housing there are likely to be tenants' associations, while in industrial cities, trades councils and chambers of commerce will seek to articulate the interests of their respective memberships. Similarly, the sort of problems encountered in the cities, associated with, for example, housing, education or old age, engender predictable patterns of group formation. In addition there are groups which reflect, on an ad hoc basis, the current policy of the council, such as plans to build roads, develop inner city areas, or change the education system in some way. These usually disappear once they have achieved or irredeemably failed to achieve their objectives.

Access to the councils is relatively open and can be made in a variety of ways including petitions, personal meetings with members, and letters. There are also formalised communication channels such as consultative councils and ex-officio membership of local organisations by councillors. Channels can be established to the local bureaucracy where, in cases where the political parties are not highly dominant, it is possible to make a far more effective impact on policy than through more overt political means. Local groups also have recourse to public opinion in seeking to change attitudes through various forms of demonstration and use of the local mass media. The effectiveness of this last expedient will vary depending on the vitality of the local organs. Generally speaking, the local radio and press in the large towns, particularly the metropolitan districts, show a reasonable degree of interest in local politics, but in the smaller towns and rural areas coverage is intermittent.

The extent to which pressure groups direct their attention towards any governmental institution is a measure of its perceived ability to influence public policy, and in the case of local authorities this is a matter of some contention. Some groups, particularly those which are branches of national organisations such as the National Union of Teachers, may prefer to direct their main attention towards central government in the belief that this is where the 'real' power lies.

THE INFLUENCE OF THE ELECTORATE

In the controversial area of central–local relations, the principal justification for local autonomy is the independent electoral base of local councils; no other agency of public administration outside Parliament can claim a similar justification. Having been elected as a political party with a manifesto, a council can claim the authority of a mandate for its policies: a condition which produces a contradiction, and a problem for central government, since it too can claim a mandate on the same basis but on a national scale. In legal terms, the central government can command the overriding authority in accordance with the doctrine of the Supremacy of

Parliament, but local government, with a history as long as central government, is able to establish a moral claim for local autonomy supported by tradition and British political culture.

The extent to which elections may be said to determine policy is questionable. We have already noted that the fixed nature of party allegiances among voters creates a tendency towards single party government in a substantial number of authorities. This may be one of the reasons for another characteristic of local elections: a turnout that is regarded by most commentators as rather low.

ISSUES AND TENSIONS

There are several tensions within the British system of local government. The relationship with central government is one of the most crucial of these, with philosophical undertones which help to form the British political culture. The decade of the 1980s proved traumatic for British local government and illustrated the central–local tension. The 'new right' agenda of Thatcherism with its determination to cut public expenditure meant that central and local government were on a collision course. Throughout the decade local government can be said to have been under assault with attempts by the centre to reduce its functional portfolio by deregulation, compulsory competitive tendering, and hiving off, often giving the function to private sector bodies or to quangos operating beyond the arm of local democracy, such as urban development corporations. At the heart of the assault were draconian financial restrictions, the most potent erosion of local autonomy. Local parties, and hence local democracy, were also under attack and the Widdecombe Report (1986) made a number of recommendations to curb the powers of elected councillors and to enhance those of the officials who were more likely to toe the central line.

In the eighteenth century Jeremy Bentham outlined a system of local government based upon his utility principle. The system was logically created, rational and highly centralised. In planning his nineteenth century reforms of the administrative machine responsible for the relief of poverty, Edwin Chadwick sought to embody Bentham's ideas, which he later attempted to extend to the administration of public health. However, J.S. Mill, whose early intellectual development was largely founded upon utilitarian principles, came to revise much of this philosophy and emphasised certain intrinsic values for the individual and the state in a system of self-government which allowed a greater degree of autonomy from the centre.

Centralism does not necessarily equate with efficiency or rationality, but in some respects there are connections which cannot be overlooked. In Chadwick's day it was true that many local authorities were inefficient, ill-funded, corrupt and, for various reasons, unwilling even to contemplate the efforts required to remedy many pressing social evils. Today this is not the case, but the nature of central government has been transformed to encompass a wider functional portfolio, including a comprehensive range of social welfare services and the management of the economy of the country as a whole. It appears to be the case that central governments find it difficult to carry out these functions effectively and efficiently without impinging on the autonomy of local authorities, which themselves shape and administer a number of social policies directly and which collectively account for a considerable proportion of public expenditure. The demands by recipients for equality, in national terms, in the provision of services is a further factor which renders problematic any encouragement of local diversity.

The contradiction posed by efficiency and equity on the one hand and local autonomy on the other is not only a central–local issue. It is sometimes argued that a large number, perhaps all, of the local government functions are essentially apolitical in character. Accordingly, functions such as policing, refuse disposal or education are best left to technical experts rather than politically motivated laypersons. Much of the academic and professional debate surrounding local government in the post-war era has centred on the subject of management and administrative efficiency, rather than on questions of democracy. Generally speaking, when the imperatives of efficiency have seemed to impinge upon the sphere of councillor activity, arguments of reformers have supported a reduction in their role. Thus the Maud Committee (1967) on management recommended the demotion of the advisory status of the majority of councillors on any council, while the Bains Report (1972) placed much emphasis on the delegation of responsibilities from councillors to officers. During the 1960s and 1970s it could be said that most authorities had adopted some form of corporate management. However, in the early 1980s a reaction set in, with councillors seeking to reassert their own authority vis-á-vis the managerialists, and the view began to gain acceptance that local authorities could not import ideas developed in other organisations without serious attention to the unique contingencies of local government.

In conclusion, it can be said that the twin issues of efficiency in local administration and the operation of a viable system of local democracy remain unresolved areas of debate. There is a continual state of tension between the various central and local agencies, resulting in a constantly shifting balance of power. In this, local government in Britain can be seen as an integral part of the wider pluralist system of government and politics.

BIBLIOGRAPHY

Bains Report (1972) *Report of the Working Group on the New Local Authorities: Management and Structure*, London, HMSO (for the Department of the Environment).

Chandler, J.A. (1991) *Local Government Today*, Manchester, Manchester University Press.

Kingdom, J.E. (1991) *Local Government and Politics in Britain*, Hemel Hempstead, Philip Allen.

Mallaby Report (1967) *Report of the Committee on the Staffing of Local Government*, London, HMSO (for the Ministry of Housing and Local Government).

Maud Report (1967) *Report of the Committee on the Management of Local Government*, London, HMSO (for the Ministry of Housing and Local Government).

Newton, K. (1976) *Second City Politics*, Oxford, Oxford University Press.

Rhodes, R.A.W. (1986) *The National World of Local Government*, London, Allen and Unwin.

Widdecombe Report (1986) *Report of the Committee of Inquiry into the Conduct of Local Authority Business*, Cmnd 9797, London, HMSO (for the Department of the Environment, and Scottish and Welsh Offices).

Chapter 3

The Republic of Ireland

M. McManus

It should be made clear from the start that this chapter is concerned with the system of local government that exists in the Irish Republic (or Eire) and does not deal with the administration within Northern Ireland, which since 1922 has been a constituent part of the United Kingdom. For the sake of convenience we shall refer to the state as 'Ireland' and to the people as 'Irish'.

PRINCIPAL INSTITUTIONS OF THE STATE

Ireland is a small country on the edge of Europe, tied to England for much of its history and, like Wales and Scotland, treated as a province. In 1922 it achieved independence from Britain though still remaining within the Commonwealth. This link was loosened somewhat by de Valera when he came to power in 1932 and was finally broken by the Republic of Ireland Act 1948, which formally constituted Ireland as a Republic. Despite this repudiation of English political control the major influence on Irish political thought and practice has been British and this is manifested quite clearly in much of the local government system as it exists today.

The population of Ireland is small: in 1981 it was 3,443,405, making it one of the smallest members of the EC. It is also the least densely populated country in the EC, with forty-seven inhabitants per square kilometre, still essentially being a rural nation heavily dependent on agriculture. The agricultural population is made up primarily of owner-occupiers of small farms, who constitute an important part of the political scene in both national and local government. Another feature of the Irish population, which is important in terms of political values and the political climate, although not necessarily affecting local government, is the fact that 95 per cent of the population are Catholic.

The system of government has been described by Chubb as 'early British Commonwealth' (Chubb 1983) in that it is parliamentary, with a

Prime Minister and cabinet government. Several innovations were introduced post-independence, the most notable and lasting of which were the use of referendums for certain matters and, more important, the use of a system of proportional representation in voting at both national and local levels, although, to be strictly correct, proportional representation was introduced before independence to help the Protestant minority, but it is regarded as a fruit of the revolution.

Ireland has a written constitution, the *Bunreacht na hAireann* passed in 1937, which replaced the Constitution of the Irish Free State of 1922. The 1937 constitution was the culmination of several years of constitutional reform following de Valera's accession to government in 1932. It was in some ways a radical departure from 1922 and in other ways a confirmation of existing practice and principle, its main difference being the repudiation of formal Commonwealth links and the elimination of the role of the Crown in the constitution, so as to stress the republican nature of the new state. This process was finally completed in 1948 when Ireland was formally declared to be a republic. The machinery of government enshrined in the *Bunreacht na hAireann* is based very firmly on the early twentieth-century Westminster model, to a large extent confirming existing structures. As de Valera explained to the *Dáil* in 1937, 'What is being done here is to translate into practice what has been done in the past . . . making explicit what was implicit all the time.' Following to some extent the British tradition the *Bunreacht* provides for a House of Representatives, known as the *Dáil Aireann*, and a Senate, known as the *Seanad Aireann*. The Irish Parliament is called the *Oireachtas* and constitutionally consists of the President as well as the two Houses.

The President is elected every seven years, though on only four occasions since 1937 has the post been contested by more than one candidate, since the various parties usually come to some agreement beforehand. The role of the President is largely that of a figurehead rather than the active political one we are familiar with in the United States of America or France. Effective political power resides in the *Taoiseach* (the Prime Minister) and the government of the day.

The *Dáil* is the more important of the Houses of the *Oireachtas* and its composition is fairly conventional, in that its members are elected by adult franchise based on geographical constituencies. The *Dáil* reflects the influence of England on Irish political structures, since it operates in much the same way as the British Parliament with many of the same problems in relation to policy making. Essentially, with a secure *Taoiseach*, a comfortable majority, and voting on party lines, the role and effectiveness of the *Dáil* in policy making is limited.

There are at present 166 deputies or TDs (*Teachta Dala*). There are three main parties, though a new party, the Progressive Democrats launched in December 1985, may upset the established trio. Fianna Fáil was founded by de Valera in 1926 as the anti-Treaty party, while Fine Gael, established in 1933, was the successor to *Cunnan na Gaedheal*, the original pro-Treaty party. The Labour Party was founded by James Connelly in 1912.

The second house, the *Seanad*, is part elected and part nominated in an attempt to provide both a balance and a check to the first House and also to provide a different kind of representation. A continuing problem has been to arrive at a satisfactory method of constituting a second house that is both democratic and yet different in kind to the *Dáil*. The solution proposed by de Valera still holds today with minor changes. The *Seanad* is composed of three groups selected as follows. Firstly, there are six senators who are elected by the two Universities and the other institutions of higher education as specified by law. Secondly, forty-three senators are elected, using the single transferable voting system, by an electoral college of 900 consisting of members of the *Oireachtas* and county and county borough councillors. The candidates for this election are nominated by five panels representing different groups of interests, which are education and culture, agriculture, industry and commerce, labour, public administration and social services, and also by members of the *Oireachtas*. The final eleven senators are nominated by the *Taoiseach* personally to give representation to any group neglected by the rest of the process and, as de Valera himself admitted, to ensure a government majority. Despite the attempt at a wide non-political representation, the reality is that the *Seanad* is still composed of mainly party politicians and presents only a limited check or challenge to the *Dáil*. However, some *Seanad* committees do have quite wide-ranging powers to investigate mis-spending and misconduct by the government, so it would be wrong totally to dismiss its power and effectiveness. With that proviso, the *Seanad* is inferior and subordinate to the *Dáil* and is treated as such in both the constitution and political life.

THE STRUCTURE OF LOCAL GOVERNMENT

Historical development

The development of the local government system in Ireland can be divided into two phases, the period under English rule when it largely followed the prevailing model in England with whatever modifications were needed for the Irish situation and, secondly, the period from 1922 to the present during which several significant changes were made to the system which the new nation had inherited. The most notable of these were the adoption of the city and county management system first evolved in the United States, the creation of the Local Appointments Commission and a marked tightening up of central control, so that the present system is not merely a variation of the English model but contains elements which are purely Irish or which derive from non-English theory and practice.

There are two traditions in the development of local government: firstly, that of civic autonomy and, secondly, that of the use of Justices of the Peace to carry out non-legal administrative tasks in the countryside. As in England there was a separation of town from country on the assumption that each had different needs that merited different administrative structures. However, the development of the local government system was not as rational or coherent as the foregoing statement might seem to imply and, in many ways, local government, like Topsy, 'just growed', lacking any philosophy of its role. This is shown in the fact that there is no positive provision for local government in the *Bunbreacht ne hAireann*, unlike the constitutions of some other countries such as France and West Germany.

The county

As Ireland is still essentially a rural, agrarian nation it seems right to outline the development of county government first. The formation and delineation of the counties is linked originally to the Norman invasion and the attempt to make effective the introduction of English law. By the beginning of the seventeenth century the 'shiring' of the country was completed and the counties have remained substantially as then delineated. The main change was the splitting of Tipperary into two ridings in 1838, a division that still exists today.

The counties were units for the territorial administration of justice, which was conducted by a system of grand juries consisting of the major property owners and the higher bourgeoisie elected by the High Sheriff. The 1836 Grand Jury Act attempted to make grand juries more accountable and democratic, as a response to criticisms of their inefficiency and corruption. The reforms never really worked and despite other attempts at reform the grand juries continued until most of their administrative duties were taken over by the county councils under the provisions of the Local Government (Ireland) Act of 1898.

The towns

Towns had existed from pre-Norman times and in the twelfth and thirteenth centuries some were granted royal charters which made them boroughs under the control of borough corporations. As in Britain, these bodies were infected with corruption and decay in the eighteenth and early nineteenth centuries, increasingly coming under the control of a patron who was only concerned with securing the return to Parliament of the right candidate. The neglect of their duties to the town and its inhabitants was recognised by the Lighting of Towns Act of 1835, which allowed towns to appoint commissioners to run the public lighting, sewerage, cleansing and other environmental services. These commissioners were elected by a restricted franchise but it was at least a limited form of local democracy. The Municipal Corporations Act 1840 was the Irish equivalent of the 1835 Act which was passed in England, though altered to suit the Irish situation. The Benthamite ideal of household suffrage was modified to require a £10 valuation franchise, but the Act did abolish all but ten of the sixty-eight boroughs then existing.

The next major legislation, the Town Improvements Act 1854, enabled town commissions to be set up and, although the legislation is largely ineffective and out of date, it is still operative in over twenty towns. The Act which shaped the present system of municipal government was the Local Government (Ireland) Act 1898, which made the urban sanitary districts into new urban district councils, while the four county boroughs were given substantially the same powers as county councils.

The Irish Poor Law

The third aspect of local government in the nineteenth century was the administration of poor relief. Although the Commission set up to investigate the problem in Ireland rejected the English Poor Law system, the government under Lord John Russell decided on, and implemented, an Irish version of the 1834 Poor Law. As in England, the workhouse system acquired many health functions during the rest of the century, which were mainly taken over by the new authorities set up by the 1898 Act. It should be noted in passing that the Great Famine had a serious effect on the system of poor relief, which was not designed to deal with a major catastrophe. The Poor Law Commission was absorbed by the Local Government Board, which was set up in 1872.

By the turn of the century, local government in its various forms covered a wide spectrum of responsibilities, including health, welfare, environmental services and the local administration of law. The Local Government (Ireland) Act of 1898 attempted to solve this administrative muddle by setting up county councils and rural district councils to take over the functions of grand juries and poor law guardians in county areas, and by creating urban district councils to deal with the same issues in the towns. It thus created a two-tier system except in the county boroughs which became all-purpose authorities.

One important aspect of the 1898 Act was the extension of the franchise to include all male householders or occupiers, so that the parliamentary electorate became the local government electorate. This, coupled with the abolition of multiple votes, greatly increased the democratic nature of local government and was to be of crucial importance in determining the role of local government in the coming struggle for independence. The last piece of British legislation in this area was the Local Government (Ireland) Act 1919, which introduced the system of proportional representation into local elections to safeguard the interests of minority groups, especially the Ango-Irish and the Protestants.

The new state and local government

Local authorities played an important part in fighting British rule and when the *Dáil Aireann* was set up in 1919 a large number of councils refused to recognise the authority of the Local Government Board and declared allegiance to the Department of Local Government which the *Dáil* established in 1920. Although this was useful in the struggle for independence, it had an untoward and harmful effect on local government, which was left weakened and inefficient as a result of these factors: first, the financial penalties levied on the recalcitrant authorities by the British government; second, the lack of finance caused by the collapse of the rate collecting system; third, the disruption which ensued from the civil war following the Treaty. The effect of all this was to bring about much greater central control by the new government, which suspended some authorities including Dublin and Cork for negligence and initiated a consideration of the whole nature of local government. Thus, the new government, for pragmatic reasons as much as any other, established a highly centralised system of local government.

The move to centralisation included the abolition of the Poor Law and the Boards of Guardians and the absorption of various sub-county bodies into the county councils. The other major changes concerned the functioning of local authorities and include what Basil Chubb calls 'Ireland's major invention in the field of local government' (Chubb 1983:

261), the city and county manager. This innovation will be examined in greater detail later in this chapter, but, in outline, the first manager was appointed in Cork in 1929 as a result of pressure from local businessmen for a more effective and efficient local government. The system was extended to the whole of Ireland by the 1942 County Management Act.

With regard to the personnel of local government, various measures were enacted to try to ensure a more professional and effective local government officer. The restrictions on mobility were lifted by an Act of 1925 and, in 1926, the Local Appointments Commission was established to select and recommend to local authorities persons for appointment to principal offices. It was hoped that this device would curb the nepotism and jobbery that was rife in local government at the time. To what extent it succeeded we shall see later in this chapter. Since 1942 there have been no major changes in the structure and function of local government, apart from the abolition of the domestic rate in 1978 and the loss of certain functions to central authority. There have been several moves, especially in the late 1960s and early 1970s, to reform local government, but none has been implemented.

Present structure

As shown in Figure 3.1, the principal local authorities are the twenty-seven county councils, the four county borough councils, seven borough corporations and forty-nine urban district councils. There are also twenty-eight town commissions, which are elected bodies with a range of functions similar to those of other authorities.

The administrative county, either a county borough or a shire county,

Oireachtas	
TIER 1	
County Borough Councils	County Councils
4	27
TIER 2	
	Borough Corporations 7
	Urban District Councils 49
	Town Commissions 28

Figure 3.1 Local government structure in the Republic of Ireland (from Chubb 1982: 296)

is the major unit of local government. The Local Government Reorganisation Act 1985 has changed this picture slightly by setting up three new electoral counties in the Dublin area to replace the Dublin County Council and the Dun Laoghaire Corporation. There are several other local bodies such as the joint burial boards which are not elected but which are the responsibility of the Department of the Environment. There are also various bodies for which the Ministry does not have responsibility, such as the Vocational Educational Committees, which involve local authorities to a substantial degree (Roche 1982: Ch. 7).

As might be expected in a centralised system such as that in Ireland, central government plays an important role in all aspects of local government. The main department with which councils communicate is the Department of the Environment. This was originally the Department of Local Government and Public Health from 1924 until 1947, when it was split into three: the Department of Local Government, the Department of Health and the Department of Social Welfare. It acquired its present title in 1977 and the name changes encapsulate the development of local government in Ireland in the twentieth century. Local authorities have relations with government departments other than the Environment, and the following are a few examples of areas of major intervention. The Department of Agriculture is concerned with the Committees of Agriculture, statutory committees nominated by the county councils. Vocational Education Committees are the responsibility of the Department of Education, while the Department of Finance is concerned with the County Development Teams and valuations for rating. Regional Health Boards, which include councillors as members, provide 'a partnership between local government, central government and the vocational organisations' (Health Act 1970) and are responsible to the Department of Health. According to Roche (1982), all fifteen central departments interact with local administrations in either major or minor ways. This gives some idea of the limitations placed upon local government in Ireland.

State-sponsored bodies

Several state-sponsored bodies are part of the local government scene, though they are not directly controlled by local councils. They act as centres of advice and information for both central and local government. The principal bodies comprise the National Institute for Physical Planning, the Library Council, the National Building Agency, the Planning and Development Board and the Local Government Computer Services

Board. There are financial links between these bodies and local government in that some of them are funded by a levy on local authorities as well as by a state grant.

FUNCTIONS OF LOCAL GOVERNMENT

There are two ways of looking at the functions of local authorities: one is to list the areas of work covered by local authorities as a whole, and the other is to distinguish between the functions of councillors and officers and, in particular, the manager.

The functions of county councils, county boroughs, borough and urban distict councils can be classified into the following programme groups:

1 Housing and Building: Management and provision of local authority housing; assistance to persons housing themselves or improving their houses; itinerant rehabilitation; enforcement of housing standards and controls.

2 Road Transportation and Safety: Road upkeep and improvement; public lighting; traffic management facilities; safety education and propaganda; collection of motor taxation; licensing of drivers, etc.

3 Water Supply and Sewerage: Public water supply and sewerage schemes; assistance for private water and sewerage facilities; public conveniences.

4 Development incentives and controls: Physical planning policy; control of new development and building; promotion of industrial and other development.

5 Environmental Protection: Waste collection and disposal; burial grounds; safety of structures and places; fire protection; pollution control.

6 Recreation and Amenity: Swimming pools; libraries; parks; open spaces; recreation centres; art galleries; museums; theatres; conservation and improvement of amenities.

7 Agriculture, Education, Health and Welfare: Contributions to the County Committees of Agriculture, Vocational Education Committees, Regional Health Boards, Joint Drainage Committees and the Unemployment Assistance Fund; public assistance; rates waiver scheme; other services of an agricultural, educational or welfare nature.

8 Miscellaneous Services: Financial management and rate collection; elections; courthouse; coroners and inquests; consumer protection measures; markets; fairs and abattoirs; gasworks; corporate estates; malicious injuries.

Public Bodies (Amendment) Order 1975

The functions of town commissions are of a more limited nature, covering principally the management of local authority housing, markets, allotments and fairs. As Roche (1982) points out, the functions of Irish local government are limited when compared with the range offered throughout Europe. Out of a possible thirty services, Irish local authorities operate eleven. A major point that needs to be made about the list of services operated by Irish local authorities is the absence of health, welfare and educational services. To all intents and purposes Irish local authorities are environmental authorities concerned mainly with material matters.

The second classification of functions is peculiar to Ireland and is a direct outcome of the adoption of the system of city and county managers. Under this system the functions of the local authorities are divided into reserved and executive functions. Reserved functions are discharged by elected members and comprise mainly major policy matters, such as making the budget, disposing of council property or nominating persons to act on other public bodies. They are defined by statute in Managerial Acts and those Acts that deal with specific services. The manager is left with any function which is not a statutory reserved function. This includes the employment of staff, the acceptance of tenders, the collection of rates and the administration of the day-to-day affairs of the community.

The restraints upon the activities of both councillors and managers are grounded in law and, as in England, the doctrine of *ultra vires* is important. The overall effect of *ultra vires* and central control is to limit the room for innovation that councillors have, though how far this legalistic picture coincides with reality is open to question.

FINANCE OF LOCAL GOVERNMENT

As with most systems of public finance there are two aspects to the funding of Irish local authorities: revenue and capital expenditure. Capital expenditure of local authorities is normally financed by borrowing from the Exchequer by means of the Local Loans Fund, which is managed by the Commissioners of Public Works on behalf of the Ministry of Finance, who sanction the loan, if the project is deemed satisfactory in technical terms and within the remit of the local authority. However, the building of an international-class airport to serve the village and shrine of Knock does seem to raise questions about the working of the system! By this means a check is supposed to be kept on public expenditure, a constant theme in all liberal democratic governments today. The effect in Ireland has been to reduce the local capital expenditure as a proportion of the Public Capital Programme from about a quarter in 1976 to less than one-fifth now.

Table 3.1 Sources of revenue

	1977 £m	%	1984 £m	%
Rates	107.4	34	126.0	12
State grants	145.7	46	660.0	64
Other	63.5	20	246.0	24
Total	316.6	100	1032.0	100

Source: Roche (1982); *Irish Year Book* (1986)

Revenue or current expenditure is met from three main sources: rates, government grants and miscellaneous receipts from property and other charges. Table 3.1 shows the amount raised from the various sources in 1977 and 1984.

The innovative feature about rates in Ireland is that since 1978 domestic rates have been abolished and have been replaced by a state grant in compensation for lost revenue. It is worth looking at this feature of local government finance since rating systems in general have come under attack in most countries where they exist.

There has been criticism of the rating system since the early 1960s. There were a number of reports from the Department of Local Government between 1965 and 1968 which recommended various changes to the system, a few of which were accepted by the government, though some were pre-empted by government action. During the election campaign of 1973 Fianna Fáil promised to de-rate domestic properties but the National Coalition parties won the election and pursued their own policies. By 1976, however, they decided, despite the evidence of a commissioned report by the Economic and Social Research Institute, that they would phase out domestic rating. Fianna Fáil, while in opposition, had planned for the total abolition of domestic rates, a policy they put into effect when they regained power in 1977. This action is all the more remarkable for the lack of evidence to support it. As Desmond Roche is quoted as saying,

> There has been virtually no rational discussion of the sudden conversion of first one and then all parties to the new faith. The move has been popular and is clearly a political master stroke.

(Alexander 1979)

Several reasons could be offered for the change, among which the most important are, firstly, that there was a deep resentment about rates in

Ireland because of the inequity that resulted from the combination of wide variations in population and rateable value, and, secondly, that the phasing out of health costs from the rating system between 1973 and 1977 showed that it was feasible to de-rate properties.

One interesting sidelight on the exercise is that the abolition of domestic rates was done initially without legislation, emphasising again the power of central government over local authorities. This power has been increased by the centralised nature of the grants system now in operation. The local authority strikes a rate but only for the still rated industrial properties, while the government acts as the domestic ratepayer and pays the authority the appropriate sum by means of a state grant. However, the government sets a limit on the amount of rates by specifying the percentage by which rates may be raised. In 1978, for example, rises were limited to 11 per cent and in 1979 and 1980 to 10 per cent. The criticism that this limits the autonomy of local authorities was answered as follows by the Minister for the Environment.

> The limit which I have imposed does not interfere in any way with the discretion of local authority to determine priorities within the rate in the pound which they strike. This remains, as before, a matter for the local authorities themselves, who must continue to exercise their best judgement on local priorities.
>
> (Alexander 1979: 18)

The continued insistence of the minister that the new measure does not limit the powers of local councils seems to miss the point, perhaps deliberately.

There is a mixture of disquiet and apprehension in local government circles that the new system not only affects the practical matter of decision making, but also, more seriously, brings into question the fundamental justification for local government, the principle of local democracy. Is it possible that the rates problem has been settled at the cost of a major change in the character of local government? The Chairman of Dublin City Council described it as a 'mortal blow to local democracy'. However, others do not see any necessary link between local finance and local government. Donal de Buitleir (1974) described it 'as much a myth as the belief that the earth is flat'. One section of the population, the domestic ratepayer, has of course expressed little disquiet about the new situation.

Grants

As a result of the de-rating, state grants now form a large part of local government revenue. There are several state grants paid by a number of central government departments. The most important grant for a long time was the Agricultural Grant given to local authorities so that they could give an abatement of rates to certain occupiers of agricultural land. The amount of grant decreased in the late 1970s but started to rise again in the first years of the 1980s. The obvious step of de-rating agricultural property is included in the programme of the present government. The other grants are a housing subsidy to meet loan charges on house building, a grant for road works to replace the Road Fund, and a sanitary services subsidy to assist water supply and sewerage schemes.

Miscellaneous receipts

The third source of finance are charges for the provision of goods and services. The main producer of income is housing, in the form either of rents or payments of house loans. In 1978 £19 million came from rents and the sale of council housing, £22.8 million from repayments of house purchase and reconstruction loans and £5.3 million from water supply and sewerage charges, out of a total income from the heading of £70 million. As a result of recent legislation local councils are now empowered to charge for refuse collection, water supply and planning applications.

INTERNAL STRUCTURE

Given the fact that most Irish local authorities are small, staff members are limited and departments are few. The numbers may vary from 70 headquarters staff in Limerick County to 350 such staff in Cork, the largest of the counties. The standard organisation of a county administration from senior to junior staff is:

1 County Manager
2 County Secretary
3 County Accountant
4 Administrative Officers
5 Senior Staff Officers
6 Staff Officers
7 Assistant Staff Officers
8 Clerical Officers
9 Clerk Typist
10 Clerical Assistants.

The lower grades, those from 4 to 10, are recruited either internally by promotion or directly to the required grade on the basis of the results of examinations such as the Leaving Certificate. Appointments to Grades 7 to 4 are made by way of promotions competitions held locally. The three senior appointments involve selection and recommendation by the Local Appointments Commission. These vacancies are publicly advertised and are open to all people who are qualified, though, since knowledge and expertise of local government are decisive factors, there is an over-whelming tendency for appointments to be made from within the service as a whole, making it difficult for outsiders, however well qualified, to break into the senior levels of the service.

The offices of county or city manager, secretary, town clerk and county surveyor must be appointed. In addition to these, most counties would have, together with supporting departments, a highways engineer, architect, librarian, solicitor, coroner and fire officer.

Committees

In most systems of local government based on the English model, committees play an important part in the running of the local administration. However, in Ireland the role of the committee has changed. One of the inheritances of the British system was the use of committees for decision making. This role was a victim of the management system and committees no longer play a major role in Irish local government in the same way as they do in Britain. Indeed, as Marshall reported to the Maud Committee, 'While some authorities make intensive use of committees, others have recourse to them intermittently and for specific projects.' An essential difference between English and Irish committees is that Irish committees do not make executive decisions, but tend instead to offer advice to the manager and to acquaint themselves with the manager's decisions and actions.

The lack of committees affects the working of councils in several ways. Firstly, the traditional position of the committee chair is absent from the hierarchy of both the council and the ruling party and thus the composition of any party caucus has to be based on different criteria to those employed in Britain. Secondly, it might also loosen the hold of the parties over the day-to-day running of the council, though this is affected to a large extent by the separation of reserved and executive functions. Thirdly, it frees the councillor from the heavy commitment of time that committee work involves. This time may be spent in a variety of ways but, given the individualistic nature of much of a councillor's work and the wide geographical spread of his or her constituents, it enables the councillor to deal far more efficiently with the workload.

The Local Appointments Commission

One of the first moves of the new Republican government was the setting up of the Local Appointments Commission, a body of three which was charged with the duty of selecting and recommending to local authorities persons fit for appointment to principal offices. The Commission is completely independent of local authorities and is only connected to central government in that its membership usually consists of such people as the Speaker of the *Dáil*, the Secretary of the Department of the Environment and the Secretary of the Department of Health. Its obvious purpose was to ensure the selection of officers on the basis of merit rather than patronage and illustrates the lack of esteem with which councillors were viewed. The feeling was justified at the time and accusations of jobbery are still prevalent today. Though the opportunities for patronage are not as wide as those available to American political bosses, patronage is still a factor in local affairs as shown by Sacks's (1976) study of Donegal.

The Local Appointments Commission covers appointments to chief executive, technical and professional posts as well as certain others. Some posts in an authority may be filled by internal promotion with the consent of the Minister, but the post of manager cannot be filled just by promotion and the vacancy has to be given to the person recommended by the Local Appointments Commision. If the council fails to appoint the nominee within three months the person automatically becomes manager. Once appointed, a manager cannot be sacked by a council, but only suspended while the case is examined by the Minister for the Environment who alone has the power of dismissal, an action never yet carried out.

The Commission system is well regarded both by the public and the professionals and has contributed much to making public administration non-political and giving it a career structure that enhances the mobility of staff. This in turn has generated a demand for training that has led to the creation of specific courses in public administration at both undergraduate and postgraduate levels.

POLICY MAKING

It is important to understand the unique position of the manager in Irish local government if one is to understand the policy making process. As already outlined, there is a legal distinction between the powers of the manager and the powers of the councillor and this is considered by Zimmerman (1972: 63) to be a distinctive feature of the Irish system. There have been slight amendments to the dividing line, most notably by the City and County Management (Amendment) Act 1955, which increased the powers of councils to direct the managers and to be consulted by them before action was taken on certain matters. In practice it has been increasingly difficult to keep the two areas apart, so that, inevitably, managers are involved in policy making. Indeed, as the main contact between central and local government they are the disseminators of national policies. This has strengthened the power of the manager, who is thus the main initiator of policies and the driving force behind local administration. To counter this, councils have acquired greater influence over the executive functions of the managers, so that the system now in operation does not correspond too exactly with the original enacting legislation. However, the manager is still in a dominant position, by virtue of being full-time, with resources and information that are denied to the unpaid councillor. This unbalanced relationship is not peculiar to Ireland but seems to be inherent in any system of local government that has both elected members and career officials, and, of course, mirrors the problem of the power of civil servants at national level. Myles Tierney (1982) in the *Parish Pump* heads his chapter on the management system with the title 'The Dead Hand', which indicates the view of at least one senior Dublin City councillor on the role and function of the manager, while Chubb describes the relationship between councillors and managers as that of 'clients seeking favours rather than that of a board of directors and their top management' (Chubb 1970: 289).

The role of the councillor in Irish local government is different from that of the pre-Republic councillor who made policy and represented and administered his neighbourhood. As Chubb says, 'The elected member is a consumer representative and more of a factor in the administration of services than a policy maker or legislator' (Chubb 1982: 305). This is a role that councillors choose to play for it brings success at both local and national level. Many councillors go on to be Deputies in the *Dáil* and it is quite usual to be both a local councillor and a deputy, in fact some would go as far as to say that it was necessary for a TD to hold local elective office. As Farrell noted:

> It happens that at least ninety-five Deputies (66 per cent) of the nineteenth *Dáil* are, or have been, members of local authorities. Approximately a quarter of these, however, only gained a place in local politics after they won their *Dáil* seat. In many cases these are relatives

succeeding to 'family' seats in *Dáil* by-elections and subsequently assuming the local authority role vacated at the same time. Clearly these Deputies see membership of the local authority as a route to the *Dáil* but also as a useful (necessary) means of maintaining the strong local connections and constituency service that Irish politics demands.

(Farrell 1971: 320)

To a great extent the Irish political system is reduced to one level including both national and local politics, and indeed local authority matters are a major concern of the TD. One effect of this is to trivialise much of the work of councillors, especially for the majority of councillors who are not TDs. Since the management system and tight central control have taken over major areas of policy, the councillor is left with individuals' requests and problems comprising the bulk of the workload. Local politics is thus imbued with a particularist style and the councillor enters into patron–client or brokerage relationships with the constituents. This has implications for both the party system and pressure groups. It is important to note that there is dispute in the literature as to the extent and significance of brokerage and clientalism in Irish local politics. The traditional picture of a patron–client relationship based on the rural peasant social system which would disappear with modernisation and urbanisation may not be valid. As Komito states: 'Brokerage was . . . a result of specific structural conditions and was not caused solely by an agrarian economy or peasant values. . . . Political brokerage may simply be the most visible manifestation of the common tendency to deal with friends' (1984: 190–1).

As to the socio-economic background of councillors, they are overwhelmingly male and middle-aged. Ireland lags behind other Western European countries in terms of female representation at both local and national level, despite the fact that women have had the vote since the start of the Republic and that a woman now occupies the Presidency. This is probably explicable in terms of both religious and socio-cultural factors concerning the general position of women in Irish society. The bulk of the councillors are middle class, being drawn from the more prosperous farmers, professionals (especially teachers), shopkeepers and other people with family businesses. It is only in the relatively small urban district that the working class is strongly represented. At the 1974 local elections the percentage of manual workers, skilled, semi-skilled or unskilled, who were elected to various councils is shown in Table 3.2.

Whether this social bias matters to the electorate is doubtful, since people tend to see the councillor as their advocate and so it is perhaps to their advantage to have someone of standing pleading their case.

Table 3.2 Proportion of councillors in manual occupations

	%
County Councils	7.7
County Borough Councils	17.6
Urban District Councils	28.3
Town Commissions	30.1

Source: Adapted from Chubb (1982: 92)

One other important feature of councillors is that they are expected to reside in or, even better, originate from the area they represent. There is a strong local patriotism in both the town and county based on the quite justified belief that it pays to have a councillor in your district. This perhaps leads to the other feature of 'family' seats, where son follows father or a seat is passed from one brother to another. An example of this at the highest level was when de Valera's daughter took over his seat on his death, a move that was not greeted warmly by all the constituents. Kinship relations are important in local politics in Ireland, to some extent emphasising the peasant culture that still permeates aspects of rural life.

POLITICAL PARTIES

Local government is dominated by the national parties in terms of elections, although in some areas this pattern is changing as community association representatives have been elected as a measure of frustration at the inability of the parties to solve problems and also, perhaps, as an expression of the Irish voter's traditional low esteem of politicians. Candidates mainly present themselves on party tickets and are voted in on this basis, but how far the party system penetrates the council chamber and the business conducted therein is more open to question. It is also noticeable that independent candidates secure more votes at local elections, around 15 per cent, than they do at national elections, where their share slips to between 5 per cent and 7 per cent (Chubb 1982: 308). They also attract a higher share of the votes in towns than in rural areas. This might be because it is easier to reach the electorate in a town and, therefore, less expensive for an individual, and also that, given the parochial nature of much of local politics, voters like a person who is aware of local issues rather than just a party hack.

At local level there are, in essence, few if any differences between the parties in terms of ideology and policy. As mentioned before, acceptance or non-acceptance of the Treaty was the touchstone for party affiliation and this traditional division still affects party loyalties. There are strong kinship bonds, so that families may vote according to traditional ties, which in some cases pre-date the Treaty and rest on groupings formed as part of the nationalist struggle. To the individual councillor the *cumainn* or ward grouping is of more importance than the national party or headquarters. This is a result of the close links between local and national representatives and the electorates' perception of the councillor and the TD as the broker for the constituency. Membership of the party may be related not so much to political views as to a calculation of the potential gain in being close to the provider of services.

> Most *cumainn* members linked the party to government benefits. First, they credit the party with the establishment of the programmes from which they benefit. But, more specifically, most *cumainn* members drew a connection between their own service to the party and their receipt of benefits.
>
> (Sacks 1976: 120)

Councillors use a mixture of kinship, religious, moral and other non-material benefits to keep their support, though the basis of the system is a transactional relationship, whether actual or potential. There is some evidence to show that the room for patronage is decreasing and that the patron–client relationship may be more a perception in the mind of the rural voters than a common reality. It is suggested by some writers that there has been a transition to brokerage rather than patronage within the increasing modernisation of the Irish state. This has had an effect mostly on the rural Western periphery of the country, though the extent of the reasons for the changes are not wholly clear (Gibbon and Higgins 1974).

The single tranferable voting system has an effect on local politics in that it is not enough to rely on a party label to be elected. Each constituency returns three or more councillors. Thus, a candidate has to compete with fellow party councillors as well as the opposition in the fight to secure preferences and eventual election. Since all party candidates fight on the same policy platform individual differences may be the deciding factor within the electorate and the building up of a coterie of personal voters is important. The effect of this is described by Bax:

> It is incorrect to look upon competition for voters as something taking place during election time only. In actual fact it is a long process of cultivating support between elections: the votes are only harvested, so to speak, at election time.
>
> (Bax 1976: 40–1)

There is, therefore, constant competition for votes and the Irish councillor needs to keep party colleagues in view if s/he is not to be outflanked.

The effect of all this is shown in the working of pressure groups who play very little part in the process of local politics. To some extent this is due to the fact that most major policy making is carried out at national level, thus limiting the usefulness of the local councillors in this area. Moreover, as the manager is likely to be the initiator of policy decisions, any attempts to influence policy would be directed there. There is, however, little evidence of pressure groups operating at local level and it has only been fairly recently that the major pressure group in rural areas, the Irish Farmers' Association, has tried to exert a corporate influence on the voting behaviour of its members.

All of this works to the advantage of the elector, especially one who is willing to play the field of candidates. It has been known for constituents to contact councillors of both parties to intercede on their behalf on the same issue, promising allegiance to both. There is a high turnout at local elections, partly as a result of the strong party presence and also because of the size of constituencies. In county council elections the average turnout since 1955 has been 65 per cent, although for urban authorities the average ranges from 40 per cent for Dublin to 67 per cent for town commissions. The community spirit that exists in many small towns and rural areas, as well as the social pressure to be seen to vote, may obviously affect the turnout.

It should be noted that despite these relatively high turnout figures, compared with Britain, for example, the proportion of the population who actively engage in politics is very small. Raven *et al.* (1976: 26) found that only 11 per cent of the electorate had ever acted to influence a decision at local level, and only 3 per cent at national level. These figures also cast some doubt on the patron–client and brokerage models of Irish politics. The most optimistic figure for party membership is 7 per cent of the population, the reality being probably nearer 4 per cent. As Chubb suggests:

> The pattern of political participation . . . is by no means unusual for a western democractic country . . . active participation in political affairs is not only for the few but for a special few: equality of opportunity to engage in politics does not exist.
>
> (Chubb 1982)

THE OMBUDSMAN

In common with other countries in Western Europe, Ireland has established an Ombudsman to deal with the problems arising from maladministration by officals. The post was set up by the Ombudsman Act of 1980 but was not implemented until January 1984. In its original form it was excluded from looking at local authorities and concentrated on the civil service and central government. However, in April 1985 the jurisdiction of the Ombudsman was extended to local authorities, a move that brought some criticism from members of local authorities on the grounds that it might interfere with their work. The Ombudsman has been at pains to point out that his role differs substantially from the traditional role of councillor as supplicant for his or her constituents. While the councillor makes representations to government departments or local authorities on direct behalf of a member of the public, the function of the Ombudsman is to investigate complaints by the public about unfair treatment and, where such complaints are found to be justified, to recommmend that corrective action be taken. It is important to note that, although the Ombudsman has wide powers to demand information, he has no power to force a body to accept his recommendations.

The Ombudsman is yet another part of the public complaints procedure that seems to characterise Irish public life, and the reference by the Ombudsman, Mr Michael Mills, to the 'level of sophistication of the Irish people' in terms of the low number of invalid complaints, might serve to show their expertise in using the various channels available to them (Mills 1985). The desire to keep the roles of councillor and Ombudsman separate is also shown by the fact that the reserved functions of local authorities, that is, those functions exercised by elected representatives, are excluded from investigation by the Ombudsman. Other than that restriction, members of the public can complain about their treatment by a local authority, provided that they have first of all tried to solve their problems with the public body concerned. The Ombudsman has extensive powers in law, which enable him to demand any information document or file from any body complained of and to require any official of that body to attend before him to give information about a complaint. Whether this new route of complaint will alleviate the burden of TDs and councillors or merely be used as an extension of the present system remains to be seen.

PROBLEMS AND ISSUES

Several of the problems confronting Irish local government have been mentioned already, such as the problem of finding appropriate methods of financing local authorities and the long-running battle over the amount of central control of services. There are a few further issues that need to be raised in order to conclude this look at Irish local government and to point to possible changes in the future.

First, there has been, over the years, a trend to larger units for the administration of services. An example of this was the creation of the Regional Health Boards in 1970 to administer the health services. It was felt that the existing system of control through the counties was too disparate and lacked cost effectiveness. Larger units, it was felt, would lead to more efficient use of resources and better long-term planning by central government. The creation of ad hoc bodies such as these was seen by some as an attack on the notion of democracy and accountability, in the search for efficiency. There has, however, been a long tradition in Irish politics of setting up state-sponsored bodies as a solution to the central–local dilemma. It is obvious, looking at the geographical spread of local authorities and functions, that some areas are too small while others are too large and this has led inevitably to some inefficiency. However, the regional solution has been implemented haphazardly and, consequently, inefficiently so that neither system works well and it is becoming increasingly difficult for a geographical system of government to contribute effectively to the national well-being. An advisory committee on local government, which reported in 1990, has argued for the creation of uniform regional, county and district tiers of local government and a clearer delineation of responsibility between these tiers and central government. It is possible that further reforms of the system are likely in the 1990s in the wake of these recommendations.

The problems of Dublin exemplify the position of local government, where an outmoded system is attempting to cope with the dynamics of growth in an urban context. The authority is seen as distant from the people, as is evidenced by the low turnout at elections, and seems to regard itself as incapable of tackling the problems it faces.

The official view is that everything will work out well, but, despite several reports and a White Paper, little has emerged in the form of positive action until recently. An enquiry into the system of local government in Ireland published in 1990 recommended the division of Dublin County into two. The sheer size of Dublin in comparison with the other towns and cities of Ireland is itself a problem. In 1979 Dublin County Borough had a population of 544,586, the nearest city in size being Cork with 138,267 and after that Limerick with 60,665. The greatest growth has been in the dormitory towns surrounding Dublin and in the overspill areas on the edge of the conurbation. Thus, the town of Tallaght has grown from 6,174 in 1971 to 43,833 in 1979 and is now regarded not as a town but as an area or suburb of Dublin (Roche 1982: 330). To give some indication of the problems facing the local authorities, in the parish of West Tallaght 72.2 per cent of the population are under the age of ten and in Tallaght as a whole the unemployment rate is 54 per cent with only 10 per cent of the population bothering to vote. This illustrates the great differences there are between the local authorities in the rural areas of Ireland and those in the area of Dublin where nowadays a third of the population lives. This increase in the population of Dublin has brought to a head the traditional problem of all local government systems of how to link a town with its hinterland, and while it is not a new problem it does seem to be causing difficulties in Ireland at the moment.

Second, the quest for administrative efficiency has led not just to larger units but to a stranglehold of central government over local authorities, so that in many ways local government is not much more than the administration of services determined and controlled by the centre. In addition the system of managers has been seen by many as the emasculation of the role of councillors and a lessening of the principle of local democracy. However, the establishment of the manager system showed the traditional distrust of the politician, and the lack of outcry at the postponement of local elections in 1965 and 1970 perhaps strengthens the claim that the Irish value efficiency more than local democracy. One of the other results of tight control from the centre is that local government has no ability to adjust to new demands and thus local initiative is stifled and neutralised.

At the heart of all the debates about structures and systems is the attempt to satisfy two competing demands, one the demand for democratic representation and the other the demand for efficient dispensing of services. This is a debate that has been carried on in most countries and in Ireland it has led to the enunciation of three main views:

1 The notion that local authorities should merely be the executive agencies of central government and that this represents the logical extension of the present system. This view is represented by the Devlin Report (1969).

2 The picture presented in *More Local Government*, which suggests that local government should be government in a local context, involving a measure of devolution from the centre and thus an adherence to the principle of subsidiarity: that is, that the state should not take over the duties and powers that should be handled by the lower authorities (IPA 1971).

3 The view expressed by the Department of the Environment, that the responsibilities of the local authorities should be narrowed down to a coherent set of functions that could be carried out without excessive reliance on the Exchequer.

Which view will win remains problematical, but the chances for change seem poor. There is little leadership from the top and the close relationship between central and local representatives seems to inhibit any move to reform. As T.J. Barrington says:

> Local government is like any other historical ruin, something that we are perhaps reluctant to see removed wholly, but which we are prepared to see moulder away.

(Barrington 1980)

BIBLIOGRAPHY

Alexander, A. (1979) 'Local government in Ireland', *Administration* 27(5), 3–27.

Barrington, T.J. (1980) *The Irish Administrative System*, Dublin, Institute of Public Administration.

Bax, M. (1976) *Harpstrings and Confessions: Machine-style Politics in the Irish Republic*, Assen and Amsterdam, Van Gorcum.

Chubb, B. (1970) *The Government and Politics of Ireland* (1st edn), Oxford, Oxford University Press.

Chubb, B. (1982) *The Government and Politics of Ireland* (2nd edn), London, Longman.

Chubb, B. (1983) *A Source Book of Irish Government*, Dublin, Institute of Public Administration.

Collins, N. and McCann, F. (1989) *Irish Politics Today*, Manchester, Manchester University Press.

de Buitleir, D. (1974) *Problems of Irish Local Finance*, Dublin, Institute of Public Administration.

Devlin Report (1969) *Report of the Public Services Organisation Review Group 1966–1969*, Dublin, Stationery Office.

Farrell, B. (1971) 'Dáil Deputies: The 1969 Generation', *Economic and Social Review* 2(3).

Gibbon, P. and Higgins, M.D. (1974) 'Patronage, tradition and modernisation. The case of the Irish "Gombeenman" ', *Economic and Social Review* 6(1), 27–44.

Institute of Public Administration (1971) *More Local Government: A Programme for Development*, Dublin, Institute of Public Administration.

Komito, L. (1984) 'Irish Clientelism: a reappraisal', *Economic and Social Review* 15(3), 35–59.

Mills, M. (1985) 'The Office of Ombudsman'. Press release by the Ombudsman's Office, Dublin, 10 May.

Raven, J., Whelan, C.T., Pfretzschner, P.A. and Borock, D.M. (1976) *Political Culture in Ireland: The Views of Two Generations*, Dublin, Institute of Public Administration.

Roche, D. (1982) *Local Government in Ireland* (2nd edn), Dublin, Institute of Public Administration.

Sacks, P.M. (1976) *The Donegal Mafia: An Irish Political Machine*, New Haven, Conn., and London, Yale University Press.

Tierney, M. (1982) *The Parish Pump*, Dublin, Able Press.

Zimmerman, J.F. (1972) 'Council-Manager Government in Ireland', *Comparative Local Government* 2, 61–9.

Chapter 4

France

M.C. Hunt and J.A. Chandler

The origins of the French local government structure are found by many observers in the reforms initiated by Napoleon Bonaparte between 1799 and 1815. So entrenched are these creations that some parts of their structure, such as the commune, have remained almost unchanged since their foundation despite the major upheavals in the nature of French government that have occurred since the beginning of the nineteenth century. This is, perhaps, not suprising. A culture of centralisation pre-dates the Revolution and owes its origin to the absolute power exercised by the monarchy. Napoleon did not devise a brand new structure but a system that streamlined existing practices, reconciling central control with local independence which had evolved during centuries of monarchy.

THE POLITICAL SETTING

Although many of the structures of the French state have changed between the First and Fifth Republics, the underlying culture of the administrative system remains essentially the same. Successive attempts at reform either by right- or left-wing parties have operated within a broad consensus about the nature of the nation-state. Article 20 of the Constitution specifically lays down that it shall be the government which decides and directs the policy of the nation. Anglo-Saxon notions of pluralism and limitations on executive power are not a traditional element of French political culture. There is an understanding that France is a centralised nation in which local institutions of government are subordinate to the centre. However, this pervasive impression of a totalitarian democracy is, at least as regards centralisation, not borne out by reality.

For modern students of French government the particular importance of the 1958 Constititution lies in the balance that it seeks to establish between strong executive dominance and democratic control. In essence the Constitution reflects a movement away from the parliamentary form of government characteristic of the Third and Fourth Republics, which had culminated in the political instability of the late 1950s. In its place is a political system with the balance of power biased in favour of the executive and, specifically, the President, who is elected every seven years by the nation's voters.

The President has the power to choose the Prime Minister, and can dissolve the Assembly, the French Parliament, provided he or she has not done so within the preceding twelve months. The power of Parliament is constitutionally limited to certain areas of policy making, leaving substantive elements of decision making to the President, especially foreign policy, emergency actions and administrative controls. Successive incumbents of the most powerful office under the state have generously interpreted these rules in their favour. The Assembly's power to supervise government activities is also constrained by limitations on the length of its sessions and on its formal opportunities to censure the government for its policies. Nonetheless, the President is not an autocrat. Most actions of the President must be countersigned by the Prime Minister if they are to be legally effective, and the Prime Minister, although selected by the President, cannot remain in office if the lower house of the Assembly, the Chamber of Deputies, refuses to ratify his or her initial selection or passes a vote of censure against him or her. The President must, therefore, have support among the Deputies in order to rule through the Prime Minister.

In practice, for most of the Fifth Republic the President has been the effective leader of the party or coalition of parties that have enjoyed a majority within the Chamber of Deputies. In such circumstances the power of the President, rather like that of the British Prime Minister, is primarily limited by his or her ability to retain the support of senior party leaders. However, from 1981 to 1987 the socialist President François Mitterand faced an Assembly with a majority of right-wing deputies and was thus obliged to select the Gaullist leader Jacques Chirac as his Prime Minister and resign to him the direction of domestic and, to a lesser extent, foreign policy. Although apparently dominated by a President, party cohesion ensures that the Fifth Republic is governed more on the lines of European parliamentary structures than that of the United States.

It is important to the understanding of French local government to stress that the French Parliament is far from being the wholly powerless organisation that is sometimes depicted in older textbooks. Parliament is principally composed of two chambers, the Assembly and the Senate. The Assembly is the most powerful and is elected currently by proportional representation. Its deliberations are checked by the Senate, which is elected indirectly from major public organisations in France but is principally composed of local government representatives. Local government is also strongly represented in the Assembly, with a majority of Deputies serving as mayors of communes. The French Parliament thus enfolds a very strong corporate interest in local government at the heart of the centralised decision making process.

THE LEGAL STATUS OF LOCAL GOVERNMNENT

The conventional concepts employed to analyse British local government are not immediately applicable to an understanding of the French system. In particular, the British understanding of local self-government with an elected council having responsibilty for the exercise of major functions within a fairly large geographical area is not easily transferable to France, where both central and local government are creatures of the state and, in that sense, local governments are not dependent upon the the state for their status and powers but can claim an independent existence of their own. At the same time, the functions of government are not provided by either local authorities or central government as in Britain, but in large part by deconcentrated offices of the central administration operating principally at the level of the department to form a hierarchy whose apex is in Paris. Through these offices, therefore, the political and administrative rulers of France are directly involved in, and able to control, many of those services normally regarded as 'local' in Britain.

A counterbalance to this centralisation is provided by the activities of the mayor and communal councils, the departmental councils and also by organisations such as the Economic and Social Committee of the Regions. Representation also occurs more importantly through the actions of deputies and senators in the National Assembly, many of whom will have strong administrative ties with the area they represent. Through these actors, the interests of the locality are represented in a way that is the exception rather than the norm in Britain, where Parliamentary constituencies for many MPs are simply a means of getting to Westminster, rather than an important link with local areas. In France these links, which safeguard and continue the unity of the state and the interests of quite small areas of the country, are an integral part of the decision making apparatus of the state. French public administration cannot, therefore, operate effectively unless it accommodates the political demands of localities.

THE STRUCTURE OF LOCAL GOVERNMENT

On a macro-organisational level France is divided for local government purposes into five tiers: regions, of which there are 22; departments (96); arrondisements (320); cantons (3,350); communes (about 36,000). Of these the arrondisement and the canton play only a limited role in government, the former serving as a geographical area for a sub-prefecture and perhaps for a road engineer, while the latter may serve as a police division but is principally an electoral area.

Communes

Communes remain the key to local government in France, having undergone only limited reform since their inception in the Napoleonic era. They are an organic element in the local government structure, having evolved over centuries around populations and areas of very varied identities. In contrast, the departments and regions are creations of central government. A commune may, therefore, be anything from a hamlet or a small village to a city the size of Marseilles or Bordeaux. From time to time it has been proposed that the small communes are merged for the sake of efficient government. However, attempts to amalgamate the smallest communes by creating joint syndicates have met with strong local opposition. Reform proposals have had limited success and left France with about 36,000 communes, of which the majority have less than 2,000 inhabitants.

For those who value efficient management above community loyalty, reform is of particular importance given the limited resources enjoyed by the communes and the varied functions that they may be required to perform. These include the construction and maintenance of minor roads, refuse disposal, and, in towns, the construction and upkeep of schools. However, it is in the provision of discretionary services that the differences between the larger communes and their rural counterparts is most keenly felt. Many towns provide libraries, theatres, public transport and tourist offices, but the smaller communes find it impossible to fulfil these functions and, indeed, may only be able to provide mandatory services by collaborating with other communes.

Departments

These form the second tier of the administrative structure initiated by Napoleon and provide the principal point at which centralised and decentralised services come together. The powers of the department as an entity in itself are limited and comprise principally the building of some roads, personal social services and the provision of tourist facilities. However, the key official in the department, the prefect, is the principal representative of centralised services, whose role is complemented by the departmental council, which comprises representatives from each of the cantons. In practical terms councils are less important than their title might suggest, meeting only for about six weeks in any year. Many of the functions of the council are delegated to the departmental commission, in effect a small executive, which normally meets monthly.

Up to the important local government reforms of 1981–3, despite the presence of an elected council, the most powerful individual within the department appeared to be the prefect. This key official in Napoleonic systems of local government is a civil servant appointed by the government, who is responsible to the Ministry of the Interior. The legal powers of prefects prior to 1982 appear to be immense. They prepared the agenda for the general council of the department and executed its policies. Communes had to offer their budget to the prefect for approval and many of their decisions could be declared void by the august presence in the prefecture. In practical terms prefects were able to exercise a high degree of personal autonomy, not least in their presentation of the agenda for council meetings, their preparation of the annual budget and their responsibility as an executive officer for the council's decisions. These, together with their state functions, ensured a degree of power for which there is no comparable British equivalent. The reforms of the early 1980s have, however, much decreased the formal powers of the prefect by giving executive control to the chair of the departmental council. The prefect was also renamed the commissioner of the Republic, but popular usage decreed a return to the title of prefect a few years later.

One of the major roles of departmental councillors is to represent the needs of their area to the prefect. Of particular significance are the functions performed by the departments for the communes. These tend to be carried out on an individualised basis by the separate services of the department, and often involve acting as a form of missionary in advising the commune on practical projects that the commune would like to develop but which it lacks both the technical knowledge and finances to implement. Individual departmental officers are, of course, able to provide advice because of their professional knowledge, and may also be able to assist in obtaining grants for projects through their administrative and political contacts in the Ministry. An important aspect of the unitary state is not, as it is sometimes seen in Britain, the imposition of additional burdens by the centre on the locality, but, more frequently, an attempt made by ministry officials to meet with representatives of the localities to help them understand their needs and, where possible, to help in the provision of those needs. This is particularly important in the rural communes, which, in most cases, lack the resources to employ technically qualified staff themselves. In this way the disparities between urban and rural areas might be minimised.

Regions

Regions are the most recent creation in the structure of local government, dating from a decree of 1964. This marked the consolidation of previous piecemeal attempts at reform by recognising the region in formal terms and by creating the regional 'super' prefect to co-ordinate this area, together with the regional mission, conference and council. Under this reform the prefect assumed responsibility for land and economic planning in the region. The decree of 1964 also states that the prefect has the function of stimulating:

> the activities of departmental prefects within his region as well as the administrative heads of field services and the chairmen or directors of public companies or mixed economy enterprises which may embrace several departments within the area and which do not have a national character.

It is difficult to be precise about the role of the regional prefects, although clearly they form a crucial link between the department and the planning commissariat. The person appointed to these duties is invariably a departmental prefect who becomes *primus inter pares* in relation to colleagues. In practice, as Ridley and Blondel (1969) observe, the role is much more open than simply being a mediator. The 1964 decree points out that the regional prefect may be invested with special powers by decree of the Conseil D'Etat.

Further reforms to the regional structure were completed by President Pompidou in 1972 and 1973. These transposed the regions into *Etablissements Publics* with the single task of carrying forward the economic and social development of the region. This was to be achieved primarily by carrying out studies to establish the economic requirements of the region, and to forward proposals for public investment policy in the area. The regional governments could then pursue these policies by generating financial support for public works projects and by undertaking projects of regional interest in conjunction with appropriate local authorities.

Although the reforms of 1972 made the regional prefect the executive officer for the region, this did not signify that the region had any real authority. The reforms were more a gesture to the idea of regionalism than a determined delegation of power, that did not constitute a means of devolving power to sub-national interests rather than providing a means of facilitating economic development. The areas did not, therefore, bear much relationship to nationalist interests in France. Only a limited amount of power was delegated to the regions themselves and they were given limited financial resources. The exact functions of the regions were not clearly defined, leaving their prefects unsure about their powers and status, while the relationship between the regional council and the economic and social committee was unclear to the extent that the powers and responsibilities of each were not adequately defined.

Inevitably, therefore, few citizens have taken an interest in the regions. Most members of the public are unable to relate to them in a geographical and cultural sense, and find that the effect of these remote institutions on daily life is marginal. The principal organs of government remain the national government in Paris, the departments and the communes. Nonetheless, the growing use of the regional prefect as a mediator between the departments and Paris on an increasing range of subjects perhaps indicates a longer term and more extensive role for the French institution. The continuing expansion of the European Community also provides an enhanced role for the region, since the Commission prefers to use such units as the base for economic planning rather than national states.

FINANCE

While central governments in many liberal democracies are progressively binding local finances to the centre, there has been a trend in France towards loosening central fiscal control. Central distrust of local expenditure was such that, although there was some measure of local determination of tax levels, it was always central government that collected and distributed local taxation. The means of raising funds were, moreover, highly complex and subject to frequent piecemeal change.

In 1984 communes spent some 293 billion francs and departments accounted for 115 billion. This amounts to over 30 per cent of public expenditure. Almost half of the revenue spent by local authorities derives from taxes and half from grants, although relatively smaller sums are obtained through charges for services.

Funding revenue spending

Levies on property have always been an important source of local revenue through direct taxation. These taxes are imposed on domestic property, equivalent to the British rates or United States property tax, and also on land and non-domestic property. French communes also raise funds through property taxes, but this does not form such a dominant element of local fund raising as in Anglo-Saxon countries. A more important source of direct taxation is a levy on businesses based on the worth of an enterprise assessed in terms of its property, turnover and employment costs. Initially termed the *patente* it was restructured in 1976 as the *taxe professionelle* to assess the property and payroll of a firm and to raise approximately half of local tax revenues. The tax has, not suprisingly, been unpopular with industry and subject to frequent changes in the form of its assessment. In particular, it is seen as detrimental to job creation and, therefore, an encouragement to increase unemployment.

In the past a major source of local revenue was the *taxe locale*, an indirect sales tax levied on retail sales and on services such as restaurants and hotels. The sales tax was generally unpopular since it provided a relatively low tax base in village or suburban areas with a limited number of retail outlets. Councils were thus forced to increase direct taxes, particularly those on land and property, which had the effect of discouraging the very retail traders that the area might need in order to increase its indirect tax revenue. With the development of the EC, local taxes on sales became illegal and, to widespread satisfaction, the tax was abolished in 1966. Loss of income from this source was replaced by an agreed system of sharing revenues accruing from specific central taxes. The principal tax used to facilitate this is levied on businesses through assessment of their employees.

In addition, some areas can impose a local urbanisation tax. Essentially a development tax, it is levied by the commune, which grants a construction permit. It is normally fixed at about 1 per cent of the value of the whole complex being developed. A subsequent related tax, introduced in 1976, adds a fine on over-construction by a contractor.

Until the 1980s French local authorities had almost no powers to determine how much they could raise through local taxation. The reforms to local government have slightly amended this restraint and permitted some discretion regarding the amount of revenue to be raised from the various tax sources. However, it is a complex procedure to use this power and it is only likely to be practised by the larger, more professional authorities.

In 1979 the government of Giscard d'Estaing established a block grant, the *Dotation Globale de Fonctionnement*, to cover some of the revenue costs of local governments. The transfer of further functions to local government has also been supported by a subsidy in the form of a block grant representing a percentage cost of the services, the *Dotation Globale de Décentralisation* (Keating and Hainsworth 1986).

Funding capital spending

Grants for capital expediture traditionally came from the government in the form of subsidies for local expenditure on welfare and public works. These were given at varying rates, depending on government assessments of the particular project being undertaken. The grant was often awarded only for work that met conditions laid down by central government and served as a further means of ensuring central control. Since the 1970s, however, efforts have been made to give local governments greater freedom over their investment and revenue policy through the development of a number of block grants.

A major new subsidy for capital expenditure, particularly for departments, is the *Dotation Globale d'Equipement* which progressively replaces specific grants by block grants, which give local authorities much greater discretion over its use. This measure added to a smaller tax implemented in 1976 as compensation for payment of VAT on building work. Not all Ministeries have been happy with this orgy of independence and so at times they have continued to promote capital developments through more tied specific grants (Keating and Hainsworth 1986: 85). Capital spending is also funded in part by loans, which accounts for more than one-third of expenditure in this area. Most loans are made by public bodies and are subject to stringent controls from the Ministry of Finance.

Problems of finance

In spite of the recent attempts at reform, some of the traditional problems of the local financial system remain unresolved. One of these obviously is the degree of control exercised by the government both over budgets and, less directly, over the amounts of money that might be raised to fund local activities. Although a limited ability to decide their own rates on some trades eases this control slightly, centralist pressures still remain extremely strong.

A second problem is the variation in the size of the communes and their diverse requirements and expectations. Too proud to wish to amalgamate, yet in many cases too small to operate many of their own services, they remain inevitably dependent on government support, which frequently requires joint arrangements with other communes. This problem may in part be alleviated by the development of local controls over finance.

A third problem, not unknown in Britain, is the tendency of central government to place additional burdens on local units without due regard to their financial ability to carry out these tasks. Even without that, the increasing expectations of the public, together with developments in services, has put severe pressures on the resources that local authorities are able to command. A particular problem has been the pressure created by urbanisation, which has frequently resulted in loans being sought from outside agencies. So rapidly have these loans grown, and so extensive have they become, that some of the loans now being taken out are being used to repay previous loans rather than to indulge in further expansion. Clearly the problems caused by inadequate internal funding may remain with local authorities for some time to come.

Nonetheless, there are hopeful signs of more liberalising trends in local government finance. In particular, the use since 1970 of planning contracts has indicated a desire not only to fund local authority development nationally but also to defer to local initiative. Under the scheme both the government and the local authority agree to a contract which establishes joint means of financing a series of projects. Apart from the certainty provided by such a scheme, the contracts allow for more comprehensive and less ad hoc developments by authorities. The limited provision that local authorities might vary their own tax rates is further evidence of this liberalising trend.

INTERNAL STRUCTURES

Communes

Decision-making powers within a commune are vested in a council which is popularly elected every six years. The size of the council will vary from 9 to 49 members depending on the population served by the commune. Given that there are over 35,000 communes, there are some 460,000 municipal councillors who compose in their own right a significant interest group defending local powers (Ashford 1982: 21). The political composition of the council is important in determining the ideological direction of the commune but its members are generally more concerned with supporting or criticising the policies enacted by their leader, the mayor, than participating in details of administration.

The mayor is elected by the municipal council following each council election. The office is much more important than its British counterpart. On election the mayor becomes far more than simply the principal politician of the council; he or she is also an agent and representative of the national state. As agent of the state the mayor ensures the execution of the laws and directives emanating from Paris, acts as official registrar of births, deaths and marriages and also has responsibility for collecting some official statistics on behalf of the government. As principal executant of the wishes of the commune the mayor must seek to establish and represent the 'general view' of the community in its dealings with the departmental prefect and with central government. His or her standing is enhanced by the generally subservient position adopted by the council of the commune, who are not usually able to exercise detailed control over the mayor's administrative decisions and are normally content to follow his or her leadership. This pre-eminent status is countered by the expectation that the mayor will act for the community as a whole and will attempt to achieve a consensus of opinion in the community before undertaking any major steps on its behalf. Wright describes the mayor as the

> gentle autocrat of the commune, its principal arbitration officer, its father confessor and the guardian of its interests. . . . He is judged largely by his ability to keep peace in the commune . . . and also by his capacity to intervene for his citizens with the prefectorial authorities.
>
> (Wright 1989: 302)

The department and the prefectorial system

Historically the department was designed as an arm of central government and not, like the commune, as a reflection of community interest. Thus, when created it was firmly controlled by its centrally appointed chief executive, the prefect. The Third Republic established within each department an elected general council which had the duty to advise the prefect, who called its meetings, set its agenda, and implemented its decisions. The council, however, became gradually more important than its subordinate legal role suggests. It tended to attract the attention of local notables who exerted power not so much from their membership of the council as from their general personal influence in other political spheres. In practice, therefore, prefects took care not to offend the council and, if they became too opposed to its more influential members, were often obliged to transfer to another department.

The 1982 reforms have changed the relationship by removing the prefect's powers as the principal member and chairman of the council. This role is now taken by a president, elected, rather like the mayor of the commune, from among the councillors. The president is, therefore, likely to assume a key role in departmental policy, somewhat akin to that of a mayor, although s/he may have to be careful not to alienate fellow notables and to cultivate a good working relationship with the prefect.

Even though it has recently been downgraded in importance, the office of prefect retains great significance at departmental level. The prefectorial system established by Napoleon represents the summit of his attempts to organise an efficient and effective state supervised from the centre. The task of prefect is still, formally, to act as a representative of the state in the department and, at the same time, to represent the government by co-ordinating the policies and activities of not only the Ministry of the Interior but also most of the other ministeries operating in his or her area. The principal exceptions are the Ministries of Justice, Labour and Education. Such demanding, complex and sometimes contradictory set of tasks requires the services of the ablest graduates from the élite civil service training school, the ENA.

Ridley and Blondel (1969: 93) summarised the principal tasks of the prefect as:

1 Acting as representative of the state on formal occasions.
2 Acting as the representative of the government in the department as well as being the representative of the Ministry of the Interior. In other words the prefect is responsible for the supervision and co-ordination of all government activities within the department. This involves political as well as normally administrative functions.
3 Representing of the Ministry of the Interior, and so responsible for public order, including functions such as public safety and public health as well as the police and security services.
4 Being ultimately responsible for all of the political problems of the area. (This is a 'political commissar' role. It describes the prefect as being rather more than an administrative arm of government, who may be involved in major industrial disputes or crises and emergencies within the department. In this sense the responsibilities go beyond any formal functions that have been handed down by statute.)

The 1982 reforms did not in practice curtail the prefect's authority as much as it may seem. The prefect before 1982 was much less of an autocrat of government decrees than these roles suggest. S/he still often acts as a mediator between the centre and the periphery, reconciling the claims and demands of each upon the other. At the same time s/he must recognise the demands made by the various interest groups and must, in order to survive, be able to secure a consensus for policies s/he decides to pursue. Although appointed by the state, s/he cannot be seen simply as its agent but must harmonise the wishes of the centre with those of powerful politicians located in individual localities.

Within the department itself there are various problems to be faced by the prefect. Firstly, there is the obvious difficulty of co-ordinating the work of officials in different departments, who may not wish to relate their own limited objectives to the wider objectives of the department as perceived by the prefect. The control by specialist officials of information concerning the activities of their department may act as an effective brake on the prefect's own attempts at overall co-ordination.

The region

The structure of regional government has, since the 1982 reforms, resembled that of the departments. An elected council determines policy for the region and is chaired by a president elected by the council. The prefect has the more subordinate role of serving as chief executive to the council and as a mediator between the central government and the regional politicians. Prior to 1982 there was only an advisory regional council and the prefect was the principal initiator of policy.

In practice the 1982 reforms underwrote existing practice. Even before 1982 the super-prefect had to pay close attention to the demands of local notables, who, at the level of the region, were normally powerful politicians with strong leverage in central government. The system of a more powerful council electing its president has ratified the power of the notable and to some extent promoted greater concentration of power in the hands of a single powerful politician, who may have less need to share any opinions with other regional notables, especially those of differing parties.

PERSONNEL, RECRUITMENT AND TRAINING

The role and status of officials at the local level reflects the fusion of centrally and locally determined services. Officials in the communes, although nominally part of a nationwide local government service, are recruited and appointed locally. Movement between communes is unusual and thus career prospects in anything other than the larger communes tend to be rather limited. The situation in the departments and regions is somewhat different. All officials are members of the national civil service although, as in Britain, the process of appointment and training is different for junior and senior grades. A more important distinction is to be made between those officials who work in an administrative capacity in the prefecture and those who are members of one of the technical services, principally industry, agriculture, education, welfare, public works and transport.

Recruits to the highest departmental administrative posts such as prefect and sub-prefect will be chosen from among the ablest graduates of the universities who, after a period of postgraduate training in institutions such as the *Ecole de Sciences Politiques*, move on to the prestigious *Ecole National d'Administration* (ENA) for a course of instruction lasting approximately two and a half years. The course includes practical experience, acquired while on secondment, often to a prefecture. The final examinations classify students in order of merit. This is of especial importance in determining future careers, since it allows the ablest students to make their choice of jobs from one of the most prestigious *corps*, the self-regulatory professional groups which vertically divide the French Civil Service. These include the prefectorial corps. The value of attendance at the ENA is enormous but of equal importance is the assimilation of a shared culture, which for this élite group makes easier the task of governing the country and acts as a barrier to those without the benefit of such privileged education.

Entrants to the technical services attend the *Ecole Polytechnique* in Paris. From here they move on to one of the specialised postgraduate schools pertinent to their *corps* and thence to a post in a ministry, which may entail being based in Paris or in a locality, or to some other public or private organisation.

Attendance at either the ENA or *Ecole Polytechnique* is theoretically open to anyone, although, inevitably perhaps, it is the middle class who dominate. The benefits and prestige conferred by such an education are immense. The reputation of the schools ensures their graduates have access to important posts within both the public and the private sector, and for many people a spell in both sectors is an accepted and understood means of developing a political career.

Membership of one of the *Grand Corps* is greatly prized. These associations operate alongside specific ministries and provide its most important personnel. Their particular strength lies in the loyalty engendered among members of the *corps*, which can lead to protracted and unnecessary disputes between members of different groups which they often abandon only when there is a common threat from outside the system. These disputes often extend to the departmental or regional level when policies are being co-ordinated between a number of ministries. It means that members of the *corps* in Paris will support a fellow member in the province. A further problem of the *corps* is their innate conservatism.

This is particularly evident in the technical *corps* whose members, although well trained for a particular and specialised profession, tend to lack knowledge or experience of management. Thus, they find difficulty in adjusting to the demands of modern public sector practice. Although some of the recent entrants to the *corps* have undertaken short management courses, the potential difficulties here are far from resolved. The nature of the *corps* and the need to protect their own professional boundaries militates against them.

INTER-GOVERNMENTAL RELATIONS

The key to understanding the nature of French local government lies in an appreciation of informal patron–client relationships that parallel the superficially highly centralised formal system. The presence of this informal arrangement may be sensed by the apparent paradox that, although the French local government system is supposed to be centralised, more than 80 per cent of the National Assembly deputies hold an office in local government (Wright 1989: 321); in Britain, where local government is supposed to have greater discretion, only a handful of MPs are local councillors.

A superficial legal explanation of French local government suggests that, at least up to the 1982 reforms, the prefect dominated departmental policy making and could, through the principle of *tutelle*, enforce central directives on the communes. In reality even the policies of central government are as much directed by local interests as local policies are directed by the centre. Dupuy (1985: 80) describes central–local relations in France as operating 'through a network of informal relationships between a certain number of state administrative services and local interests, based on an interdependence of the roles played by their leaders'.

The crucial factor sustaining these links is the potential power of the centre. Because, legally, so many aspects of local government can be controlled through a network of officials directed by the Ministry of the Interior, it is of value for local politicians to be represented in the centre in order to influence central decision making in favour of their locality. As a Deputy or Senator a politician with local interests can threaten or cajole ministers and senior civil servants to favour his or her parochial demands. Politicians also gain considerable local electoral support through their ability to bring resources from the centre to the locality. Hence a patron–client arrangement lies at the heart of French local government. Local notables gain and keep national office as a consequence of their ability to use their influence at the centre on behalf of their locality. The most successful patron secures not only his or her election but that of fellow travelling lieutenants from the area.

Politicians not only held jointly the offices of mayor and Deputy (or Senator). The most powerful political figures amassed a powerful array of posts including positions in departmental and regional government and often in ad hoc agencies. The local notable also is a dominant figure in the policy making committees of his or her political party. The obvious difficulties in attending to a large number of offices through this tendency, referred to as the *cumul des mandats*, led in 1985 to legislation restricting individuals to holding only two elective offices. The local notables, however, still retain power in many organisations through their control over factions in their political party.

Among the most outstanding examples of politicians at the apex of these central–local patron–client networks are Chaban Delmas, the long-standing mayor of Bordeaux, who is also a leading Gaullist politician who has held the post of Prime Minister. Jacques Chirac was simultaneously Prime Minister and mayor of Paris. The architect of the 1982 reforms, the Socialist Party Minister of the Interior, Gaston Defferre, was at the same time the long-standing mayor of Marseilles.

As a consequence of this system it is impossible for a prefect to impose policies on a commune without risking an immediate appeal to the mayor, who may well be a member of the Assembly capable of creating serious difficulties for the adventurous prefect through contacts with superiors in Paris, or through raising awkward questions in the Assembly. Even in small communes the mayor, although unlikely to be a Deputy, will often be close to, and even a client of, the Deputy for the constituency.

The prefect, even before the 1982 reforms, was, therefore, never a dictator or simple agent of central government. Much of his or her task was as mediator between the interests of central government and local demands as articulated by leading local 'notables'. In larger towns and cities this often took the form of the prefect acting as a channel for facilitating change, while in the many smaller communes the prefectorial office was regarded as a source for obtaining technical help or expertise that was beyond the resources of a small community.

PARTIES AND PRESSURE GROUPS

The image so far depicted suggests a central–local arrangement in France built on mediation and facilitation of local demands through negotiation between united peripheral interests and the central government in Paris. France is, however, like all European nations, strongly divided on ideological lines and the central–local nexus is shaped by such conflict. The principal ideological division both at national and city government level is between right and left. Since the inception of the Fifth Republic there has been a gradual consolidation of left-wing influence within the Socialist Party to the detriment of the once larger Communist Party. The right, formed into a cohesive unit in the early 1960s as a support for General de Gaulle, has now fractionated into two groups led respectively by Giscard d'Estaing and the more Thatcherite mayor of Paris and ex-Prime Minister, Jacques Chirac. The once powerful group of centre parties has declined to an almost insignificant rump.

At the local level, elections in most larger cities are, at least superficially, fought along party lines. There are some cities such as Grenoble in which the balance between right and left is evenly weighted and contests are genuine struggles over the party political stance of the local council. Most cities, however, are more obviously balanced firmly towards the right or left and usually in the direction of the left given their more industrial character. Thus, it would be remarkable if cities such as Marseilles, Lille or Amiens fell to the right. There are, nevertheless, some major cities such as Bourdeaux or Lyon that have continually returned right-wing councils.

Within the cities with a pronounced left- or right-wing bias, local elections may still be sternly fought contests, ostensibly between on the left Communist and Socialist parties and on the right followers of Giscard or Chirac. However, these contests may also have an added dimension of local rivalry between pretenders to major political influence within the cities, as different patron–client groups within a dominant party seek to gain political control over the area. A major sensation was created in the run up to the 1989 municipal elections over the fierce contest within the Socialist Party to control Marseilles. The city had for many years been led by Gaston Defferre, but the ageing leader, who died in 1988, had been facing a challenge from a younger rival. The subsequent election was a bitter contest between supporters of the Defferre faction and the supporters of the new pretender. Such internecine strife on occasion leads but to the ruination of a Party's hopes in that area. For some years Grenoble returned a centre right council as a consequence of divisions among the more numerous left.

Although party strife may be very intense, there are, nevertheless, pressures in France that can cut across party loyalty and create effective working relationships between parties. This is particularly the case in inter-government relations since party division does not always transcend local loyalties. Competing parties within a community may often join together to pressure the centre for greater resources. The *Association des*

Maires de France is a highly effective interest group despite its multi-party composition. In central government, as is argued above, ministers recognise and defer to the local interests and the role of deputies and senators over and above party interest.

Pressure groups

While political parties form a significant element in French local politics, pressure groups are comparatively much less important organisations. Representative sectional groups are viewed with suspicion as vested interest intruding on the established communal consensus. The interest group is, therefore, as much subject to demands that it should tailor its needs to that of the community as that the community should adapt to its needs. Thus, although sectional interests such as chambers of commerce, trade or farming unions are well established, they are rarely major components of the policy making process. They are expected rather to dovetail their values with that of the national government.

Although interests groups are not, in general, particularly influential in France, those groups which have by their structure a foothold in the political system may through corporate links wield considerable power. The representative bodies of local authorities are by this means able to have considerable powers to shape the local government system. Foremost among these groups is the *Association des Maires de France* representing the communes, which is paralleled by similar bodies representing the presidents of regional and departmental councils. Their influence derives from an ability to bury party differences and because their members often wield great influence through their personal position within the centre of the political system as members of government, deputies or senators.

ISSUES AND PROBLEMS

Local government in France has for many years faced demands for modernisation but has proved highly resistant to pressure for change. The 1981–3 decentralisation reforms were remarkable not so much for the scale of change but for the fact that there was any change at all. In comparison with the root-and-branch restructuring of British local government in the 1970s and the subsequent centralisation of the 1980s the French reforms are small beer. French resistance to change, in part, represents the entrenched power of notables but is also a reflection of major divisions among political élites over what direction any change should take.

On one hand it can be claimed that the system of communes is wholly outmoded for a modern developed industrial society. Many small units of government are unable to muster the resources to make a serious impact on the government of their areas and are largely reliant on financial and technical help from the department. However, those resisting change in this area can claim that the structure of French local government encapsulates local values and traditions in a manner wholly absent from Britain. The system is flexible, allowing large conurbations to be governed as a unit, while retaining for small rural villages a sense of political identity. Cooperative working agreements between small communes ensure viable provision of local services in rural areas. Efficiency can be gained without dispensing with a sense of local community. Given the effective informal links between centre, department and commune, efficiency can still be maintained in practice.

The informality that lies at the heart of central–local relations also gives rise to complaints that there is a lack of clear definition between the functions of each tier in the system. It is by no means as easy as in Britain to read off from legislation the exact function and powers of competence of a department as opposed to a region. This criticism is, however, not so serious in practice as it appears. Provided an understanding of local influence and competence is known and accepted in the locality it matters little if it appears an unintelligible relationship at the centre.

A more pertinent critique of the French system is that, for all its localism and flexibility of practice, the structure is not particularly democratic. While it allows citizens access to the decision making system so that élites may circulate, it places power largely in the hands of small local élites who govern their territories through both local and national influence as, in some cases, personal fiefdoms. It is a system much more based on paternal central direction, and hence far less open to interest group involvement or popular pressure. The local interest may be that of the local notable who may not necessarily encapsulate the popular general will.

BIBLIOGRAPHY

Ashford, D.E. (1982) *British Dogmatism and French Pragmatism*, London, Allen and Unwin.

Dupuy, F. (1985) 'The politico-administrative system of the department in France', in Y. Meny and V. Wright (eds), *Centre–Periphery Relations in Western Europe*, London, Allen and Unwin.

Hayward, J.E.S. (1983) *Governing France: The One and Indivisible Republic* (2nd edn), London, Weidenfeld and Nicolson.

Keating, M. and Hainsworth, P. (1986) *Decentralisation and Change in Contemporary France*, Aldershot, Gower.

Machin, H. (1977) *The Prefect in French Public Administration*, London, Croom Helm.

Ridley, F. and Blondel, J. (1969) *Public Administration in France* (2nd edn), London, Routledge and Kegan Paul.

Wright, V. (1989) *The Government and Politics of France* (3rd edn), London, Unwin Hyman.

Chapter 5

Italy

R.E. Spence

In many ways Italy is a country of enormous contrasts and contradictions. From a climatic point of view the regions of northern Italy have more in common with the continent of Europe than regions such as Sicily or Calabria in the south, which are closer to North Africa. Similarly, the social life of a city such as Milan more closely resembles that of Zurich than Naples or Palermo, which could almost be on another continent. The linguistic differences which were so important in the past have been removed by the spread of mass education and culture, though even now there are those who consider Italian almost as a second language.

Similar contradictions can be found in economic and political spheres. The economic triangle based upon the northern cities of Turin, Milan and Genoa was the home of the industrial revolution in Italy. It has been, for most of the twentieth century, part of the wider European industrialised world of the north. Many regions of the south, on the other hand, are still predominantly agrarian and practise farming methods which in some areas have not changed at all since the last century. The uneven development between north and south has led to mass internal migration, resulting in overcrowding in the cities of the centre and north and depopulation in many areas of the south. Despite massive investment of both public and private capital, the south still lags a long way behind the north and the gap does not seem to be narrowing.

On the political front, the present system of government is based upon the constitution which came into effect in 1948. The constitution is divided into two: the first deals with the rights and duties of the ordinary citizen, the second with the establishment of the legal, political and administrative organs of the state. More cynical observers suggest that the real split is between those parts of the constitution which deal with concrete proposals, and those dealing with pious hopes.

The system of government to which the constitution gave rise was one clearly based on the supremacy of Parliament. Cabinet government of a sort does exist, but power is fragmented owing to the fact that no government since the constitution was ratified has been anything other than a coalition of often very antagonistic parties. A whole new journalistic vocabulary has developed to describe the different types of coalition which have emerged. Centre-right, centre-left, national unity, organic centre, convergence, limited spectrum, enlarged spectrum and total spectrum are some of the translatable terms used to give meaning to different coalition formulae. Such a rich vocabulary results from the fact that the average life-expectancy of an Italian government is about ten months.

The fragility of the Italian executive has introduced into the political system a degree of immobility which is, perhaps, unique in Europe. Urgently needed reforms are delayed or lost completely because of the need to satisfy a large number of political actors. The immobility is further exacerbated by a state bureaucracy which is notorious for its inefficiency and lack of responsiveness to the needs of modern administration. The government-sponsored Bozzi Commission has recently delved into the whole problem of streamlining the government apparatus. The report, which became the subject of quite intensive debate both in parliament and the media, has resulted in very little by way of change. The Bozzi Commission itself, in fact, fell victim to the very immobilism it was trying to eradicate, since there was no agreement among the parties which made up the commission as to exactly what its recommendations should be. This then, briefly, is the background in which the system of local government operates.

THE STRUCTURE OF LOCAL GOVERNMENT

Historical background

In Italy local government has a tradition which goes back well beyond the period of national unification. It is not uncommon for historians to trace the development of the commune as an almost unbroken process beginning in the twelfth century and continuing into the present day. During the period of the *Risorgimento*, for instance, the communes were considered to be the heirs of the autonomous cities of the middle ages. Attractive as this view may be, the reality is somewhat less romantic. The present communal structure is a much more recent phenomenon which has its origins in the early nineteenth century. Between 1802 and 1814, Italy, like much of continental Europe, fell under the domination of Napoleonic France. The resulting application of French administrative practices to the whole peninsula proved to be the *coup de grâce* to any vestiges of medieval self-government. The French imposed a system of government based on rigorous political and administrative centralisation formed by uniform laws and regulations, which took no cognisance of specific local traditions, needs or differences.

These arrangements remained intact until the period immediately after unification in 1861, when a debate opened up concerning the question of how much autonomy should be given to the communes and provinces within the new political system. Two diametrically opposed views emerged. On the one hand there were the 'centralists' who argued that the newly created state was far too fragile a structure to permit the luxury of any dilution in the sovereignty of the central government and, on the other, there were the 'autonomists', who wished to see the re-emergence of the concept of local independence, a return, in other words, to the so-called golden age. Not only did the 'autonomists' wish to create a system of communal government to achieve these objectives but they also considered it essential to establish regional levels of government in order that the different linguistic and cultural traditions would find expression in the new political structures. It was the former centralist position that triumphed. The system that emerged and, with a few modifications, remained intact for the next century was based upon strong centralisation in which the powers and functions of local government were rigorously fixed by central government. No concessions were made within the framework which governed the activities of the communes to either population or geographical differences.

The present structure of local government is the product of a vast amount of legislation, which has accumulated over the 125 years since unification. Each political regime has added its own layer of laws to those already in existence, so that the system cannot be said to be the product of one particular political style. The major innovation introduced by the new republican constitution after the war was the creation of a three-tier system of local government by adding regional governments to the already existing communes and provinces.

The regions

The constitution makes provision for the establishment of five regions of 'specific statute' and fifteen of 'ordinary statute'. They were created in 1970, the year in which the Italian Parliament passed the necessary financial laws to make them operational. The first councils for the ordinary regions were elected in the same year with the task of drawing up the regional statutes which were subsequently ratified by Parliament in 1971. The delay in creating the fifteen ordinary regions was due to a large number of factors, which all in one way or another relate to the political requirements of the Christian Democratic Party (DC). Fear of Communist Party (PCI) control of the regions in the red belt, the area of greatest PCI support, and the need to maintain a centralised system of political patronage conspired to delay their creation. There was also the widely held belief that the regions would simply create another expensive tier of bureaucracy. In the first five years the regional governments were handicapped by the fact that the central government was reluctant to transfer to the regions the necessary authority to undertake these tasks, which were very clearly allocated to them in Article 117 of the constitution. Not until 1975, when law no. 382 was passed, were the first steps taken to delegate powers to the regions. Further delay in transferring the necessary functions to the regions resulted in the passing in 1977 of an emergency measure, Presidential Decree no. 616.

The legislative powers of the regions are determined by their status as special or ordinary regions. The powers of the special regions can be described as a combination of exclusive, complementary and integrative with regard to national laws, while those of the ordinary regions are restricted to the last two. According to the constitution the regions were to be granted responsibility for a large number of administrative and political tasks, which can be divided into three broad areas. First are community and social service matters such as health and welfare, local transport, libraries, museums and a very limited role in education, mainly in the restricted area of students grants. Secondly, the regions have a number of responsibilities which can be grouped together under the broad heading of land use policy, comprising urban and regional planning, water supply, and forestry. Thirdly, there are the economic issues of a purely regional nature such as tourism, agriculture, local commerce, and fishing. The role of the central government was to be in those areas of specifically national concern such as foreign affairs, monetary policy, industrial policy and education.

The Italian system of regional governments forms a half-way house between the unitary system, which is so characteristic of the British system of government, and the West German federal system. Many of the responsibilities outlined above are concurrent powers shared with the national government. They are also dependent on the central government for most of their finance, and a government commissioner with the power of veto over all regional legislation is present in each region. Finally, the constitutional court is the arbiter in disputes between the regions and the central government. The rather restrictive interpretation which the court placed on the concept of regional autonomy did much to retard the development of the regions, at least during the first five years of their existence.

The provinces

The provinces, unlike the communes, cannot lay claim to a glorious history, since their creation was the product of the post-unification period. They have always had a rather ambiguous existence. On the one hand, they have served as units of local government with their own elected assembly and *giunta*, while, on the other, they have served as geographical or field units of central government. These two often contradictory functions have only been able to coexist for such a long period because the former role has always been subordinated to the requirements of the latter. As units of local government their powers have never been very extensive and have been under the closest supervision from the centre. As units of field administration their responsibility has been that of controlling the activities of the communes, through both the *giunta provinciale amministrativa* (GPA) and the prefect, and the maintenance of public order. Most provinces' functions have, in recent years, been transferred to the communes and the regions. In many respects the province is typical of many other organisations on the Italian political landscape in that it continues to exist long after its original *raison d'être* has disappeared, mainly for political rather than administrative reasons. It still performs a very valuable role within the system of political patronage.

The communes

The most striking feature of the system of communal government is its chronic fragmentation. The present number of 8,066 communes is a relatively recent phenomenon, as the number has fluctuated quite substantially throughout the life of the unified state. The present total was reached in the early 1960s. The most significant fact about the communes is not their number but their geographical and sociological heterogeneity. The larger communes such as Milan, Turin or Naples have populations of over a million; Rome has almost three million. At the opposite extreme are communes with populations measured in hundreds with around 8 per cent of the communes having populations of less than five hundred.

Equally striking are the variations in geographical size. The average size is about 37 km^2, but some are smaller than 0. 1 km^2, while others, like

Rome, cover over 1,000 km². The smaller communes, whether measured by population or area, tend to be concentrated in the north. Piedmont, for example, in the northwest, contains 1,209 communes (15 per cent of the total), of which over 900 have populations of less than two thousand.

The function of the communes

Despite their long history, the communes have never performed anything other than a marginal role within the Italian administrative system. The major reason for this has been the tendency for successive political regimes to allocate a large number of their administrative functions to 'special agencies' or to the field agencies of the central bureaucracy. The position of the 'special agencies' is of particular significance, since it has been against them that most of the proposals for the democratisation of administration have been aimed. There is little agreement on just how many 'special agencies' there were in existence, though the general consensus seems to centre around a figure of about 60,000. The special agencies or *enti pubblici* were most numerous within the administration of welfare, but they were by no means confined to such tasks, being involved as they were in every aspect of Italian life.

The combination of these special agencies and the field administrations of central government meant that there were very few areas in which the communes could act without duplicating a service that was already performed for them by some other agency. It was not uncommon, for instance, for one of the special agencies, the *Casa per il mezzogiorno* (the now defunct Southern Development Fund), to take major investment decisions without first consulting the affected communes. This was particularly so in cases where the commune was ruled by parties which formed the opposition at the centre.

Legislation in the mid-1970s abolished many of the special agencies and transferred their function to either the regions or the communes. This was the now famous Presidential Decree of 1977, no. 616. The abolition of many of the special agencies was heralded as a victory by the left, which had for a long time been campaigning for the democratisation of the administrative system. As a result, the functions currently carried out by the present system of municipal government are broadly similar to those undertaken by the other municipal governments of Western Europe.

Once again, it is difficult to present an accurate picture of the functions of the communes since size plays such a dominant role. If we take as our model the tasks performed by a middle-sized or large commune, we would see three broad categories: those which may loosely be defined as social services, those relating to economic services and economic development, and those relating to land use. Included within the social services are health care, personal social services, housing, a limited educational role within the sphere of educational assistance and grants, and many matters pertaining to the cultural life of the commune. Economic development activities concern matters such as the control of commercial activities and the promotion of tourism and agriculture. Items such as urban planning, public works, pollution control and municipal public transport make up the third category.

Not all these tasks are carried out directly by the *assessorati* (communal departments). Many of the functions are 'hived off' to municipal enterprises with the object of subjecting them to commercial pressures. The municipal enterprises have a history dating back to before unification. The city of Genoa, for instance, created a municipal gas service in 1845. By far the vast majority of municipal enterprises are, however, post-second world war creations. Although ostensibly operating in a commercial environment, they were created to provide services efficiently rather than to make a profit. Most, in fact, make a loss, and in doing so have contributed quite substantially to the 'fiscal crisis' of the communes. The most important of such operations in terms of scale and deficits are the municipal transport agencies (*Azienda Tranviaria Municipale* – ATM). Others are involved in the supply of gas, electricity, dairy products and water, as well as street cleaning and pharmacies. Since the municipal enterprises are almost exclusively restricted to the larger communes, they provide yet another factor which serves to increase the heterogeneity of the communal system of government. As in many other European countries the communes have, in recent years, begun an extensive process of privatising communal services through the procedure of contracting out services either to the profit-making sector or, in the case of many welfare services, to voluntary organisations. The Italian communes are still far from being simply 'enabling' bodies, leaving service provision to third parties, but the trend toward contracting out municipal services has become more noticeable in recent years, even in staunchly left-wing authorities such as Bologna.

Neighbourhood councils

As a result of law no. 278 passed in 1976, there began a process which led to the establishment of *consigli di quartieri* (neighbourhood councils). Their creation constituted an attempt to decentralise the decision-making process in the larger urban communes where the administrative structure had remained unchanged for over a century, during which time their populations and functions had increased enormously.

Though the concept received legal recognition in 1976, many communes had been experimenting with the idea of neighbourhood councils for some time. The idea behind their creation was to bring the administration of the large urban centres closer to the ordinary citizen, and in so doing to increase popular participation in the decision-making process. There was also the hope that the communes would use the opportunity to experiment with new forms of internal administration by delegating many of their functions to the new neighbourhood councils.

The law of 1976 enabled the communes to establish the councils either by direct election or by delegation. The vast majority of communes had, by 1980, chosen to elect these councils through direct popular participation. The functions of the neighbourhood councils are predominantly consultative. In performing this function they must be consulted by the commune before it draws up its budget, before it makes any investment or economic plans and before a number of other acts specifically mentioned in the 1976 law. Some communes have chosen to add a large number of other subjects upon which the neighbourhood councils must be consulted before any decision can be taken. These may include cultural and educational issues, social services, health care, and sporting and recreational concerns.

For those who considered the neighbourhood councils to be a panacea for all the ills of the large urban centres in Italy, or as instruments for transforming the nature of Italian democracy, the experience of the councils has not been particularly encouraging. To start, the use of the English word 'neighbourhood' is a little misleading. Rome, for instance, is divided into twenty councils each with a population approaching 150,000; Milan's neighbourhood councils each have a population of 84,000. Turin, which initially created twenty-three councils each with a population of 50,000, subsequently reduced the number of councils and in so doing increased the population size to well over 110,000. Bologna, seen by many as the cradle of the neighbourhood councils, reduced its eighteen councils to nine and doubled the population from 26,000 to 52,000. The so-called neighbourhood councils are themselves the size of small cities. Any increase in participation has taken place through the established party channels with the communes remaining the real centres of power. The success of the neighbourhood councils has been in their facilitating greater access to community and voluntary groups, particularly within the sphere of social services. Nevertheless, the functioning of the neighbourhood councils has fallen far short of the expectations of the urban movements of the 1970s which inspired their creation.

INTERNAL STRUCTURES

Political and administrative structures

One of the major changes brought about by the regions with regard to local structures has been the breaking of the traditional power of the prefect and the *giunta provinciale amministrativa*. Now stripped of the more political aspects of the role, the once all-powerful prefect performs what is essentially a law-and-order role. The powers once enjoyed by the prefect are now exercised by the regional control councils (RCCs). Located within each region the RCC consists of five members, three of whom must be administrative experts, chosen by the regional council. The other two consist of a regional administrative judge and a government commissioner. The powers of the RCCs are quite extensive and cover the 'legitimacy' of communal activity, that is, whether the communes are acting *ultra vires* or whether full legal procedures have been followed in the passing of communal legislation, and the 'merit' or 'utility' of communal proposals, that is, whether they conform to the dictates of sound administration.

Despite the enormous variations in population and size, the communes have the same institutional structure and, at least on paper, the same powers. The three political organs of the commune are the council, the *giunta* and the mayor. The council is directly elected every five years. One of the few concessions made to size is the number and method of election of councillors. The larger communes elect up to 80 councillors, the legal maximum, and the smallest elect the legal minimum of 15 members.

The method used to elect councillors varies according to whether the commune has a population of over or under 5,000. In those communes with more than 5,000 inhabitants the method of electing councillors is the same as that used in national elections. The system is one of the most representative of any electoral system currently in use. It is a list system, in which the elector chooses his or her desired party and then selects from among the party's candidates through preference votes. Each party receives a number of seats strictly proportionate to the percentage of popular votes it receives. The successful candidates are those who receive the highest number of preference votes.

In the communes with less than the required 5,000 inhabitants, the election is conducted according to the majoritarian principle, but with a difference. The difference lies in the fact that no party or grouping is allowed to present to the electorate a list containing more than four-fifths of the seats to be won. This ensures that there will be representation on the council for the minority party or parties.

·   To be eligible to stand for election, a candidate must be able to read and write and be resident in a commune of the Republic though not necessarily the one for which he or she is standing. However, certain individuals are disqualified because of the positions they hold. Employees of the commune and those employed in other organisations which exercise a controlling function over the communes are disqualified. So too are those who, because of a special relationship with the voters, might be able to influence unduly the outcome of an election: this applies particularly to both priests and judges active in the commune. The law also prevents members of the same family being elected to a commune, or an individual being elected to more than one commune. Finally, the law also prevents people presenting themselves as candidates if they have a special business relationship with the commune.

Once elected, the council's task is to elaborate the policies of the commune, to approve the communal budget, to enact municipal legislation and to create and control the other two organs of local government. To comply with the law, the council need meet only twice a year, once in the spring, to consider the previous year's expenditure, and again in the autumn to pass the budget for the following year. These ordinary sessions of the council can be supplemented by special sessions, which can be called by the council itself, the *giunta* or the mayor.

The *giunta* is a collegiate body elected by the council and consisting of *assessori*: that is, the heads of the administrative departments. Though the council is formally responsible for electing the *giunta*. the council role is, in most cases, merely one of 'rubber stamping' a decision already arrived at by a protracted process of bargaining between the parties that form the governing coalition.

In formal control of the activities of the commune is the mayor, who directs the work of the *giunta*, represents the commune in its dealings with third parties, ratifies all the communal acts and regulations and signs all the contracts entered into by the commune. The Italian mayor is a Janus-like figure, since s/he is, at one and the same time, a locally elected chief executive and a representative of central government. The latter role involves him or her in such matters as public security, public hygiene and the registration of births, deaths and marriages. As with the *giunta*, the formal role of the mayor is modified by the relationship between the political parties present within the assembly. The mayor's role can be reduced to one of a figurehead, who simply ratifies decisions already taken within the party apparatus.

The power relationship between the organs of the commune can vary quite considerably, depending upon the size of the commune. Giannini has pointed out that small communes tend to be dominated by the mayor, the middle-sized ones by the council and the large ones by the *giunta*, or, to be more precise, by the individual heads of department who constitute the *giunta* (Gianinni 1967).

Ad hoc agencies

Perhaps the major problems facing the regional governments from the moment of their creation were the result of the central government's failure to reform the system of communal government at the same time. The heterogeneity within the local government system made it almost impossible for the regions to devise a framework for dealing with the communes. The region of Lombardy alone was faced with the problem of how to establish relationships with no fewer than 1,500 communal governments. The regions were also faced with the problem of how to devolve planning and service functions to communes which were far too small to undertake the tasks required of them.

The response of the regions to these and similar problems has been to create new intermediate tiers of administration between themselves and the communes. Not all the organisations about to be discussed owe their origin to the regions. Many were in existence long before the regions themselves. However, the proliferation of these intermediate organisations is the result of the regions trying to cope with twentieth-century tasks in the face of a communal system more appropriate to the nineteenth century. There are two broad categories of intermediate organisations, those created as planning organisations and those created to undertake a particular service or group of services.

The planning bodies are typified by the activities of the *comprensorio*, a decentralised unit of regional administration charged with responsibility for promoting the economic development of the area under its jurisdiction. The *comprensorio* has its own council comprising representatives drawn from participating communes and provinces. Despite the hopes of many people that the *comprensori* might become a new tier of local government, they have remained only advisory in capacity and have in no way altered the traditional role of the communes.

The intermediate organisations created for the provision of services are the *consorzi*. They predate the creation of the regions and have formed the basis of communal administration for some time. They are, in simple terms, groups of communes which join together to provide a particular service to the public which, on their own, they would be unable to undertake. In the past they would have been spontaneous creations of the communes themselves. In recent years they have formed an integral part of both state and regional legislation. The most recent addition has been the establishment of the Local Health Authority, the *Unità Sanitaria Locale* (USL), as a result of the health care reforms of 1978.

In principle the creation of the *comprensori* and the *consorzi* was a positive step, offering, as it did, a way of overcoming the totally inadequate communal system of government with which the regions had to cope. Unfortunately, the reality has not been quite so positive. Their creation has led, in the opinion of many observers, to a process of 'hyper-institutionalisation'. Instead of creating multi-purpose *consorzi*, many regions have chosen to create one for each task that it wished to perform. Alongside the USLs there are others dealing with traffic issues, still others with education, with transport, with the environment, and so on. Each has its own organisation, finance, legal status and distinctive boundary. This, by and large, is the result of a lack of collective government at the regional level. Each regional department creates its own *consorzi* without any reference to another department. Instead of offering an alternative layer of government to the outmoded communes, the creation of intermediate organisations has merely served to add a further layer to what is already an administrative jungle.

FINANCE AND EXPENDITURE

In recent years Italian legislators have behaved in an almost schizophrenic fashion with regard to their legislation concerning the communes. On the one hand, as we have already observed, the legislators have introduced a large number of reforms which have greatly enriched the functions of the communes, by allocating to them a vast number of tasks previously performed by state and para-state organisations. On the other hand, the same legislators have passed measures which have denied the communes real autonomy in the way they are able to respond to the new challenges by refusing the communes the right to raise their own revenue. The result has been that a very large number of communes have found themselves unable to provide quite basic services or have burdened themselves with massive debts.

The financial problems of the communes are due, in the opinion of most observers, to a series of measures which were introduced in the early

1970s. The most important was the fiscal reform of 1972, which effectively denied the communes the power to finance their services through local taxation, by abolishing a number of taxes on housing, families, goods, services and businesses. These changes robbed the communes of something in the region of 92 per cent of their income. The changes were justified on a number of grounds, in particular the need to rationalise the Italian taxation system in order to avoid taxing the same subjects twice, as was the case with the family tax, and to bring the taxation system into line with the rest of the EC with regard to VAT. Despite the obvious consequences for local autonomy, the changes gave rise to very little dispute between the political parties. There appeared to be a consensus that the centralisation of government expenditure was necessary to overcome class and regional inequalities. The result of the transfer of financial responsibility from the periphery to the centre was that Italy had one of the largest system of transfer finances in the western world (Martinotti 1981).

Whatever the merits of the concerns for social and regional equality, the impact on local budgets was a disaster. For a limited period of five years between 1972 and 1977, transfers to the communes from the centre would be based upon the so-called 'historic income' of the communes: that is, the income the communes could have expected from their local taxes prior to the reform. To this the government added a figure of between 7 and 10 per cent to take account of inflation. What the figure could not take into account was the ability of the central government to pay on time. A combination of delays in getting annual budgets through parliament and the inability of the central bureaucracy to keep to deadlines ensured that the communes had to incur massive short-term debts simply to keep the most basic services functioning. In 1972 just over 50 per cent of communes had to seek loans to cover their budget deficits. By 1976 the figure had risen to just over 60 per cent. In many central and southern regions over 90 per cent of communes had incurred massive debts (Dente 1985). In certain cities, most notably Rome, income was barely sufficient to pay the interest on cumulative debts.

The response of the central government to the financial problems of the communes was one of placing ever-increasing central controls on the local authorities in order to prevent the indebtedness before it could arise. These took the form of forcing the communes to balance their budgets and, to make this easier, the central government placed severe restrictions on both current and capital expenditure. The degree of central control of finance and expenditure is such as to separate Italy from the mainstream of central–local relations in the western world.

Expenditure

After a brief period in which communal expenditure as a proportion of total government expenditure rose rapidly, it has, in recent years, fallen back slightly. In 1975 the proportion stood at about 14.7 per cent, rising to 19.7 per cent in 1985. Between 1985 and 1987 it fell back to 16.7 per cent. Within the total of communal expenditure the balance between current and capital expenditure has also undergone a significant change. Current expenditure in 1984 stood at 41.6 per cent of the total. By 1987 the proportion had risen to 61.1 per cent. Both the above changes can be explained by the severe restrictions the government placed upon the ability of communes to finance their expenditure through bank lending. Given that most of the lending went into the capital account it not only reduced total spending but shifted the balance of spending from the capital to the current account.

The figures in Table 5.1, while interesting from the point of view of gross expenditure, conceal an enormous amount of variation between the communes. One obvious variation will be dictated by the size of the communes. Dente has observed that the per capita expenditure on interest repayments in the larger communes is greater than the total spent by the smaller communes on the whole of their services (Dente 1977.).

Although the relationship between size and expenditure may be obvious, the relationship between political control and expenditure is less so. There has been quite an intense debate in recent years concerning the question of whether politics matters in determining expenditure patterns of communes under different political control.

Table 5.1 Communal expenditure (in billion lire)

Service	Current	%	Capital	%
Administration	8,895	20.7	1,653	5.2
Law and Order	2,068	4.7	281	0.9
Education and Arts	8,359	19.4	2,785	8.7
Housing	591	1.4	2,308	7.2
Social Services	13,689	31.8	7,817	24.4
Transport	5,145	12.0	6,027	18.8
Economic Policies	1,944	4.5	1,410	4.4
Unclassified	2,286	5.5	5,066	15.8
Loan Repayments	—	—	4,633	14.6
Total	42,977	100.0	31,980	100.0

Source: SPS *Rapporto* (1989)

Much of the early research into this question tended to arrive at the conclusion that the nature of political control of local government had only a minor impact on financial policy. This was certainly the conclusion arrived at by the *Istituto Cattaneo* of Bologna. After studying the financial policies of a sample of provincial capitals throughout Italy, the Institute's conclusions were that there was very little difference in either taxation or expenditure policies between local authorities controlled by the DC and those controlled by the PCI. An almost identical conclusion was arrived at by Fried after a study of the financial policies of 31 cities with populations in excess of 100,000. The major determinant of the financial policies of these cities was, in Fried's opinion, their latitude rather than the nature of the dominant party. In other words, the fact that the cities were located in the north or the south had a greater impact than the political ideology of the controlling party (Fried 1971).

More recent research has tended to suggest that the issue is much less clear-cut than this. Giorgio Brosio and his collaborators have reached entirely opposite conclusions. After a study of fifty-seven provincial capitals in the centre and the north of the country, in which all the possible determinants of financial policy were isolated, Brosio arrived at the view that there was indeed a marked difference in the expenditure policy between the left-wing and right-wing-dominated authorities, particularly with regard to current expenditure (Brosio 1975). Later studies by the same author in collaboration with others served to confirm the view that politics was indeed important in explaining financial policy (Brosio *et al.* 1978). The conclusion of a study published in 1982 has further tended to confirm Brosio's conclusions. M. Aitkin and G. Martinotti, after their study of 325 communes with populations in excess of 20,000, concluded that the left-wing-dominated communes, defined as those with a strong Communist presence, consistently spent more, and that their expenditure was much more likely to be dominated by welfare functions than was the case with communes without such a strong left-wing presence (Aitkin and Martinotti 1982).

COALITIONS AND COUNCILLORS

Perhaps one of the most widely discussed aspects of local government in Italy is the chronic instability of the governing coalitions which form the *giunte*. In a survey of the governing coalitions of Italy's provincial capitals stretching back over a period of eighteen years, F. Cazzola, one of Italy's leading experts on local government, has identified the different types of coalition and their duration. Out of a possible total of 904 *giunte*, the total number for all the provincial capitals during the 18-year period, 303 belonged to the pentapartiti (the five-party coalition forming the centre-left, the PCI–PSI–PRI–PLI–PSDI); 33 were formed from a two-party coalition of DC–PSI; 116 were formed by the DC along with either some or all of the lay parties, that is, PLI–PRI–PSDI; 140 consisted of a PCI–PSI coalition; the PCI–PSI combination formed another 114 *giunte* in coalition with the lay parties; 84 were single-party administrations formed by the DC; a further 18 single-party administrations were formed by the PCI; 12 were formed by the so-called 'anomalous administrations' which derive their name from the unusual nature of the coalition, such as the combination of DC–PCI. The most unstable of the provincial capitals had more than fourteen *giunte* in the eighteen-year period. The most stable averaged around eight during the same period. The instability is even more apparent if we look more closely at the figures. Of the same 904 *giunte*, 307 lasted for one year or less; 352 for two years; 127 for three years; 46 for four years; nine lasted for the full five years permitted by law. The impact of the instability cannot be exaggerated. It produces a culture of 'short-termism' among the *assessori*. Only those projects which can be brought to an early conclusion will be embarked upon. Nobody wishes to set in motion a project for which another politician will gain the credit, particularly, as is most likely, if that politician is from another party (Cazzola 1991). The danger which such chronic instability carries with it is the possibility of creating a gulf between the local political élites and the people in whose name they claim to govern. A survey carried out by one of Italy's leading newspapers, against the background of a prolonged political crisis in the communal government of Milan, discovered that over 78 per cent of respondents had no idea which parties had formed the new *giunta* or what had led to the breakdown of the previous *giunta*. The overwhelming impression that the survey left was the almost total exclusion of the ordinary citizen from the manoeuvres being carried out in their name (*Corriere della Sera*, 13 August 1988).

Another interesting phenomenon to emerge from the wealth of research into the local political élite is what has been described by Barberis (1978) as *la funzione agglomerante del potere*, that is, the extent to which certain parties are able to claim a higher proportion of the powerful positions in the communes than their level of electoral support would suggest. This applies particularly to the DC. Out of a total of 149,865 communal councillors, of whom just over 40,000 held the post of *assessore* and just over 8,000 that of mayor, 69,860 were held by the DC. The dominance of the DC is due to the fact that the party is extremely strong in small rural communes which form a very high proportion of the total;

according to Barberis about one-fifth of all councillors represent these small communes. Whereas the DC lays claim to 53 per cent of the vote in rural communes, the figure declines to 32 per cent in the urban centres. However, the dominance of the DC becomes more significant if we turn to its control over the posts of *assessore* and mayor. From a base of 47 per cent of council seats the party is able to occupy 50 per cent of the posts of *assessore* and 55 per cent of the posts of mayor. This is so because of the key position the party enjoys within the formation of coalitions. This advantage is not, however, confined to the DC, but is applicable to any party which can occupy the centre ground in the game of coalition politics. Claudio Petroccioli, writing in the Communist Party weekly *Rinascita*, has demonstrated how the PSI, with 14 per cent of the seats in the major cities, is able to participate in over 79 per cent of the *giunte* of the major towns and cities, while the PCI, with over 20 per cent, participates in less than 37 per cent. The PSI gains such an advantage because it is the only party which stays in power if a commune changes its coalition (*Rinascita*, 13 May 1983).

In his analysis of the socio-economic background of councillors, Barberis demonstrates the increasing tendency for councillors of all parties to be drawn from the tertiary sector of employment in general, and the public sector in particular. More recent research for the year 1987, conducted by CENSIS, showed that 8.9 per cent of councillors were drawn from agriculture, 24.8 per cent from industry and 56.5 per cent from the service sector. Of the latter, 45 per cent were employed within the public bureaucracy and amounted to 25.8 per cent of the councillors. The presence of public employees becomes even more marked if attention is turned to the leading positions in the communes. Public employees hold 30.0 per cent of *assessorati* posts and 37.9 per cent of mayoral positions.

One of the major reasons for the dominance of public employees in the corridors of power at the local level is to be found in a whole series of laws and regulations concerning the rights of employees to gain leave of absence from their employers to undertake council business. Prior to 1985, when the regulations were changed, there was a marked bias in the rules governing leave in favour of public employees. Legislation dating from 1966 provided for paid leave of absence if public employees were elected regional councillors, provincial presidents or *assessori* (in provinces with over 700,000 inhabitants). This also applied to mayors of communes which were either provincial capitals or had populations of over 50,000, *assessori* of communes with over 100,000 inhabitants or representatives of mountain communities. For the rest, paid leave was permitted only to undertake tasks necessary for fulfilling their mandate. Many private employers interpreted the latter point to mean only meetings of the communal council. Despite a number of attempts to have the rules declared unconstitutional because of the unequal treatment they encouraged, the disparity of treatment remained until 1985 when the privileges of the public employees were removed.

Perhaps one of the major factors to emerge from Barberis's research is the extent to which women are under-represented in local councils. Despite the many changes which have occurred in recent years concerning the status of women in Italian society, women are still excluded from positions of power at every level of political life. Only 6.6 per cent of local councillors are women. The position of women worsens the higher one goes up the local political hierarchy. Women account for only 5.4 per cent of *assessori* and 2.6 per cent of mayors. The exclusion of women from positions of power at the local level is, according to Barberis, one of the major failings of Italian democracy. Taking these and other findings relating to the age and educational achievement of councillors, Barberis concludes that power at the local level in Italy is exercised by males over females, by the educationally qualified over the unqualified, by the middle-aged over the young and old, and by those employed in the tertiary sector, in particular in the state bureaucracy, over the manual workers and liberal professions.

The local bureaucracy

Bureaucracy in Italy does not enjoy a particularly wholesome reputation, whether at the national or local level. To the ordinary citizen it appears to be inefficient and often corrupt. Anyone coming into contact with the local bureaucracy will immediately be aware of its repetitive, complex and highly frustrating procedures. A visit to any local government department results in an endless round of unnecessary form filling. However, unlike the bureaucracy at the national level, which is said to be culturally separate from the political class in terms of the southern background of its members and its predominantly legalistic training and outlook, the local bureaucrat is more likely to be drawn from the locality in which s/he works and to have a similar social background to that of the local politicians. Indeed, given the previously discussed tendency for local politicians to be drawn from the public bureaucracy, the chances are that many local bureaucrats are also politicians.

Positions within the local bureaucracy must be filled by open competition in accordance with the constitution. The competition may involve a formal examination or some other assessment of the candidate's ability in cases, for example, when the applicant has filled a similar post in another authority. For new recruits entering the service, no special training is required, the typical entrant being a graduate in law or political science. Until quite recent times no special training was required once a person was in post. In more recent times, however, large numbers of local bureaucrats are being seconded for short periods to the burgeoning business and management schools.

A typical bureaucratic structure does not exist since so much is dependent upon the size of the commune. In only the larger communes do organisational structures exist which would be familiar to students of British local government. The typical organisation of a larger commune would consist of: a health department providing environmental and preventative medicine; a technical department concerned with urban planning and public works; a finance department responsible for the raising of finance and the control of expenditure; a department of finance charged with the drawing up of the municipal budget; a veterinary department concerned with the controlling of abattoirs and public protection in all matters concerning animals.

Within the smaller communes no such departmental specialisation occurs. They employ so few administrative staff that the divisions would be meaningless. Because of the undifferentiated nature of the small communal administrations, the administrator has to be a jack of all trades. The more able administrators are de-motivated owing to the quite often anachronistic tasks they have to perform or because they lack the necessary technical support to carry out their tasks adequately.

The relationship between politicians and administrators at the local level has changed quite substantially in recent times. Until the end of the 1950s the relationship between the two groups was considered to be one of 'partnership' – a partnership in which the politicians were responsible for broad strategic policy choices, the politicians and administrators together would determine short-term tactical policies, and the administrators would be left to implement the policies and undertake internal management tasks. This *modus vivendi* began to break down in the late 1960s when the political nature of the ruling *giunte* swung in favour of the parties of the left. The major changes occurred in the wake of the 1975 local elections when a large number of urban communes came under left-wing control. A number of factors reflected the changed relationship. Firstly, the administrative departments of the communes took on their present title of *assessorati*. This involved more than just a change of name: it reflected the fact that the new departments became almost independent centres of decision-making. Dominated by the political head, the *assessore*, the departments now became little more than extensions of the party apparatus. Secondly, with the dominance of the political head, the role of the full-time departmental heads was undermined, and what had once been a climate of partnership became one of conflict. Thirdly, this conflict was reflected in the practice of mayors and *assessori* employing an informal departmental staff in the form of a kind of ministerial cabinet drawn from the ranks of the party or party faction of the political head. Fourthly, as a result, the full-time officials became marginalised from the process of policy-making within their departments, in many cases also usurping the function of internal management. The reason for the changes in style within local administration was the desire by the parties of the left to adapt to the changing demands of administering the new welfare policies which were being enacted during this period. Not all the changes were beneficial, however. The result was often a lack of coordinated decision-making due to the *assessorati* being in different political hands as a result of coalition governments and an extension of the process of *sottogoverno*, the process which lies at the boundary of patronage and corruption.

Before leaving this discussion of the local bureaucracy, it is necessary to consider one post which they all have in common, the communal secretary. In the right circumstances the communal secretary can have a profound effect upon how the commune is run. The communal secretary is something of a hybrid figure. He is the administrative head of the commune, by which he is paid, but at the same time he is an employee of the central government, which recruits him and determines his salary and career prospects.

The reason for dwelling on the role of the communal secretary lies in the fact that this was, along with the office of prefect, one of the major instruments through which central government controlled the activities of the communes. Foreign observers of Italian local government often overlooked the role played by the communal secretary, mainly because it has always been a much more surreptitious form of control than that exercised by the prefect. The communal secretary is the extension into the communes of the central bureaucracy. His role is that of providing expert, mainly legal, advice to both the politicians and the administrators. This could place him in an extremely important position, particularly in the vast majority of communes which, because of their size, would have little access to other sources of expertise. The communal secretary can dissuade the politicians from adopting a particular course of action, not acceptable to central bureaucracy, by declaring it to be not legitimate. Advice could be given to the commune in such a form that policies would be difficult to elaborate or execute. In other words, the communal secretary could dislocate the local bureaucracy from the local politicians and, in so doing, distort the power structure of the communes. The communal secretary's power in the large communes has declined substantially owing to the political changes outlined above, but in the small communes the role remains a very important one.

POLICY MAKING

Central–local relations

Recently two eminent Italian scholars have lamented the fact that the study of local government in Italy was backward in comparison with the state of the literature in other European countries and the USA (Dente 1977; Catanzaro 1979). More precisely, their concern centred around the absence of detailed studies of policy making and the relationship between the centre and the periphery. The reason for this state of affairs was, in their view, to be found in the overpowering dominance of the administrative law traditions in Italian universities. Those studies which did concentrate on the political dimensions of local government were, by and large, the product of foreign observers. Over the last six years, the situation has changed dramatically, so much so that Italian scholars have carried out what is perhaps the most extensive and detailed study of central–periphery relations to have been undertaken anywhere (Dente 1984).

In the past, most studies of local government in Italy tended to the traditional, administrative law approach. The stress was placed upon the overriding power of central government. Little, if any, role was allotted to the units of local government themselves in influencing policy. According to Dente, the traditional approach suffered from three major defects. First, it tended to view central government and individual units of local government as if they were single unified organisations rather than as groupings of separate and often competing organisations. The administrative law approach, in concentrating on the regional relationship between the two poles of government, tended to ignore the activities of non-governmental organisations. The major concern of the research conducted by ISAP (*Istituto per la Scienza dell' Amministrazione Pubblica*) was to discover the impact which organisations such as the church, political parties, trade unions, the mass media and so on, had upon the relationship. Secondly, the traditional approach had always tended to view relationships between the central and local governments as a kind of zero-sum game. Once again, as Dente has observed, the elected representatives who occupy the two poles of the system are members of the same political parties and have ideologies and interests in common, producing bargains and compromises which benefit both. Thirdly, local government is a vast reservoir of expertise, without which central government would find it extremely difficult to govern. It is unrealistic to assume that local governments are not able in some way to influence and modify the policies which affect them (Dente 1984).

In a recent article covering the same issues, Zariski has identified four approaches to autonomy in Italy. At one extreme he identifies the 'legalistic' approach, which is the same as the above-mentioned 'administrative law' model. This is followed by the centre–periphery approach, which still views the relationship in hierarchical terms but which also stresses the extent of cooperation between the two levels of government. The third model is identified as the 'integrated administration' approach. Here the emphasis is placed much more upon cooperation than hierarchy, and powers are seen as being shared rather than 'rigidly separated and jealously preserved against intruders'. The final model is described as the 'partial government' approach. Here the distinction between the various levels of government disappears altogether and we see the use of terms such as 'disintegrated administration' or 'partial government'. Within this approach politics is seen not as the relationship between different levels of government, but rather as a series of 'systems of interactions revolving around specialised problem areas'. The traditional concerns surrounding central–local relationships are almost irrelevant since there is no identifiable local interest (Zariski 1985).

The role of parties

Perhaps the most widely researched aspect of the political dimension of centre–periphery relationships has been that concerning the role played by political parties. In the past, the literature dealing with the subject of political parties has tended to emphasise their centralising tendencies. Researchers concentrated on the extent to which the parties robbed local elections of their significance by using them as opinion polls for future national elections or as testing grounds for coalitions later to be adopted at the national level, as was the case with the experiment with centre–left coalitions in Milan in 1960. More recently, commentators have emphasised the extent to which purely local issues are dominating politics in the periphery. This is demonstrated by the difficulty which the DC is encountering in trying to impose the national five-party coalition on communal administrations. Most observers trace this change to the landslide victory of the left in the 1975 local elections, during which the number of large communes under left-wing control rose from 419 to 656, and the number of people under left-wing administrations rose from just under 8 million to almost 17 million.

A vast amount of research has been undertaken in recent years, demonstrating the extent to which the Italian parties have modified the highly centralised legal framework under which the communes operate. Sidney Tarrow, among others, has stressed the role which the political parties play in channelling demands from the periphery to the centre. In this respect, he contrasts the experiences of French and Italian mayors. The French mayor is able to rely on an efficient administrative structure to transmit his demands to the centre. The Italian mayor, on the other hand, faced with a notoriously inefficient administrative system, has to rely on his party connections to gain resources from his locality (Tarrow 1977).

In similar vein, Angelo Panebianco has observed that there is a difference in behaviour between countries which have national parties that have penetrated the periphery, as in Italy, and those countries in which the parties are either overwhelmingly local, as in the United States, or overwhelmingly national, as in France. In the Italian case, the parties act as a glue between the centre and the periphery. In the case of France and the USA, the mediation between the centre and the periphery is conducted through semi-autonomous agencies, such as the bureaucracy and the federal system respectively (Panebianco 1984).

Dente makes the point that, despite the centralised nature of the Italian political parties, there appears to be little dictation of policy other than the already mentioned attempts to influence the nature of the local coalition. Indeed the contrary appears to be the case, in that parties act not so much as hierarchical instruments for specific policies, but as a resource of information, advice and sometimes influence for a relationship going from the bottom to the top (Dente 1985).

No discussions of the impact of political parties on central–local relationships would be complete without some mention of the impact of clientelism on the relationship. Clientelism, in its broadest sense, is a process through which consensus and electoral support are exchanged for political and administrative protection (Graziano 1979). In the past the patron–client relationship involved a political boss, on the one hand, and the individual citizen on the other. Within the highly complex political system of modern Italy these roles are now performed by the political party or party faction, and social or professional groups respectively. Nevertheless, there is still the need for the individual broker in the form of the mayor, Member of Parliament, or government minister.

Clientelistic relations take many forms and vary quite considerably from one region of the country to another. At its loosest, it may take the form of a particular Member of Parliament acting on behalf of a municipality, often regardless of political allegiance, if both parties stand to gain by the exchange. One form of such an exchange is through the publication of posters announcing that the 'municipality of X is most grateful to the MP whose intervention in Rome secured money for a new school building'. In more covert fashion, the exchange may involve the municipality in the fulfilment of promises such as the selection of candidates acceptable to the MP. Once again, Dente observes that the most successful forms of clientelistic intervention are those which do not require the gaining of large sums of public money but rather which are aimed at overcoming frustrating and time-consuming legal procedures (Dente 1985).

PROBLEMS AND PROSPECTS

For over two decades now the problems of local government in Italy have been at the top of the political agenda. Faced with enormous institutional obstacles to a comprehensive reform of the system of local autonomy, Italian legislators have responded with a great number of emergency measures which have done little to tackle the underlying problems. These problems can be summarised as a lack of adequate finance and financial autonomy, a lack of proper political accountability, governmental instability, a lack of a clear division of responsibility between the political organs of the communes, and chronic fragmentation due to the failure to adapt the number of communes to changes in the economic and social basis of the country. However, things are about to change. The law which the Italian legislators passed on 8 June 1990 will transform the nature of local government in Italy. In terms of its effects it will probably go down as the most important piece of institutional reform in the history of the post-war republic. Much, however, will depend upon how successful the law is in being transferred from the statute books into concrete reality. Previous major reforms such as the creation of the National Health Service and the establishment of the regional governments have shown that the transition is not always easy or successful.

The reform addresses most of the problems identified above with the two exceptions of electoral reform and local finance. Both of these items would have had much more far-reaching effects than the other aspects of the reform. In particular, too radical a change to the system of voting would have had clear implications for the system of proportional representation at the national level. The failure to tackle these two issues has led to a great deal of criticism and to suggestions that the whole reform process may founder as a result.

Most of the reform proposals will need further legislation by both the national and regional governments before they can become operative. Two far-reaching measures have come into force, however, following the local elections in May 1990. One involves the stipulation that the *giunta* and the mayor must be selected within 70 days of the election result being announced. Failure to comply involves the regional government in taking direct responsibility for the affairs of the commune. The other involves the so-called motion of *sfiducia costrutiva*. Defeat in a council vote no longer leads to resignation of the *giunta*; instead, this occurs only if there is an alternative *giunta* readily available. In other words a motion of no confidence must be accompanied by a proposal for an alternative *giunta*. Both are designed to solve the problem of coalition instability.

The major significance of the total reform package is that it removes the controls placed upon the communes by over a century of restrictive legislation. The uniformity of communal legislation alluded to above has been removed. The individual communes now enjoy a great degree of autonomy in designing their own administrative structures. The absurdity of the same organisational structure being imposed on communes regardless of the size will, in future, no longer apply. Another major consequence of the reform will be the creation of metropolitan councils in the large urban centres. With the exception of Britain, Italy is the only country in Western Europe not to have a metropolitan level of government which, given the fragmentation of the communal system, has caused immense problems for planners as conflicts over jurisdictional competence hindered decision-making. The designation by the interested regional governments of the areas to be covered by the new metropolitan councils is, at the present time, causing a few problems. In Lazio for example, the new metropolitan council centred on Rome will control two-thirds of the region's population. What this will mean for relations between the regional and the new metropolitan authority one can only guess.

Few areas of Italian local government will be left untouched by the reforms. There will be change: the dimensions of the communes; their internal organisation; their functions; the ways in which they deliver their services; the rights of citizens to participate, to gain access to council meetings and information; the controls exercised over them by superior bodies. Perhaps most of all it will provide a test of the ability of the Italian political and administrative system to transform a major piece of legislation into concrete reality – something which, in the past, it has not had a great deal of success in achieving.

BIBLIOGRAPHY

Aitkin, A. and Martinotti, G. (1982) 'Sistema urbano. Governo della città e giunte di sinistra nei grandi comuni Italiani', *Quaderni di Sociologia* 30 (2,3,4).

Barberis, C. (1978) *La Classe Politica Municipale*, Milan, Franco Angelli.

Brosio, G. (1975) 'Comportamento politico e comportamento di spesa degli enti locale Italiani', *Economia Pubblica* 10.

Brosio, G., Hyman, D. and Santagata, W. (1978) *Gli Enti Locale fra Riforma Tributaria Inflazione e Movimenti Urbani*, Turin, Fondazione Agnelli.

Catanzaro, R. (1979) *Participazione, Potere e Sviluppo*, Catania, Pellicanolibri Edizione.

Cazzola, F. (1991) *Periferici Integrati*, Bologna, Il Mulino.

Dente, B. (1977) 'Il governo locale in Italia', in R. Mayntz, L.J. Sharpe and B. Dente, *Governo Locale in Europa*, Milan, Edizione di Comunità.

Dente, B. (1984) 'Sogegeti e Potere', in ISAP, *Le Relazioni Centro–Periferia*, Milan, Editore Giuffre.

Dente, B. (1985) *Governare La Frammentazione*, Bologna, Il Mulino.

Fried, R.C. (1971) 'Communism, urban budgets and the two Italys', *Journal of Politics*, 33.

Giannini, M.S. (1967) *I Papporti fra Organi Eletivi*, Milan, AA. VV.

Graziano, L. (1979) *Clientalism e Mutamento Politico*, Milan, Franco Angelli.

Martinotti, G. (1981) 'The illusive autonomy', in L.J. Sharpe (ed.) *The Local Fiscal Crisis in Western Europe*, London, Sage.

Panebianco, A. (1984) 'I Partiti', in ISAP, *Le Relazioni Centro–Periferia*, Milan, Editore Giuffre.

Sistema Permanènte di Servizi (1989) *Rapporto sullo Stato dei Potere e dei Servizi Locale*, Rome, SPS.

Tarrow, S. (1977) *Between Centre and Periphery*, New Haven, Conn., Yale University Press.

Zariski, R. (1985) 'Approaches to the problems of local autonomy', *West European Politics* 3.

General books in English

Allum, P. (1973) *Italy: Republic without Government*, London, Weidenfeld and Nicolson.

Batley, R. and Stoker, G. (1991) *Local Government in Europe*, London, Macmillan.

Hood, C. and Schuppert, G.F. (1987) *Delivering Public Services in Western Europe*, London, Sage.

King, R. (1987) *Italy*, Cambridge, Harper and Row.

Nanetti, R. (1988) *The Growth of Territorial Politics*, London, Pinter.

Page, C. and Goldsmith, M.J. (1987) *Central and Local Government Relations*, London, Sage.

Spotts, F. and Wieser, F. (1986) *Italy: A Difficult Democracy*, Cambridge, Cambridge University Press.

Zariski, R. (1972) *Italy: The Politics of Uneven Development*, Hillsdale, Ill., Dryden Press.

Chapter 6

Germany

A.R. Peters

CENTRAL AND STATE RELATIONS

The West German state dated from 1949 with the election of the first post-war government led by Konrad Adenauer. The reunited German state has largely been formed through the extension of the West German structures to the former communist areas. The technical distribution of power within the political system is delineated by the constitution known as the Basic Law (*Grundgesetz*) drawn up by a Constituent Assembly in 1948. The format adopted has been widely seen as reflective of the determination of the western occupying powers to establish a system of government firmly grounded in the principles of liberal democracy and with a clear-cut separation of powers. To this end, a federal system of government was adopted with legislative and administrative duties dispersed between ten states (*Länder*) and a federal government (*Bund*), currently installed in Bonn. Although elected assemblies have been created at both the state and federal level, legislative power lies largely with the federal assemblies. Under article 73 of the *Grundgesetz*, the *Bund* holds exclusive right to legislate in areas such as defence, foreign affairs, currency control, rail traffic, postal services and telecommunications. Although technically the *Länder* are free to legislate in all other areas, there is also a provision for concurrent powers whereby the federal government reserves the right to legislate in areas of national interest. Through the use of this wide-ranging power, federal legislation now effectively covers the legal system, economic management and most aspects of social welfare. In addition, through the establishment of framework legislation whereby the federal government lays down the broad policy guidelines but gives wide discretion to the *Länder* in the implementation of policy, the federal government has extended its influence into further areas such as higher education and land use.

Although the elected assemblies at state level only hold exclusive powers of legislation in a restricted number of areas, such as education, control of the police and the organisation of local government, the *Länder* are guaranteed a voice in federal affairs through the creation of a bicameral legislature incorporating a directly elected chamber (*Bundestag*) from which the Chancellor and his cabinet are drawn, and a second chamber (*Bundesrat*) composed of delegates from the *Länder*. The extensive power of the *Bundesrat* to scrutinise and reject vast areas of federal legislation, particularly in the fields of finance and constitutional reform, ensures that the interests of the *Länder* are fully represented in the policy-making process.

The constitutional position of the states is reinforced by the existence of a Federal Constitutional Court (*Bundesverfassungsgericht*), which is the sole body empowered to interpret the *Grundgesetz* and to which the *Länder* can appeal if attempts are made to erode their constitutional position. In reality, however, the strength of the *Länder* lies in the reliance of the federal Government on the states for the provision of most services. Except in limited areas such as the railways, inland waterways and postal services, where federal ministries have created their own national structures, services are actually provided by the *Länder* or units of local government acting on their own behalf or more commonly as agents for Bonn. The vast majority of civil servants in West Germany are, therefore, employed at state or local government level, and the autonomy of these units is bolstered, to an extent, by the provision that they receive automatically a set percentage of revenue derived from taxation in addition to federal grants.

The West German federal system is, therefore, often termed 'cooperative' in that, although the power of initiation lies firmly with Bonn, in practice the role played by the *Länder* is extensive. Certainly the establishment of a vast network of agencies and committees to provide coordination between Bonn and the states has been indicative of the federal government's reliance on the *Länder* for policy feedback and the appreciation that the *Länder* provide the administrative backbone of service provision. To an extent the relationship in the past decade has been symbolised by the creation of 'joint tasks' in fields such as higher education and regional economic development. The projects are jointly funded, with federal ministries establishing national guidelines, but the actual implementation is the preserve of the *Länder*. In this context it is the discretion afforded to the *Länder* in administrative matters alongside their constitutional rights that has resulted in the creation of a working relationship rarely marred by open conflict.

THE STRUCTURE OF LOCAL GOVERNMENT

Legal status

Local democracy in Germany has a tradition that can be traced back to the rights granted to medieval cities, although the modern format is largely credited to the measures initiated in Prussia by Freiherr von Stein in the first decade of the nineteenth century. Although the franchise was restricted primarily to the middle class until 1918, as Gunlicks notes, the reforms outlined by von Stein:

> created a national system of well ordered and state supervised local government that enjoyed considerable autonomy in an otherwise authoritarian framework of central administration.
>
> (Gunlicks 1981: 169)

The system that emerged was heavily influenced by the Hegelian distinction between the state and society, with a marked peference for strong executive leadership based on the role of officials as guardians of legally defined adminstrative practice. The autonomy of local government was severely curtailed during the National Socialist era; therefore, given the collapse of German society in 1945, the establishment of an effective system of local government was one of the central goals set by the Allied powers in the political and administrative reconstruction of occupied Germany. The basic unit of government below the level of the state established to fulfil this role is the municipality (*Gemeinde*), of which there were originally some 30,000, ranging in size from 8,000 to 1,000,000 citizens. Rationalisation of the *Gemeinden* in the past two decades, however, has reduced their number to just under 9,000 and it is now unusual for a unit of local government to exercise authority over an area containing less than 10,000 inhabitants.

The right of the *Gemeinden* to direct their own affairs is explicitly stated in article 28 of the *Grundgesetz* which guarantees:

> the right to regulate under their own responsibility and within the limits of the laws all the affairs of the local community.

In effect, this gives the *Gemeinden* sweeping powers to act in all areas not specifically reserved for the *Bund* or the *Länder*. *Gemeinden* have made full use of this freedom and often provide a wide and varying range of services to the community. The organisation of local government, however, is not explicitly outlined by the *Grundgesetz*, other than that it should conform to the principles of a republican, democratic and socially just political system. The actual format of local government is determined, therefore, by the individual states, with the legal status and structure of the *Gemeinden* being established by the constitution of the *Land* within which they operate. While, therefore, there is an element of uniformity – for example, the affairs of the municipality will be run by a council (*Gemeinderat*) elected by a system of proportional representation drawn from party lists – the frequency of elections and the distribution of power between elected and appointed officials varies between states.

All of the *Länder*, however, have basically a three-tiered system of elected government. Operating at an intermediate level between the *Gemeinden* and the *Land* is the county or *Landkreis*. The affairs of the *Kreis* are generally directed by an official (*Landrat*) selected by the elected body (*Kreistag*), although once again there are variations on this format, particularly in Bavaria. The role of the *Kreis* is to act as a general supervisory body over the *Gemeinden* within its area, with the exception of many of the larger cities which, due to their size, have effectively been granted county status. Over one hundred cities hold the status of *Stadtkreis*, which gives them freedom from county direction and confers powers equivalent to those held by the *Kreis*. Some of the largest cities are divided into districts (*Bezirke*) with elements of administration delegated to each district. Within this network of organisations one further anomaly must be noted. Bremen, Hamburg and West Berlin hold the distinction of enjoying the status of both *Gemeinde* and *Land* and combine both functions.

STRUCTURES AND POWERS

The *Gemeinden* in the Federal Republic operate a wide and startling variety of services in comparison to many of their counterparts in Britain. Yet, while the number of services offered is indicative of the premium placed upon freeing local initiative, the vast majority of local responsibilities are, in fact, delegated from either the *Bund* or the *Land*, with the *Gemeinden* acting as administrative agents. The degree of supervision of the operation of these services, however, varies considerably. In areas such as public health, organisation of elections, taxation and various forms of licensing, particularly of buildings, local government acts on behalf of the *Länder* and is closely supervised. In other areas of delegated responsibility, however, while minimum standards are established by law, the *Gemeinden* have considerable discretion in the implementation of their responsibilities. Services covered in this category include the major public utilities, water, electricity, gas, the provision of school buildings, public transport, health care and fire services, in addition to the construction and maintenance of housing and certain categories of roads. To this list can, occasionally, be added the organisation of a local police force, although in most instances, along with the appointment of teachers, this is a responsibility reserved for the *Länder*. While all of these services are subject to an element of regulation and are partially dependent on financial assistance from the *Land*, the format adopted and the extent of provision can vary markedly between communities.

In addition to this vast array of responsibilities the *Gemeinden* are given a free hand to move into areas which are not the particular reserve of the *Bund* and *Länder*. In most instances they have made full use of the opportunity with the provision of transport networks, shopping facilities, social services and a vast array of recreational and cultural facilities. It is the enterprise and innovation displayed in this latter area which distinguishes local government in the Federal Republic from many other countries. As might be expected, however, the finance necessary to provide many, even basic, services is beyond the means of the smaller *Gemeinden*. In order to overcome this problem several solutions have been adopted. In some instances neighbouring *Gemeinden* have been amalgamated into larger units termed *Samtgemeinden* or *Verbandsgemeinden* in order to pool their resources, while it is not unusual for a particularly expensive service, such as the provision of water or electricity, to be delegated to an ad hoc agency formed by agreement between groups of *Gemeinden*.

Frequently, even the creation of such organisations is inadequate to sustain a satisfactory level of service provision, and the past decade has witnessed a steady drift of responsibilities away from the *Gemeinden* to the *Kreis*. Unlike the *Gemeinden*, the *Kreis* can only administer those services assigned to it by law. Yet, while technically this gives the *Kreis* only a limited range of functions, in practice financial necessity has led to the *Kreis* increasingly adopting responsibility for the provision of such services as hospitals, secondary education, gas, electricity and water. The *Kries*, therefore, plays a dual role in that it provides services beyond the financial means of the *Gemeinden* in addition to supervising and coordinating the range of responsibilities undertaken by local government. In this sense the *Landrat* acts as an agent for the Ministry of the Interior of the relevant state, ensuring that the *Gemeinden* work within the legal framework and that adequate services are provided.

The extent of *Land* supervision of the *Gemeinden* does not stop with the *Kreis*. In the six largest states there also exists a number of administrative districts (*Regierungsbezirke*), each run by a District President appointed by the *Land* and responsible to the Ministry of the Interior. The District

President and staff are members of the *Land* civil service and hold considerable power in their supervision of the *Kreise* and *Gemeinden*. In addition to controlling the police within the district, the *Regierungspräsident* will seek to ensure that local government acts within the law. Furthermore, representatives of the *Land* ministries at District level will closely scrutinise the activities of the *Gemeinden* where they are acting as agents of the *Land* (*Fachaufsicht*). When these duties are considered alongside the role of the district as the main agency for the dispensation of *Land* funds to the *Gemeinden*, it is evident that the ability of the *Regierungspräsident* not only to coordinate but also to direct the work of local government is considerable.

The relationship between state and local government, therefore, in many ways parallels the linkages established between state and central government. While the power of initiation lies firmly with the centre, local agencies are given a great deal of freedom to interpret the format of service provision and are provided with the opportunity to innovate in areas not already reserved for other agencies. It has to be noted, however, that the power of the state to regulate and direct local government is far greater than the ability of central government to control the state. Therefore, although local government has maintained a remarkable degree of autonomy, the growing financial burden of providing a wide range of services has significantly reduced its freedom of action. It is this development that has led observers to fear for the future role of the *Gemeinden*. Increasingly the responsibilities of local government have been progressively eroded, owing to their reliance on central finance and to the proliferation of specialised field units, organised by the *Länder* and federal agencies for the operation of major projects in the areas of housing, regional development and health care.

FINANCE

The legal status of the *Gemeinden* is clouded by the fact that, although under the provisions of the *Grundgesetz* they are guaranteed a degree of autonomy, with the right to make decisions concerning the administration of their own affairs within a legal framework established by Bonn and the *Länder*, in effect the organisation and format of the *Gemeinden* are determined by the provisions contained within the constitutions of the individual *Länder*. This position is also reflected in the financing of the *Gemeinden*, with the establishment of the principle of budgetary autonomy, while in reality the financial base is determined by the *Land*. Until the mid-1960s the chief source of independent revenue widely granted to the *Gemeinden* lay in the receipts from taxes levied locally on property (*Grundsteuer*) and the production and capital investment of local business (*Gewerbesteuer*). Given the determination of central government to assist construction programmes by limiting the level of property tax and granting immunity to many public housing projects, the main burden of revenue fell in the *Gewerbesteuer*. Taxation receipts were supplemented by fees charged for the provision of services such as transport, water, sanitation and electricity. In addition, compulsory services administered by the *Gemeinden* on behalf of the *Land* or *Bund* were financed by the parent body. The lion's share of taxation, particularly income tax, was reserved for the *Land* and Bonn, although the *Länder* were charged with redistributing an element of their taxation receipts to reduce the inequality that existed between the revenue bases of individual *Gemeinden*.

Yet, given the wide range of responsibilities assumed by most local authorities, which accounted for approximately 60 per cent of all public investment in the Federal Republic, the level of services could only be sustained with the provision of a network of grants and subsidies provided by the *Bund* and *Land* to assist the *Gemeinden* in areas such as housing, welfare programmes and education. Even with this assistance, many of the *Gemeinden* ran heavily into debt and were forced to raise loans on the open market in order to finance programmes of capital investment.

In order to tackle this problem the taxation system was significantly revised in 1969, with the result that, although the *Gemeinden* now surrender 40 per cent of the *Gewerbesteuer*, to be divided equally between the *Bund* and *Land*, in return they receive 15 per cent of locally raised income tax. Yet, despite the injection of income tax receipts, most authorities still derive over 40 per cent of their taxation revenue from the *Gewerbesteuer*. This clearly disadvantages the rural communities and generates fluctuations in revenue according to the level of economic activity. Therefore, despite the measures implemented in 1969, only three-quarters of local government expenditure is covered by taxation and fees received from the community for the provision of services. In a climate where there are continual demands for more schools, hospitals and roads, the financial viability of the *Gemeinden* is still perilous. The same situation is also to be found in the *Stadtkreise*, which are financed on a similar basis to the *Gemeinden*.

The chief source of financial aid to local government has traditionally been assistance provided by the *Land*. This aid has generally taken the form of fees received by the *Gemeinden* for the compulsory provision of services which are the responsibility of the *Land*. In addition, various specific grants and subsidies are provided to promote programmes of public utilities where minimum requirements are established but the effective extent of provision is at the discretion of local government. In the past decade, however, even the *Länder* have felt the onerous burden of financing such projects. The trend has been towards the increasing involvement of the *Bund*. Although traditionally the *Bund* has always dispensed funds to the *Länder*, where they were acting as agents for the administration of federal responsibilities, the initiation of major programmes, particularly in the fields of housing and welfare, has seen the flow of funds from the centre to local government, via the *Länder*, increase considerably. In addition, the launching of the programme of common responsibilities (*Gemeinschaftsaufgaben*), with federal funds providing 50 per cent of new investment in further education, regional economic restructuring and agricultural improvements, has further increased the role played by the *Bund* in the investment policy pursued by local government.

In this light, despite the taxation reforms, many units of local government are heavily in debt and ultimately are reliant on grants and subsidies from other agencies in order to maintain their level of services. Observers have been tempted to suggest that the reforms, although outwardly establishing the financial base of the *Gemeinden*, have actually reduced their autonomy and have tied local government into a network of revenue-sharing with the *Länder* and Bonn. In certain areas the financial autonomy of the *Gemeinden* has been clearly curtailed. For example, as a result of the fiscal reforms of 1969, local government along with other tiers of government is required to prepare a medium-term fiscal plan. While the ultimate goal is to coordinate overall public sector expenditure levels, the spending guidelines, although not legally enforceable, represent an attempt by Bonn to curb the autonomy of the *Gemeinden*. In addition, as a result of the Economic Stability Act of 1967, designed to mitigate problems generated by economic trade cycles, Bonn and the *Länder* now have the power to veto or freeze expenditure on major projects by the *Gemeinden* as a means of controlling the overall levels of expenditure in the economy. Certainly, within this framework, despite the outward autonomy enjoyed by the *Gemeinden*, control of finance appears to be gravitating slowly, yet steadily, to the centre.

INTERNAL STRUCTURES

The internal structure of local government, although uniform within each of the *Länder*, does vary considerably between states and, in particular, between the northern and southern states.

Gemeinden

The main representative body of each *Gemeinde* is an elected council (*Stadtrat* or *Gemeinderat*). The size of the council can vary considerably but will be dictated by the state constitutional law and be related to the size of the community. Elections for the council are generally held every four years, execpt in Bavaria and Baden-Wurttemberg where half the council seats are contested every three years. The form of election is usually a closed list system of proportional representation. In most of the northern *Länder* the elected council is headed by a mayor (*Bürgermeister* or, in the bigger units, *Oberbürgermeister*), who is elected from within the council for a fixed term. However, executive and administrative authority in the larger units is vested in an official appointed by the council (*Stadtdirektor*). This system is largely to be found in the former British Zone of occupation, with a distinct division between the political and administrative agents. While, to an extent, this move has been successful, in that the *Stadtdirektor* is appointed by and responsible to the elected body, s/he is generally given a degree of latitude and adopts the role of a city manager. In the smaller *Gemeinden* the post of *Stadtdirektor* is dispensed with and the *Bürgermeister* clearly emerges as the chief executive, with considerable influence in that councils are generally smaller than their British counterparts and curtail the number and influence of their committees and sub-committees. In both instances, however, ultimate authority rests with the elected body which appoints senior administrators, generally on fixed-term contracts.

In southern Germany the position, however, is slighty different in that there is effectively the fusing of administrative and political functions in the form of a *Bürgemeister* or *Oberbürgemeister* who is directly elected for a period of six years. The *Oberbürgemeister*, although accountable to the *Stadtrat*, clearly emerges as chief executive, as s/he is chairman of the council, head of the administration and representative of the polity as a whole. In most large units, therefore, the *Oberbürgemeister* is a full-time position supervising the work of the administrative sub-divisions (*Referate*) and assisted by two or more deputies. While technically the *Oberbürgermeister* must carry with him or her the *Stadtrat*, which appoints each senior administrator (*Referent*), it is clearly expected that the *Oberbürgermeister* will play a major role in policy formation and the day-to-day running of the *Gemeinde*.

Kreis

The organisation of the *Kreis* effectively parallels the *Gemeinden* in that in most of the northern states the *Landrat* is chosen from within the elected body (*Kreistag*) and is assisted by a full-time administrator (*Oberkreisdirektor*) appointed by the *Kreistag*. In Bavaria, once again, the position of *Oberkreisdirektor* is dispensed with in favour of a directly elected *Landrat* combining political and administrative functions. One further case should be noted in the form of Hamburg and Bremen, which, as two of the Federal Republic's largest cities, enjoy *Land* status. Both cities have adopted a bicameral legislature with an upper house chosen by the popularly elected lower house and granted executive powers. In these cities, the mayor, who is selected from within the governing senate, holds a position that can be equated with the relationship established between the *Bundestag* and the *Bundeskanzler*.

Local government has traditionally been beset with the problem of combining efficiency with democracy. Prior to the creation of the Federal Republic the tendency was to solve this problem by opting primarily for efficiency, with local government officials seen as representative of a perceived community interest above sectional conflict in society. This highly legalistic and, at times, élitist interpretation of the role of local government is still reflected, to an extent, in the position of the *Stadtdirektor* and *Oberbürgermeister*. Since 1949, however, the provisions established by the *Grundgesetz* clearly indicate that ultimate authority now lies with the elected bodies.

PERSONNEL AND TRAINING

In comparison with Britain, the term 'public servant' is used in a different context in West Germany in that it refers to all those who are employed by the state. With the inclusion of groups such as postal workers, teachers and railway workers, approximately 12 per cent of the working population can be classified as public servants, the vast majority (80 per cent) being employed by either the *Länder* or local government. In general, public servants fall into three categories, officials (*Beamten*), white-collar workers (*Angestellen*) and blue-collar workers (*Arbiter*). Within these categories the *Beamten* quite clearly constitute the bureaucratic élite, dominating most senior administrative posts. Approximately 40 per cent of public servants are classified as 'officials' and of these 40 per cent are employed by the *Länder* and 13 per cent by local government. The *Beamten*, therefore, are equivalent to the higher echelons of the British civil service and employment in this area has traditionally been much prized in Germany, not only for the status derived from holding a position of responsibility but also for the rewards attached to the post in the form of a job guaranteed for life and a generous non-contributory pension scheme. To most intents and purposes the *Beamten* reflect the Prussian bureaucratic tradition, with recruitment conditioned by rigid educational qualifications and a period of training heavily based on the study of law. The German civil service outwardly conforms to the model of a classic bureaucracy, with a rigid hierarchical structure based on strict delineation of duties, little interchange of personnel and respect for a legalistic interpretation of its administrative role.

One of the central considerations in the construction of the West German state was the determination to ensure that the lessons of Weimar were accepted and that the civil service was clearly seen to be subservient to its political overlords. Therefore, although the civil service is still basically a conservative force in society, it is now far more politicised than its pre-war counterpart. The debate surrounding the *Radikalnerlass* in the 1970s was a reminder of the stipulation within the *Grundgesetz* that the loyalty of officials is to the constitution and, through the primacy given to political parties in the *Grundgesetz*, to the ruling coalition. This condition has brought quite a considerable change to the role and outlook of the civil service. Public employees are now free to join political parties and hold elected office. As a result, civil servants are well represented in locally elected assemblies although, in general, an employee would not be allowed to serve on the body by which he or she was employed. In addition, senior appointments at all levels of the public sector are now seen as political appointments. While naturally the selection of a *Bürgemeister* or *Landrat* would be expected to reflect the wishes of the dominant political coalition within the *Kreisrat* or *Gemeinderat*, the appointment of a *Stadtdirektor* and senior administrators is also likely to be influenced by political considerations. This principle would apply even to what might be considered non-political posts such as within the field of education or management of a municipal opera house or theatre.

In a situation where party credentials, or at least a sympathy with the goals of the controlling political *Fraktion*, can be a determining factor in appointment, it is not surprising that doubts have been cast over the efficiency and integrity of the administrative system. The potential for political patronage is undeniable, yet it does not seem to have reduced the faith of the population in the effectiveness of the administration. In part, this is due to the acceptance that officials should be politically sympathetic to the goals of the elected body. In addition, no doubt many were not sad to see the stranglehold of the career civil servant loosened on senior positions and a channel opened for increased mobility and the use of external expertise. More particularly, however, the potential for corruption has been reduced by the detailed scrutiny of local government by both elected officials and the administrative officials of the *Land*. Furthermore, the existence of administrative courts at district, *Land* and federal level provide further avenues where redress can be sought against administrative practice.

POLICY MAKING

Intergovernmental relations

The formal status and role of local government in the Federal Republic was clearly outlined within the *Grundgesetz*, although its actual structure was dictated by the constitution of the individual states. In this sense, the pattern of intergovernmental relations is technically fashioned by reference to the constitution and, in particular, to the local government acts (*Gemeindeordnungen*) for each of the *Länder*. If, therefore, a unit of local government feels that its powers are being infringed by another agency, such as the *Land*, it has the power to appeal initially to the *Land* Constitutional Court and ultimately to the Federal Constitutional Court (*Bundesverfassungsgericht*), which is the guardian of the *Grundgesetz*. In addition, complaints against the activities of a particular agency of local government can be referred initially to the immediate supervisory body of the agency concerned. For example, complaints lodged against a *Gemeinde* would be dealt with by the relevant *Kreis*. If, however, this route fails to produce satisfaction, the complaint can be referred to the administrative courts which operate at district, state and federal levels. The courts are empowered to deal with all cases of an administrative nature although issues, such as taxation, will be referred to a separate network of specialist courts such as the Revenue Courts.

The framework of judicial review of the administration is, therefore, well established in the Federal Republic and the review mechanism has been bolstered in Rhineland-Pfalz by the introduction of an Ombudsman (*Bürgerbeauftragte*) at state level. Yet if the constitutional rights of the *Gemeinden* and *Kreis* are acknowledged, it has not prevented the increasing influence of both federal and state government in their affairs. While the *Bund* has traditionally minimised its connections with the *Gemeinden* by dealing primarily through the *Land*, the last decade has witnessed the steady encroachment of central direction in local affairs. Although the

Gemeinden, through retaining an element of budgetary autonomy, have been quite successful in resisting attempts by Bonn to impose public expenditure guidelines, federal influence is felt through its powers of legislation and the increasing reliance of both the *Länder* and the *Gemeinden* on financial assistance from the *Bund*. The leverage provided by the establishment of Joint Tasks and the wide-ranging power to dispense funds to projects of national value has allowed Bonn to establish extensive influence in the fields of regional economic development, welfare and education. In this context the influence of the federal ministries plays an important role in the affairs of both the *Gemeinden* and the *Länder*.

The focus of intergovernmental relations, however, is the understanding achieved between the *Länder* and local government. In this sphere, in addition to the levers of financial control, the *Länder* also force local government to operate within a fairly rigid framework of law. Under the general control of the Ministry of the Interior and through the supervision of both the District President (*Regierungspräsident*) and the *Landrat*, the activities of the *Kreise* and the *Gemeinden* are very closely scrutinised. If, therefore, the *Gemeinden* enjoy a certain degree of flexibility in the implementation of their responsibilities, they do have to work within a broad framework dictated and enforced by the *Land*. To an extent, however, through the mechanism of the law, the *Gemeinden* are able to prevent the formal erosion of their powers. The disturbing element in this relationship, therefore, is the reliance of the *Gemeinden* on funds provided by the *Land* in order to maintain their level of services. While the dispensation of such funds is naturally used to encourage the coordination of services within the *Land*, they symbolise a channel of influence that is progressively reducing the latitude available to the *Gemeinden*. The *Gemeinden* are not, however, without formal or informal channels of influence. At a national level representatives of local government are involved alongside other agencies in determining guidelines for government strategy in relation to future expenditure patterns and the management of the economy. In addition, the extent to which the *Gemeinden* acting on their own initiative or as agents for the *Land* or Bonn are the primary focus for the provision of services has necessitated the creation of a vast network of planning and coordinating bodies to monitor and direct service provision. Within the constant interaction between different levels of government the *Gemeinden* exert extensive influence by virtue of not only the discretion afforded to them in the level of service provision but also the reliance of both the *Land* and Bonn on the *Gemeinden* for feedback to enable the review of existing policy and the formulation of future strategy.

On a more formal level, further channels for pressure are provided by the election of local deputies to assemblies at both the state and national level. While the lobbying of deputies is often undertaken by individuals and organised groups, local government as a unit is often well represented and influential in the calculations of the *Länder* and Bonn by virtue of the fact that most larger units of local government are dominated by the major political parties. Certainly the use of the party caucus, particularly at state level, can be a valuable lever in ensuring that the state machinery takes note of local issues.

PARTIES AND PRESSURE GROUPS

One of the most remarkable features of the two decades following the creation of a Federal Republic was that, while there was widespread satisfaction with the political outputs generated by the governmental process, there was little suggestion that the population identified with either of the political parties or the overall system of government. Indeed, there was a distinct tendency to shun political activism. This suspicion of the political process was, however, not transmitted into the sphere of local government in the form of either apathy or non-participation in the electoral process. It was evident, however, that there was a marked determination to resist overt politicisation of the local government arena and particularly penetration of the electoral process by the national political parties. Most *Gemeinden* were, therefore, controlled by independents and loose local associations, which competed in closed list elections under the broad heading of Citizens Associations. It appeared, therefore, that personality rather than party affiliation was the key factor in local elections, and this was acknowledged by the major parties who often attempted to recruit leading figures in the community as their representatives.

The situation has, however, changed considerably over the past decade. While this pattern is still relevant for many of the rural *Gemeinden*, the reorganisation of local government into larger units has seen the role of personality and local groups progressively challenged by the machinery of the national parties. Within the urban and larger *Gemeinden*, the electoral process is now dominated by the major political parties. In this context, the *Oberbürgermeister*, while still a far more powerful figure than the British mayor, is now likely to be either a member of, or at least sympathetic to, the ruling political party. The party caucus, therefore, plays an important role in policy deliberation, particularly in the *Stadtkreise* and increasingly in the *Gemeinden*. Yet, in the absence of an acrid ideological battle between the Social Democrats and the Christian Democrats, collaboration and consultation between rival party groups is not unusual. Indeed, in a study of larger cities, it has been contended that there was little to distinguish CDU and SPD controlled cities in terms of commitment to expenditure on welfare and housing programmes. This perhaps can be explained by the constraints imposed by reliance on funding from the state and federal levels. It has been suggested, however, that continuity and stability are also provided by the prominence of pressure groups in the process of local government.

Pressure group activity is an accepted part of the policy-making process at all levels of government in West Germany. The organisation of occupational groups into national associations controlling recruitment and maintenance of standards has a long tradition in German society, and the right of such associations to represent the interests of their members in decision making is widely accepted. Certainly, at the local level, economic and business groups have extensive ties with the major political parties and will be expected to play a prominent role in the policy-making caucus. The encouragement of group activity has led several observers to style the decision-making process as neo-corporatist. While such a label may be an overstatement, the consensual style of post-war party politics has certainly assisted the establishment of a tripartite relationship between local government, business interests and organised labour. In the past two decades, however, this relationship has been eroded somewhat by the increasing role played in local political parties by members recruited from the bureaucracy. The bureaucracy is now a major force in local government and this explains, in part, why proposals to restructure radically the format of local government or reduce the extent of its activities have been resisted. It has been suggested that the role played by bureaucrats has been the primary reason why German local government has largely failed to respond to the problems presented by economic recession. Certainly the focus of local government attention on campaigns to lure new industry to the depressed areas rather than the regeneration of existing units or the promotion of small enerprises indicates a need to re-establish links with the business community and to adjust to a changing economic climate. Yet, in this context, it has to be admitted that the affairs of the *Gemeinden* are subject to considerable influences from the state and federal level. While pressure group politics is important at the local level, the focus of much organised activity is directed towards either the *Land* or Bonn with the sponsorship of elected representatives and the establishment of links with the major ministries.

ELECTORATE

David Conradt (1989) has argued that in the past decade citizens' identification with the political superstructure has increased markedly. It would seem, therefore, that the debate now focuses not so much on the acceptance of a liberal democratic framework but rather on the format of the framework. In this sense, the extent and level of political debate has increased, and those stating a positive disinterest in politics have fallen from approximately one-third to one-tenth of the population. The suggestion is, therefore, that attitudes to government, at all levels, are changing and there is growing willingness to accept political involvement. If this is so, it represents a rejection of the passive acceptance of 'administration in the national interest' in favour of a more politicised and volatile decision-making process.

This change, however, has not been reflected in membership figures for the major political parties, which, while exceeding their British counterparts, have not risen notably in the past decade. It has to be admitted, though, that there has been a substantial increase in political activity at the level of local government. Initially, activity took the form of groups formed to promote particular parties or candidates. This base, however, has been expanded to encompass a vast variety of local interest groups (*Bürgerinitiaven*), which mount campaigns over issues in such areas as education, housing, welfare rights and the environment. This re-awakening of interest in grass-roots politics has been one of the most remarkable features of post-war Germany. In many areas it has forced the established political parties to acknowledge that the electorate is no longer satisfied with the steady consensual politics of the first two decades of the Federal Republic. The rising concern over issues such as the protection of the environment, welfare policies and defence, alongside a willingness actively to press demands on local government, has forced the existing political parties to revise their traditional standpoints in an attempt to harness the wave of local protest. The next decade will be a particularly testing time for local government, since the existing parties, having encouraged grass-roots liberal democracy, must now adjust to its demands or face extensive opposition from new political groupings, such as the Greens, seeking to lever themselves into office.

PROBLEMS AND ISSUES

The system of local government in the former Federal Republic is a complex interweaving of distinct and often competing agencies. The individual is at any time subject to five layers of administration: federal, state, district, county and municipality. Although the *Gemeinden* are guaranteed an element of autonomy by the provisions of the Basic Law, in most instances their role in service provision is as an agent or representative for the *Land* or *Bund*. Given the complexity of the network of agencies involved in the provision of services, there has been an increasing demand for the reorganisation of local government. The position was further exacerbated by the mounting financial difficulties faced by the *Gemeinden*, which resulted in the financial reforms in the latter half of the 1960s, and a significant territorial reorganisation of the units capable of local government to create fewer but larger units able to maintain an adequate level of service provision.

The reforms, however, failed to address themselves to several central questions surrounding the future of local government. In particular, there is still an ongoing debate surrounding the question of whether the *Gemeinden* should restrict their activities purely to the provision of services not adequately catered for by the market or engage in extensive intervention, seeking to equalise opportunity and wealth between different groups in society. Traditionally, 'municipal socialism' has been widely resisted in Germany, but the problems generated by economic recession have led to local campaigns for the provision of a wider range of welfare facilities to cater for the needs of an increasingly vocal electorate. Certainly it has been suggested that the electorate is no longer content with the *Gemeinden* concentrating their attention on economic regeneration and on the allocation of resources, and greater attention will have to be paid to the maintenance of housing and welfare programmes.

To some extent, there has been a response to this situation with the increase in federal aid to promote economic and welfare programmes. While, on the one hand, financial assistance is welcomed, it has been suggested that the trend towards the reliance of the *Gemeinden* on specific grants from other tiers of government has significantly weakened their autonomy. It can be contended, however, that the financial leverage exerted by the *Land* and Bonn is countered, to an extent, by their continued reliance on the *Gemeinden* for the implementation of services and policy feedback. In addition, it is clear that any attempt to erode the constitutional position of the *Gemeinden* will be actively resisted. In certain areas, however, the reforms of the 1970s seem to have missed their target in that it has been suggested that territorial reform has not been accompanied by a rationalisation of the distribution of functions between the various tiers of government, while attempts at improving coordination and planning simply led to the establishment of a further tier of administration that in most instances was rapidly dismantled. Furthermore, the creation of larger units of government has increased the role played by the major parties but, in general, has reduced popular participation levels. It has also been suggested that the amalgamation of small units of local government into new financially viable bodies has generated a more efficient vehicle for the provision of services, but arguably it has been achieved at the price of local self-determination.

Most seriously, however, despite the financial reforms, the position of many of the *Gemeinden* is still perilous and only sustained by loans negotiated on the open market. In most areas it would appear that the reforms of the 1970s have been largely cosmetic, and the question surrounding the identification of the appropriate agencies for service provision and the establishment of an adequate financial base have still to be tackled.

One suspects, however, that the barriers to change lie not in the difficulties of reforming the constitutional position of local government but in the opposition of those groups who have a stated interest in maintaining the status quo. In particular, the bureaucracy, which is heavily entangled with the major political parties, will continue to be influential in opposing a radical restructuring of the various tiers of government. It would seem that the best that can be achieved in the immediate future will be further financial reforms, which will guarantee local government a more equitable share of the revenue cake. In the long term, however, this will not cure the problem faced by local government. The one bright point on the horizon is the reawakening of interest in local politics, which is likely to ensure that the campaign for change and reform is not ignored.

A final question concerning local government in Germany is the integration of the Democratic Republic into the Federal Constitution. It is too early to evaluate the facility with which formerly autocratically controlled communities in the East will develop successful local democracies on the lines of the former Federal structure. In particular, finance may be the greatest problem for the former East German *Länder* as technologically underdeveloped areas compete with the wealthier communities of the West. Aid programmes may for a time ease the burden on local communities, but they will also require a sounder domestic economy if they are to provide services similar in standard to the established local governments of the wealthier sections of the country.

BIBLIOGRAPHY

Childs, D. and Johnson, J. (1981) *West Germany: Politics and Society*, London, Croom Helm.

Conradt, D. (1989) *The German Polity* (4th edn), London, Longman.

Gunlicks, A.B. (1981) 'The reorganisation of local government in the Federal Republic of Germany', in A.B. Gunlicks (ed.) *Local Government Reform and Reorganisation*, Port Washington, NY, Kennikat Press.

Johnson, N. (1973) *Government in the Federal Republic of Germany*, Oxford, Oxford University Press.

Johnson, N. and Cochrane A. (1981) *Economic Policy Making by Local Authorities in Britain and West Germany*, London, Allen and Unwin.

Kloss, G. (1990) *West Germany: An Introduction* (2nd edn), London, Macmillan.

Pasley, M. (ed.) (1982) *Germany: A Companion to German Studies* (2nd edn), London, Methuen.

Roberts, G.K. (1972) *West German Politics*, London, Macmillan.

Schweitzer, C.C. (1984) *Politics and Government in the Federal Republic: Basic Documents*, Leamington Spa, Berg.

Smith G. (1982) *Democracy in Western Germany*, London, Heinemann.

Smith, G., Paterson, W.E. and Merkl, P. (1989) *Developments in West German Politics*, London, Macmillan.

Chapter 7

Sweden

Bernard Jones

Sweden is a unitary state. The *Riksdag's* laws apply throughout the whole state territory and can cover all aspects of the affairs of the Swedish people. In practice there is a degree of local autonomy, which shows itself partly as the freedom of local authorities to interpret a skeleton or framework law in ways appropriate to the locality and partly as the freedom of local authorities to make their own regulations on minor matters such as car parking. It would be a mistake, however, to suppose that local government in Sweden is nothing more than this. Local government also has the freedom to take initiatives in any way not specifically reserved to another authority and to proceed with these initiatives until successfuly challenged by a local resident through a quasi-legal process. This major freedom arises from the constitution. Local government is warmly regarded and a serious matter to the Swedes.

The liberal democratic constitution of Sweden has developed steadily from the early nineteenth century. There was a period of parliamentary government in the eighteenth century, followed by a short spell of royal absolutism, but the constitution of 1809 placed restraints on the King and, since 1975, although titular head of state, he has no formal political powers. The government has been responsible to the *Riksdag* since 1917 and Sweden is, therefore, a parliamentary democracy typical of the Western European model.

The unicameral *Riksdag* has 349 members, 309 of whom are elected from constituencies. The remaining 40 seats are allocated so that proportional representation of the parties can be achieved. Any party which gains at least 4 per cent of the overall vote or 12 per cent in any one electoral district will be represented in the *Riksdag*. In practice this system has operated within a five-party system in which the left-of-centre Social Democrats have been in control from the early 1930s to the present day, apart from a few short breaks which include the period from 1976 to 1982.

Although, on occasion, the Social Democrats have held an overall majority they are often obliged to govern in coalition with the small Communist Party. In opposition on the centre–right of the political spectrum are the Centre Party, formerly the Agrarian Party, the Liberals and the Conservatives.

There is little direct democracy in Sweden. The *Riksdag* can call for a referendum, but its status is only advisory. The Swedes were given a choice between alternative pension plans or a nuclear energy policy and their preference was accepted. They were also consulted on the change from driving on the left to the right but, although a clear preference was to retain the former, and their wish was respected for a time, the government eventually ignored the referendum and made the change.

The institutions of government and law are held in high repute by the Swedes. Laws are not seen as an erosion of civil liberty; the government is not seen as something to be resisted. Rather, the rule of law is seen as supportive of the community and society in which individuals can hope to fulfil themselves. The constancy of Social Democratic support over such a long period, set against a background of neutrality in international affairs, has meant that Sweden is often held up as the model of a welfare state created by popular will expressed through the parliamentary process. With electoral turnout figures usually over 90 per cent, the legitimacy of government cannot be questioned from a liberal democratic perspective. The welfare state provides protection from 'the womb to the tomb'. The standard of living is the highest in Europe and, indeed, in some respects, Sweden is Europe's materialist counterpart of the USA, with the added feature of a much more even distribution of wealth and income.

The growth in the welfare state has in recent years been at a faster rate than industrial expansion and this has led to increasingly severe budgetary deficits. These in turn have placed severe financial constraints on welfare. This forms the major problem for the Swedish state and has led to the rather more precarious condition of Social Democrat control since 1970. Although Scandinavian states have been termed 'consensual democracies' it appears that the liberal–left consensus is less strong than it was under the impact of these financial difficulties.

The politics of consensus in Sweden is reflected in an elaborate system for policy making and implementation that is not found outside Scandinavia. Legislative proposals are first made the subject of a board of enquiry, which includes both government and opposition members and representatives from major interest groups with a concern for the issue in question. Before the conclusions of an enquiry are put before Parliament they are sent to all interested organisations for their comments and criticisms. Major interest groups such as the Labour Organisation or the Swedish Employers' Federation are, through such procedures, recognised as powerful and important agencies that should be consulted at all stages in the policy-making process. The significant role given to major interest groups in Sweden reflects a strong corporatist dimension within Swedish politics, and the system has been criticised as being responsive to large, well organised interests to the exclusion of non-represented individuals. However, few Swedish citizens are not members of a major pressure group that is representative of their economic and social interests and these groups have in general received loyal support from their members.

Alongside this corporatist decision-making system there is also a division of powers and incorporation of interest groups into the process of policy implementation. The ministerial departments are small units of government in terms of their personnel and are largely concerned with advising the minister on policy. These departments do not directly concern themselves with putting policy into practice; this role is given to state boards, which are independent of direct ministerial control. The boards are often chaired by politicians who are likely to support the government, although their membership consists largely of civil servants and representatives of relevant interest groups. The boards, along with local government, are principally agents for public policy implementation and, therefore, between them employ the greatest number of public sector workers.

Despite the important and innovatory procedures for policy making and implementation, the office of government within Sweden that has attracted the greatest attention within other liberal democracies is that of the Ombudsman. The holders of this office, created in 1809, have been able to aid citizens in the redress of grievances against the administration. The Swedish Ombudsman in reality consists of four departments, each with particular spheres of jurisdiction. They have considerable powers to initiate an investigation with or without a complaint from a citizen and about one-third of their cases arise from their own initiative.

THE STRUCTURE OF LOCAL GOVERNMENT

Legal status

Local self-government is an important theme of the Swedish constitution. The Instrument of Government, which forms a central element of the constitution, begins:

All public power in Sweden emanates from the people. The Swedish democracy is founded on the freedom of opinion and on universal and equal suffrage and shall be realised through a representative and parliamentary polity and through local self-government.

The pattern of provision has arisen through a variety of powers. The Local Government Act of 1977 reaffirmed the right of local authorities to conduct their own affairs. The interpretation of this right depends both upon precedent and upon principles which are clearly established within the Swedish tradition. These principles may be briefly summarised as indicating that council actions should be in the public interest, not speculative, not *ultra vires*, not inconsistent with existing statute law and not oppressive. This gives a wide degree of discretionary powers. In certain cases, where the issues were unclear, enabling acts have been passed. An Act passed in 1984 further increased local autonomy by permitting some local governments to obtain additional powers, subject to the approval of central government, in order to experiment with new ideas emanating from local initiatives. On top of these general powers there are statutory powers amounting to instructions to local authorities to perform certain duties. These powers are usually backed up by grants-in-aid from central government.

This constitutional commitment to local government has been realised in practice by the Swedish people, partly because of a long history of local government that was closely linked to the parish system of the established church, and partly because of their firm adherence to the constitution, the law and the practice of democracy. Somewhat more than 3 per cent of Sweden's adults are concerned with the political aspect of local government either as councillors or co-optees on to specialist boards.

STRUCTURES AND POWERS

The primary unit of local government is the municipality or commune, of which there are now 284. This number evolved through a process of amalgamation which began in 1952 when there were more than 2,500. At first the principle of amalgamation was voluntary, but in 1969 a compulsory element was introduced and a reduction to 278 was effected by 1974. Since then some merged municipalities have been redivided, but this process is unlikely to be much extended, partly because of the financial complexities involved and partly because the Social Democratic government is less sympathetic to pleas for separation. The motive for the rationalisation was to provide adequate populations in each commune to support an elementary school of satisfactory size. This minimum population was set at 8,000.

Birgersson (1977) notes that these reforms should be seen as a transition from a local government system with features of direct democracy to a modern, functionally organised representative system. Anton (1974b) argues that, although there was resistance to the changes in some quarters, the reforms should not be seen as an example of central government imposing its will on the local government system. The Swedish legislature was at that time bicameral and the upper house represented regional interests. In effect it was county politicians, many of whom had strong municipal links, who supported the reforms. Jonnson (1983) notes that most of the reductions in the number of local governments took place in the form of a larger municipality taking over one or more smaller municipalities. In order to protect the interests of their inhabitants, many of the smaller governments indulged in capital spending sprees just before amalgamation, astutely borrowing the money required so that the new municipalities would share the burden of repayment.

The secondary unit of local government is the county or region, of which there are twenty-four including Stockholm with its population of 1.5 million. Two large towns of historic importance, Malmö and Gothenburg, and the island of Gotland are excluded from this system and are effectively municipalities that can exercise county powers. All the counties are governed by a council, which exercises authority over their functions. The mean population of the counties, excluding Stockholm and Gotland, is 300,000, which is regarded as adequate to support the health care and medical services which are their main responsibilities.

In parallel with the county councils and co-terminous as far as boundaries are concerned is a system of county administrative boards which are the regional arm of central government, responsible for the regional administration of centrally provided services. The county or regional governor is a government appointee who presides over the board, which is made up of members nominated from the county council. This board is thus a hybrid with responsibilities both to central government and the county. In practice it has been found to work well, but the distinction between the elected county council responsible to the electorate for certain services and the nominated board responsible to the government and the council for the administration of other services must be understood.

FUNCTIONS

Central government maintains responsibility for the traditional areas of foreign policy, defence and the maintenance of internal law and order. The police are the responsibility of central government, although local controls can be maintained through their attachment to the county boards. Much of the infrastructure is administered by central government, either directly, such as long-distance communications, or indirectly, through state-controlled enterprises such as LKAB, a mining corporation, or NJA for steel. The economic infrastructure including economic policy, the labour market and social insurance is administered centrally, as is the important area of higher education. The *Riksdag* is also responsible for the laws that form the contextual framework within which local authorities work.

The major activity of the county councils is the provision of medical care and health services, together with many associated services such as training for nursing and looking after the mentally retarded. In addition, the county also has several social service functions, including providing fostering services and family counselling. There is a joint responsibility with central government for vocational rehabilitation.

County councils share a number of responsibilities jointly with municipalities. There are federations of local authorities for local and regional communications, instituting, for example, passenger transport executives to provide a variety of bus, streetcar and local train services. Another example of the cooperation between municipality and county lies in the folk high schools. These are a form of adult education college, which provide a variety of courses, many for mature students. Those courses, which are vocational in nature, are financed by the county council. Other courses are financed by the municipality. The dividing line is blurred but funding is divided approximately equally between the two authorities.

It must be remembered that the county council nominates members to the boards which provide the regional level of administration of central government departments. This provides a significant level of power and influence to the county without budgetary cost, given that the board administers several important functions in its area. These embrace responsibility for law and order, which includes the administration of the police and of local judicial systems. The boards also have an important role in regional planning and are charged with co-ordinating the ideas and policies of the various local governments within a county. As an agency of the state the boards also have several prefectorial powers of supervision over the public health and welfare interests of local governments and can act as a first instance tribunal in cases where citizens dispute the decisions of a local authority.

The municipalities are allocated the majority of services that are, in most countries, attached to local government. Most costly is responsibility for compulsory education up to the age of 16 in the comprehensive schools and for much of the 16 to 18 education in the high schools which, although not compulsory, have a 90 per cent take-up rate. Housing, and some social services, including payment of social assistance, also absorb a considerable proportion of the budget. Fire services, roads, and sports, arts and leisure facilities also are municipal charges. In addition to these functions the municipality has productive as well as consumption roles and in particular regulates gas and electricity supplies, with some larger municipalities generating their own electricity.

The 1984 legislation that permitted communes to develop new functions subject to central approval has somewhat widened the capacity of local governments to gain new functions. These powers have been used in particular for planning and economic development and also for establishing more flexible procedures for schools, such as changing the hours and numbers of days for pupils' attendance in some rural areas. While the changes are more in the nature of amendments to existing powers, they nevertheless are a tendency to move away from rigid implementation of uniform dictates from central government.

FINANCE

The pattern of local government revenue and expenditure is best understood by reference to Table 7.1. For both municipal and county administrations taxation forms the chief source of revenue with grant-in-aid from the state forming an important contribution. Both municipality and county raise about one-sixth of their revenue from charges.

The tax referred to is an income tax. This is a flat rate percentage in contrast to the progressive state income tax, and is levied on the taxable income of residents within a local authority and upon 'legal persons', that is businesses, that operate in the area. The municipal rate of tax has practically doubled since 1952 and is now about 17 per cent. The county rate of tax has more than trebled in the same period and is now approximately 13 per cent. The combined tax rate is thus 30 per cent. The tax is assessed and collected by the state taxing authorities as part of their routine duties and the local authority portion is returned. The level of tax is the sole responsibility of the local authorities, and the levels cited above

Table 7.1 Sources of Swedish local government revenue in 1981 (as a percentage of total)

Source	County	Municipalities
Taxation	62	42
State grants	16	25
Charges	17	18
New loans	1	6
Other sources	4	9

Source: A. Gustafsson (1983: 109)

conceal variations of from 10.6 per cent to 19.6 per cent for municipalities and from 11.5 per cent to 14.5 per cent for counties. These variations would be larger were it not for the grants paid by the state.

The total state grant, which forms 25 per cent of municipal income and 16 per cent of county income, is made up of three elements, an equalisation grant designed to even out differences in tax bases between the authorities, grants for consumption expenditure basically covering running costs, and grants for investment which largely cover capital costs. These grants in total amounted to 24.3 per cent of the Swedish central government's expenditure in 1977/78 and must, therefore, be seen as a significant element in any exercise of restraint by central government over local.

The pattern of expenditure for municipal and county councils can be seen from Tables 7.2 and 7.3. The importance of the health services for the counties is well illustrated, as is the importance of social welfare education and environmental spending on energy, water, refuse disposal, land and housing for municipalities. In general terms, about 75–80 per cent of local government spending is an obligation, since the local authorities are fulfilling a state-imposed duty. About 17 per cent of municipal spending is classed as capital, corresponding to about 8 per cent for counties. This is reflected in the higher new loans figures for municipalities. However, the borrowing figures are both low so that the inference can be drawn that capital spending in Sweden is much more likely to be financed from revenue directly than from loans. Local government borrowing does not, therefore, form a significant proportion of the total public borrowing as it does in, for example, the United Kingdom. This, of course, eases the pressure on central planning by making local government, at least in this respect, less obtrusive.

The actual fixing of the tax and planning of spending is done on an annual basis through a detailed budget, which local authorities must

Table 7.2 Expenditure of Swedish county government by sector during
1981 (in percentages)

Sector	
Health services and medical care	76
Care of the mentally retarded	9
Other activities	6
Education and cultural services	5
Central administration	3
Social activities	1

Source: A. Gustafsson (1988: 119)

Table 7.3 Expenditure of Swedish municipalities by sector during 1981
(in percentages)

Sector	
Social welfare	25
Education	24
Energy, water, refuse disposal	15
Land and housing	7
Recreation and cultural amenities	7
Joint municipal administration	7
Environment, health, social protection	6
Communications	5
Employment and enterprise	4

Source: A. Gustafsson (1988: 118)

complete, preferably in November but by early December at the latest,
before the fiscal year begins. The budget is drawn up in the context of
increasing attention to longer-term planning. Checks on expenditure are
performed by auditors who are appointed for three years by the local
authority and who work closely in association with auditors from the
Swedish Association of Local Authorities. Their function is not so much
to check on financial misdemeanour as to see that council decisions have
been effectively and efficiently implemented. The auditors produce an
annual report.

INTERNAL STRUCTURES

In the days of a multitude of often tiny municipalities, when local
government had little power and responsibility, there were nearly 200,000
elected representatives and rather fewer local government employees.

Many of the elected representatives undertook, voluntarily, work of a routine nature, especially in the smaller communes which were little more than parishes. The position has now changed completely. There are currently only 70,000 councillors and they are far outnumbered by local government employees who, if teachers are included, exceed a million. The work of all municipalities and counties demands a structure of committees, each served by salaried officials, with all except the very smallest having at least one salaried councillor, who is termed a commissioner. The largest authorities, such as Gothenburg, Malmö and above all Stockholm, have complex administrative patterns and several commissioners.

Councils must consist of an odd number of members, with a minimum of thirty-one, while Stockholm, the largest, has 101 members. All councillors have alternates, who substitute for them when they are indisposed. There must be at least four meetings annually, although most authorities meet monthly and some even more frequently. Meetings are open to the public and are advertised in, and reported by, the local media, especially the press. The council debates and decides major policy, especially the budget, taxation and charge levels. Matters of principle or of great importance cannot be delegated to committees. The chair of the council is an influential figure, although he or she is not a mayor in either the British ceremonial sense or that of the French political boss.

In practice, of course, much of the preparatory work for council meetings is done by committees. There must be an odd number of councillors, at least five, on these committees which are elected by the council. If a minority on the council so demand, these committees must be constituted proportionately to party political strength. The council also elects the committee chairs, who will usually, but not always, be from the majority party or party grouping. Each committee member, including the chair, has an alternate who substitutes when necessary.

The central committee, which will attract the most influential councillors, is the executive committee. This is required by law and exercises leadership and co-ordinating roles. It can demand information from other committees and can make suggestions to them. It is responsible for setting priorities and for co-ordinating both the planning and the operation of the council which it can do through its responsiblity for budget. It is usual for the executive committee to consist of the chair of the major committees. Its chair is a highly significant political figure, who will often also be the chairperson of the council. Committees meet in camera partly to facilitate full and frank discussion and partly because personnel matters are frequently discussed.

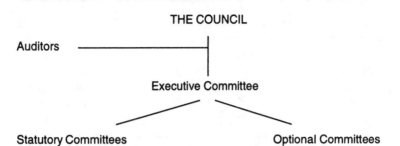

Figure 7.1 Outline committee structure for Swedish councils.

The structure of committees for both municipal and county administrations is set out in Figure 7.1. It should be noted that certain committees are statutory (for example, education for municipalities, health and medical for the counties), while others are optional and will be chosen according to the needs of the council. Municipal councils have the option of devolving some of their deliberations but not decisions to special district committees. This option is taken up mainly by the larger councils. These sub-municipal committees can discuss such matters as day nurseries, schools, libraries, sports grounds and sheltered housing, reporting to the appropriate statutory committee.

Most committees will have an apparatus of officers and permanent accommodation. The function of the committees is formally to draft business for council consideration, to implement council decisions and to undertake certain delegated administrative duties. It is expected that members will participate in the administrative process. The corporate nature of Swedish administration demands not only horizontal integration between service departments, but also a vertical integration within those departments with policy and administration not being separated.

A recent development arising from the 1977 Local Government Act is the emergence of the commissioner, a salaried full-time elected councillor, of whom there are now more than 500 in municipalities and counties. Most of the municipalities have at least one commissioner, even if only part-time, while medium-sized municipalities will have two or three and larger municipalities between four and ten. As paid politicians they are usually extremely influential in the policy-making process.

Two other matters may be mentioned in concluding this section on administrative structure. The first is the special problem of Stockholm which, because of its size, its position as capital city and its physical proximity to national government, demands an even more complex organisation. The second is the fact that municipalities and counties have at least a part stake and often a majority holding in a variety of enterprises. There are 1300 of these, employing 40,000 people, which is 4 per cent of the local government workforce. Areas include housing, property administration, electricity supply and district heating. The management of these enterprises is integrated into the council structures in appropriate ad hoc ways.

INTERGOVERNMENTAL RELATIONS

Anton (1974b) notes that the Swede is not so much worried by the question of who governs but much more concerned with the question of whether they govern well. Questions, which may occur to a British or a United States observer, regarding the relationship between central and local government in terms of the tension between centre and periphery and the gradual establishment of central prominence, do not occur in the same form to the Swede whether s/he be an academic, governed or in government.

In conformity with the corporate basis of Swedish democracy the generally cordial relationship maintained between central government and local authorities is based on the mediating role of the two Swedish local authority associations. On all general matters concerning local government the local authority associations will be consulted by the centre, which can be assured that the constituent members of the associations will abide by the decisions reached on their behalf.

As might be expected, the two associations have a political complexion but tensions are to a large extent avoided by having the Congress elected and its executive selected proportionately to the political situation in the municipalities and counties. The legitimacy conferred by this process helps to make them very effective in the roles which they have to play vis-à-vis central government. Of course, all is not sweetness and light, and the increasing resource constraints of the last few years have produced some signs of a more dominant attitude by central government and more aggressive responses by local government.

The Swedish local authority associations have already been mentioned in the context of personnel recruitment and training. In addition to this role and their mediating function, the SALA (Swedish Association of Local Authorities) and FCC (Federation of County Councils) act as a collective in the labour bargaining process with local authority employees and as information centres for local authority employees and councillors.

Since Sweden is a unitary state the local government authorities are not autonomous. Ultimately the state has jurisdiction, but the political culture of the Swedes, together with certain demographic trends, have ensured that the state is certainly not seen as an onerous overseer of local government. Indeed, the official Swedish portrait is just the reverse. Local government has expanded in relation to the central state and the powers of the state over local government have been rarely used in times of economic expansion, although there are indications that the last few years have seen at least a partial reversal of this trend.

If the relative importance of the respective spheres of government is measured in financial terms, the predominance of municipal government is clearly seen. By 1981, 35 per cent of the GDP was accounted for by central and local government: 12 per cent by the state, 15 per cent by the municipalities and 8 per cent by the counties, principally on the health service. The total local government expenditure is thus nearly twice that of central government. These figures are reflected in the working population. Out of 4 million employed persons, about 1.6 million (40 per cent) are employed by the public sector. This figure splits into one million (25 per cent) in local government, and 0.3 million (8 per cent) for each of the central government and public utilities. Thus, cultural disposition and democratic provisions have, at least in times of expansion, reinforced the importance of the local cornerstone of the Swedish constitution. There are, of course, both principles and mechanisms by which the central government can influence the local authorities, and these will be discussed further when the restraints upon local government are considered, but first an account of the various functions of local government will be given, together with an outline of the financial structure.

The general drift of responsibility has been from the state to the municipality. The chief examples contrary to that statement are the movement of employment and labour market affairs from county to state in the 1940s and 1950s and policing and magistrates' courts from municipality to the state in the 1960s. It should be noted that these movements were before the major reform of municipal administration. Since then, and with the larger municipalities better able to cope with government delegation, other powers, notably education, have passed to the local government sector.

The reasons for the prominence of local government are threefold: first, the principle of administration, which holds that decisions affecting individuals should be taken at the lowest possible level consistent with equity and the achievement of minimum standards; second, the power granted to local authorities in 1862 to raise income tax without restriction as to rate; third, the neutrality of the Swedish state militarily.

The impact of these three factors may be illustrated quite briefly. The health service, administered regionally, is the responsiblity of local government. This immediately reduces both the central budget and state control, while correspondingly increasing the importance of county government. The Swedish population is now over 80 per cent urbanised, an increase of 30 per cent in the last fifty years. This, coupled with the great reduction in the number of municipalities and the corresponding increase in political and administrative cohesion, has meant that the delegation of tasks from central to local government has been easier as the new units have been more able to cope with the demands. Finally, the neutrality of the Swedish state has meant both relatively small state spending on military affairs, and, perhaps more important, a less centralist attitude to matters such as planning, which are only loosely connected with strategic and military needs.

THE ROLE OF POLITICAL PARTIES

Political parties play a significant part in the policy-making process of local government. For national elections political parties, financed at a rate of 110,000 kr per seat, need to break through a 4 per cent barrier to be represented in the *Riksdag*. For local elections a barrier of 3 per cent applies for the counties and there is no barrier for the municipalities. It might be thought, therefore, that, especially in the municipalities, small local parties would be well represented on councils. Such a supposition would be wrong. In the 1983 elections, out of 13,500 local seats, only 201 went to small local parties. The Christian Democratic Party gained 129 seats while the major five parties gained 95 per cent. With the seats went the money, typically 40,000 kr per seat. Thus the local party system conforms to the national pattern, so that Moderate, Centre, Liberal, Social Democratic and Communist parties have sufficient funds to organise successfully at the local level and maintain their grip on the councils and committees of Sweden.

Whatever form of coalition arrangements are entered into, and this obviously depends on the exact disposition of seats within an electoral area, there tend to be two spheres of co-operation between, on the one hand, the two socialist parties and, on the other, the three non-socialist parties, often referred to as the 'non-socialist bloc' or the 'bourgeois bloc'.

In the majority of municipalities, especially in those where the left bloc calls the tune, there is a well organised system of party group meetings. At these meetings the 'party line' will be determined for later transmission to the council. Where there is a party bloc with an overall majority, which is the case in over 80 per cent of Swedish municipalities, there will be little scope for 'maverick' behaviour by politicians who depend upon their party for their place. This is one of the results of the reforms in the size of local government units, which has promoted a switch from a more direct form of democracy to a more representative system.

The party at local level will usually be in harmony with the party at national level. There is a considerable intertwining of the networks of local/national politicians and hence the differences that sometimes occur in, for example, Britain between local and national policies of the same party are few and far between. Resource constraints are, however, reducing to some extent the automatic support which, for example, a Social Democratic majority can be expected to give to its party colleagues in central government. In the larger municipalities, and it is here that local Social Democratic parties are strongest, there is the additional factor of the sub-municipal committees. They can exert pressure by requests for specific local spending, often trivial in themselves (for example, the provision of children's play park equipment), that in total place a not inconsiderable pressure on budget makers. It is an open question if this community political pressure will be absorbed into an existing large party or will find its expression in the formation of successful new political parties.

The situation at the moment is, however, quite clearly that the major parties depend upon a well organised and well disciplined party group system within the councils and committees to realise their policies. This system is rather stronger within the municipalities than in the counties.

THE ELECTORATE

Gunnel Gustafsson (1980) argues that in the more direct democracy of the pre-reform era there was greater popular participation and representation of a wider section of the population. About 3 per cent of the population actually participate in councils and their committees. This is certainly not enough to justify any claim that Sweden has a participatory system. There have been local referenda on such matters as municipality names following mergers, and individual projects such as building a bridge or closing a railway. The turnout for these has been in the order of 60–70 per cent, but they are infrequent and usually return a vote favouring the status quo.

The system is also criticised for failing to provide a good cross-sectional representation. Women and younger people are under-represented on the councils in all parties, while the higher socio-economic groupings are over-represented. Only to a limited extent in the Social Democratic Party is there any significant blue-collar representation. Stromberg (1977) writes: 'as the communes become larger and more urbanised, their councils are progressively dominated by a well educated middle class'.

Gunnel Gustafsson (1980), nevertheless, maintains that the representative democracy model is sustained by the existence of high electoral turnouts and a well-established party system. Swedish elections take place for state, county and municipal constituencies on the same day. In recent years there has been an increase in split voting. As many as 10 per cent of the voters are prepared to support a different party in the municipality from their choice in the *Riksdag*. There are thus good reasons to suppose that councillors will heed the electorate's preferences.

Stromberg (1977) shows, however, that there is a divergence between the opinion of the electorate and the opinions of their representatives. On the whole the councillors are prepared to be more munificent than the electorate and the gap increases with the size of the municipality. There is also a difference in priorities between the councillors, who view town planning, employment and water supply as more important, and the electorate, who rate highly the more obvious services such as education and social welfare.

It would seem, therefore, that Swedish local government is likely to be responsive to the wishes of the electorate only in so far as it needs their electoral support. Well-educated councillors who understand the need for non-visible infrastructure need to respond to the electorate only to a limited extent. Over 90 per cent of a party's local popularity depends upon that party's national popularity and it is suggested that the variation is due to protest votes against the national government rather than local politicians (A. Gustafsson 1983).

But this is in keeping with the Swedish way of looking at things. It has already been remarked that the Swedes are less worried about who governs than about how they are governed. Swedes have extensive opportunity to find out the effectiveness of the governors. All public papers except those concerned with national security or respecting an individual's personal privacy are open for all to inspect. Municipalities provide information secretariats and offices, and the local media provide extensive coverage of the activities of local government; thus it should be widely known when significant errors are made. There is no evidence of serious and widespread breakdown of public confidence in local government councillors or officers, although there is some dissatisfaction with the increasingly polarised party system.

The relatively recent phenomenon of district and sub-municipal committees has often resulted from dissatisfaction with post-merger situations where a former authority feels hard done by following take-over. Experiments, such as those at Örebro, Eskilstuna, and Umea, have worked well, providing better motivation for party members, giving greater chance of contact with the elected representative and increasing scope for individual involvement.

PROBLEMS AND ISSUES

So far, we have characterised the local government system of Sweden as rational and efficient in keeping with the political and cultural values of the Swedes. There are, however, indications of strain, which may cause changes in the later years of the century as the system adjusts to the two major stresses of the 1980s.

The foci of stress are, first, the party system, which at local level has had a stronger grip since the reforms of the 1970s and, second, the economic situation, which has caused the first signs of serious rift in the consensual approach to intergovernmental relations within the consensual democracy *par excellence*. The economic problems can be traced to the oil crises of the 1970s. It may well be that the two stresses are related, as inherent weaknesses in the consensus are forced to the surface by major problems of political economy.

The economic problem is simply that, following the oil crises of the 1970s and, in line with the depression in Europe and in keeping with the structural changes forced on the West by rapid economic expansion in the East, the Swedish GDP has been unable to keep pace with the increasing demands of the social welfare system set up and developed by the Swedes in more prosperous times.

Walters (1983) documents this, demonstrating the serious budgetary deficit resulting in public sector borrrowing of up to 10 per cent of the GDP in order to make ends meet. Richardson and Kindblad (1983) characterise the period under discussion as one in which resource expansion changed to resource squeeze. The first response of the authorities was the rational one of effectiveness audit, for which systems had already been set up in cooperation with the local authority associations. Elvender (1981) discusses the budgeting policy in Uppsala County Health Authority. Previously an incremental approach had been adopted without question, but central government restraints on spending were forcing the budget-makers into a more comprehensive planning system. Such planning would seem ideally suited to the Swedish disposition.

Gustafsson and Richardson (1984) argue that the rational approach of the Swedes, while characteristic of the past expansionary era, is now giving way to a period of more ad hoc decision making to which the Swedes are not accustomed. Whereas previously it was satisfactory to characterise the cultural values in terms of rationality, consensus, long-term orientation and

common effort, now the Swedes have to accept unpredicted developments and achieve their consensus by deferring conflict. The symptoms,
in terms of the political system, are increasingly sophisticated lobbying and
the gradual emergence of a more polarised party system, effectively a
modified two-party system.

The political system's response to the economic problems is discussed
by A. Gustafsson (1983), who cites the increasing dominance of the
majority party in some areas, as instanced by a tightening grip on
committee chairmanship. Culture and constitution provide for consensus
and cooperation but climate is producing conflict. The increasing use of
the advantages of majority is putting the minority at a disadvantage.

There is a corresponding decrease in legitimacy. A. Gustafsson (1983)
points to a decline in public confidence in the political parties who are
finding it difficult to recruit young people into their ranks. It is also proving
difficult for the parties to retain their councillors. Up to a third of
councillors will resign after a term of office. It is not clear whether this is
due to the stresses of the demanding job (even though this may be made
more acceptable by increasing levels of remuneration), the stress of public
pressure or the stress of the discipline of the party group. The outcome of
the decrease in confidence can be seen in three ways: the growth of local
non-party action groups, the local sub-municipal committees already
noted, and an increasing tendency for the public to approach officers
directly without recourse to a member as intermediary. There is another
pressure, internal to councils, which has arisen from the provisions of the
1976 Co-determination Act, which gives workpeople, through their
unions, considerable rights in determining not only considerations of
service but also the general thrust of their employment. The full effects of
this have yet to be felt in local government.

But whether the people are satisfied with their councillors is a different
question from whether they are satisfied with their policies. We have
already noted Stromberg's analysis of the differential munificence of the
electorate and the elected. Birgersson (1977) discusses what he calls the
'service paradox': that 'citizens appear to be more satisfied in the
communes where the services are lower'. The study suggests that high
demands and a high level of provision go together, but that the provision
lags behind the demands. But which comes first? Do the high demands
cause the provision or does the provision stimulate the demands? Some of
the innovation is due to contact between the services providing
professionals, some of the demand is due to active and well-educated
people who are interested in politics and capable of articulating their
demands.

There remains, finally, the question of how autonomous local government can remain, inasmuch as it has ever been truly autonomous. Until the mid-1980s most commentators observed the increasing influence of the state as discussed by Greenwood (1979), mostly in the municipal context, and by A. Gustafsson (1983), in the county context. It is clearly very difficult for local government to remain in charge of its spending when constraints on grants and borrowing powers may force up local taxes to an extent which the local electorate either will not or cannot afford. Gustafsson and Richardson (1984) point to the dysfunctionality of high taxes and a highly developed social security system, in asking the question whether Sweden can afford its level of service provision in a time of containment.

The development of the free commune experiments has suggested a considerable concern to reverse a trend towards centralisation and allow local governments greater innovatory powers. However, it is questioned whether these schemes have effectively provided real autonomy for local authorities, since the new powers sought by participating councils are subject to central approval and reflect as much the approach of a wise manager who allows subordinates a measure of freedom to innovate but, nevertheless, ensures that these changes conform to managerial aims and objectives.

Local government has certainly tried measures to assist in the recovery of the economy. Councils have considerable employment powers in conjunction with the private sector, for example through the joint enterprises already discussed. Some councils (A. Gustafsson 1983) have been making direct subsidies to the private sector in an effort to prevent unemployment. This power has been further enhanced by the free commune experiments. Nevertheless the efficacy of employment creation schemes can be challenged on theoretical grounds, while the legality and propriety of this can be challenged politically. It is an area where economics and politics come together. The ability of local and central spheres of competence in sorting out the problems arising from a static economy will prove the test for Swedish local democracy in the 1990s.

BIBLIOGRAPHY

Anton, T.J. (1974a) *Governing Greater Stockholm*, Los Angeles, California University Press.

Anton, T.J. (1974b) 'The pursuit of efficiency: values and structures in the changing politics of Swedish municipalities', in T.N. Clark (ed.) *Comparative Community Politics*, New York, Halsted Press.

Birgersson, B.O. (1977) 'The service paradox: Citizen assessment of urban services in 36 Swedish communes', in T.N. Clark (ed.) *Comparative Community Politics*, New York, Halsted Press.

Elvender, N. (1981) 'Barriers and opportunities for primary care delivery systems: a case study from the County Council of Uppsala, Sweden', *Scandinavian Political Studies* 4, 295–305.

Greenwood, R. (1979) 'Relations between central and local government in Sweden', *Public Administration* 57, Winter 1979.

Gustafsson, A. (1983) *Local Government in Sweden*, Uddevalla, Swedish Institute.

Gustafsson, A. (1988) *Local Government in Sweden*, Stockholm, Swedish Institute.

Gustafsson, G. (1980) *Local Government Reform in Sweden*, Umea, CWK Gleerup.

Gustafsson, G. and Richardson, J.J. (1984) 'Sweden', in F.F. Ridley (ed.), *Policies and Politics in Western Europe*, London, Croom Helm.

Jonnson, E. (1983) 'Measures undertaken by municipalities undergoing amalgamation', *Scandanavian Political Studies* 6, 231–52.

Richardson, J.J. and Kindblad, B.M. (1983) 'Programme evaluation and effectiveness: auditing Sweden: the changing Swedish policy style', *Scandanavian Political Studies* 16, 75–85.

Stromberg, L. (1977) 'Electors and the elected in Sweden', in V. Ostrom and F.P. Bish (eds) *Comparing Urban Service Delivery Systems*, New York, Sage.

Walters, P. (1983) 'Sweden's public sector crisis before and after the 1982 election', *Government and Opposition* 18, Winter 1983.

Chapter 8

The United States of America

J.A. Chandler

The United States has an image of brash modernity, although it is the oldest liberal democracy considered in this book. The institutions of central government, outlined in a constitution that has changed relatively little since its inception, have been able to absorb huge increases in territory, population and wealth. There are many systems of local government in the United States, and some of these have structures and practices that can be traced back to the eighteenth century. Since the 1920s, however, the systems have changed very little, in contrast to those of many European nations, and it may be seriously questioned whether they have successfully absorbed the pressures created by social and economic change.

THE POLITICAL SETTING

The framework of the federal system is outlined in the succinct constitution, which was designed to ensure a balance of power between the major institutions of government. The document lists a limited number of powers that are the province of the federal government. These concern management of currency, raising an army, diplomatic and foreign policy and waging war. The federal government is also able to regulate inter-state commerce and, through this device, has become in the twentieth century increasingly involved in detailed regulation of social and commercial activities throughout the Union. Outside this framework, the states are free, within the confines of the Bill of Rights, to govern their communities as they see fit. They consequently have complete authority over the form of local government within their territories, as well as many elements of civil and criminal law, policing, public works, education and planning. They could, if they wished, own and control industries or manage a comprehensive health and social security system as is the practice in the mixed economies of Western European states. An important but rarely considered problem concerning the states is, therefore, why they do so little rather than why they do so much.

Both the federal government and the states have similar policy-making structures, owing to a convergence of ideology rather than any central government imposition. At the federal level, the President, and at the state level, the Governor, are elected by all registered voters for four years in office as head of state and the government. The President chooses his senior departmental staff, subject to approval by the Senate, and also relies on help from a team of personal advisers. Within the states the Governor is somewhat less in control since many departmental heads may be directly elected. Although the President has an important role as a policy initiator, legislation and the budget must be approved by Congress. The legislature, divided into the House of Representatives and the Senate, will also initiate legislation. Any bill that is passed can, however, be vetoed by the President, although this power can be overriden by a two-thirds majority within both Houses. All state legislatures, except that of Nebraska, are bicameral and have a similar balance of power between themselves and the executive as is found at the federal level. In the case of conflict over the interpretation of the federal constitution the issue, if not settled in a lower court, will be referred to the Supreme Court, which consists of nine judges selected for life by the President. Within each state similar arrangements are made for the adjudication of disputes concerning its own constitution.

Checks and balances in theory exist in European parliamentary systems but are, in practice, swept aside when the chief executive is the leader of a united party commanding a majority within the legislature. The dominant Democratic and Republican parties of the United States are, however, more a federation of loosely connected state parties than a national organisation. They retain many aspects of caucus parties, defined as groups of notables linked together for mutual interest rather than ideological commitment. The President cannot, therefore, rely on the support of his party colleagues in Congress and to enact policy must win support through the worth of his arguments or buy it with favours. Within the states there are considerable variations in party unity but, given a similar structure to the federal system, there are generally few pressures on party members to vote together in order to sustain their executive in office. Policy making in the states, therefore, usually follows a process of trading favours, as is the case in Washington.

THE STRUCTURE OF LOCAL GOVERNMENT

Legal status

Local government is a creature of the states. The national constitution makes no reference to local government and therefore allows the states full authority to manage their internal divisions of government and administration, subject to their remaining within the current interpretations of the federal constitution. This arrangement is legally affirmed through a ruling in 1868 of John Dillon, Chief Justice of Iowa, who maintained that the legislature of a state 'breathes into [municipal corporations] the breath of life, without which they cannot exist. As it creates so may it destroy. If it may destroy it may abridge and control.'

John Dillon is also cited as the legal authority through which states maintain that municipalities can only carry out acts that are expressly granted to them by state laws or necessarily flow from the exercise of these powers. Thus, with the exception of home-rule cities, local governments in the United States cannot take on any functions or powers that are not sanctioned by state legislation. Such a restriction is, of course, not unique to the United States and lies at the heart of intergovernmental relations in most liberal democracies.

States establish units of local government through a variety of procedures, although a distinction is made between municipal corporations, which are formed as local government units at the request of an area's inhabitants, and divisions that are imposed by the state. Municipal corporations, usually termed cities, come into being after residents within a community petition for such status and the assent of the majority of its inhabitants is received following a local referendum. The area will then be granted a charter which is, in effect, the constitution of the city. In some states, older cities are incorporated through a specific charter applying to that community in particular, but, in most cases, cities will be subject to general legislation establishing charters for all cities of a particular type within the state. Many states classify cities according to population and provide a charter with considerable powers for larger communities and more restrictive arrangements for smaller populations. A few states, including Ohio and Massachusetts, permit cities to choose from a number of alternative charters.

The largest cities in many states have a greater measure of autonomy through the grant of a home-rule charter. The idea was first adopted in 1875 for St Louis by the state of Missouri and has now been accepted in over half the states. Home rule in theory reverses Dillon's rule by allowing the city to undertake any activities unless they are forbidden by its charter or by state law. In practice, states usually draw up home-rule charters that restrict these cities almost as severely as if they were subject to a general charter. Many towns able to take advantage of such a provision have not done so, although two-thirds of cities with populations in excess of 20,000 are governed by this provision.

Outside the cities, the states establish county governments throughout their territory, through either general legislation or their constitution. The county is normally a unit of administration for rural areas and most, though not all, of their powers are ceded to the city governments where these are established. Although the county is subject to an elected council or board, it is for many purposes regarded as an agency of the state and administers a number of services on its behalf. A few counties have, nevertheless, been given charters similar to the home-rule provision of cities. Outside New England and, in particular, among eastern states, townships may administer small communities that have not petitioned for city status or have failed to qualify for such a role. These units have relatively few executive powers and act principally as local pressure groups. The New England township is, however, a more important unit of local government and within this region takes over most of the powers normally handled by counties in other areas of the United States. In addition to counties and townships, most states create a variety of special districts which are local administrative organisations governed by an elected board with the authority to undertake a specific function. The most widespread and important of these bodies are the school boards, which administer primary and secondary education within all states.

Structures and powers

It has already been shown that in most states local government can be divided into cities, counties and special districts. Although each of these units may carry out functions in an area administered for other purposes by another type of local government organisation, the United States does not have tiers of government in the style of France or Britain. Each unit is independent, although all are subject to control by the state. A diagrammatic representation of the system (see Figure 8.1) can, therefore, be very simple.

The powers of city governments may vary widely from state to state and even within states, where a variety of different charters are in operation. Most cities will have some authority for street maintenance, parks and recreation, police and fire services, and zoning (town planning in British idiom). Many cities will provide water and drainage facilities,

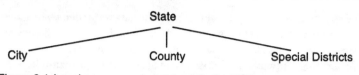

Figure 8.1 Local government structures in the USA.

although these tasks can be placed in the hands of a private company. They will also license the operations of utilities and cable television companies and, on occasion, provide these services directly. Many cities run libraries, museums and, more occasionally, theatres and art galleries, although these facilities are often operated by semi-charitable public bodies. Larger cities may also be responsible for public hospitals and public transport and may even maintain a university.

The county, in its capacity as a unit created by the state, has a number of administrative functions which it undertakes on behalf of the state throughout its territory, regardless of any city government. These include the assessment of property values for taxation purposes, registration of births, deaths and marriages, and licensing of vehicles. Outside the cities the county maintains smaller rural roads, leaving major highways to the state; keeps law and order through the office of sheriff; provides recreational facilities; zones land, and may, on occasion, like the cities, maintain libraries and museums and, in a few cases, such as Cook County in which lies Chicago, operate hospitals.

The special districts, true to their ad hoc nature, can be formed to deal with a wide range of problems. All of the fifty states have established school boards whose boundaries often bear no relation to those of other local government units. These boards usually raise much of the revenue required by local schools and supervise the more detailed elements of educational administration in their areas. Major policy on education, such as the organisation of the schools system, teachers' salaries and, on occasion, the purchase of textbooks, is determined by the state. Special districts may also be established to administer water supply and drainage in rural areas, irrigation schemes, burial grounds or pollution control.

If a list were made of all the functions undertaken somewhere in the United States by units of local government, it might well be more extensive than that of any other liberal democratic state. Certain activities, such as the management of universities or provision of social welfare benefits, are, for example, rarely the province of local government in most European countries. It would, however, be very misleading to suggest that most local governments in the United States are important and powerful organisations within their communities. Management of hospitals and universities may be open to a considerable number of cities and counties, but is undertaken by only a few. On the other hand, several responsibilities common to European local government systems, such as the provision of public housing or personal social services, are practised on a relatively small and localised scale even by the larger cities.

The majority of city and county governments in the United States are incapable of operating their services, because they are such small units in terms of population. In 1972 there were within the United States 18,517 cities, 3,044 counties, 28,668 special districts and 16,000 townships, amounting to 78,269 units of local government (Dye 1985: 227). The variation in population size between units is enormous. New York City encompassed a population in 1980 of 7 million, while in Kansas the median population of its city governments, which in theory are all able to operate their own police force, is 504 (Drury 1980: 283). Among counties the largest is Los Angeles with over 7 million inhabitants, while Loving County, Texas, had in 1982 ninety-one souls. Variation in the size of local government units is dependent upon the states and there is a wide discrepancy between the number of units per head of population among the fifty states. Illinois heads the list with 6,500 local government units, while at the other extreme Hawaii has less than twenty.

Local government in the United States has, with regard to the size of its units, much in common with France and Italy. The majority of units emphasise the interests of local communities, which are, in many cases, too small to be able to undertake any but the most basic of services. Most metropolitan areas are sectioned into small local government units which frequently surround a larger inner-city authority. A few of these inner cities can, however, be among the largest local government units within liberal democracies and may also undertake a wide range of services. It was, after all, the city of Los Angeles and not the state of California, let alone the federal government, that staged the 1984 Olympic Games.

FINANCE

Local governments in the United States pay for their activities through various forms of local taxation, municipal enterprise, borrowing and grants from federal sources. Table 8.1 provides some indication of the relative importance of each source of revenue, although it must be borne in mind that figures for the country as a whole give no indication of the major diversity regarding the source of revenue within individual local governments.

Table 8.1 Local government receipts (USA)

Raised by local government (%)		Grants (%)	
Taxes	Enterprise	Federal	State
42	16	8	34

Source: Lorch (1983: 340)

Most local governments rely on property tax as their main source of directly raised income, although in some states it is possible for them to impose a sales tax on certain goods and services. New York City, for example, imposes a surcharge on hotel room bills. In Pennsylvania and Ohio, cities may impose a local income tax on residents. Although property tax is widely used throughout the world by local governments, many criticisms are levelled against its use. The system is an inequitable means of raising revenue and this problem is further complicated in the United States, since the property of states, of the federal government and of charitable organisations has been exempted from payment. Cities with a choice of means for raising revenue nevertheless prefer to rely on this tax since it is relatively inexpensive to collect and less open to fraud and evasion than most alternatives. Many states are, moreover, reluctant to allow local governments to use a general sales tax, since this is one of the principal means through which they generate their own income.

The amount that may be raised by cities and counties through direct taxation is frequently circumscribed by the states. A limit is often placed on receipts from property tax by preventing local government units from raising from a property more than a specified percentage of its value as assessed for taxation purposes. In recent years some states have compounded these restrictions by placing limits on the assessment value of property. It is, however, possible in some areas for city governments to raise more than the normally permitted revenue from taxation, if they get the assent of a majority of their citizens to such action through a referendum. Rarely is such assent given. Similar limiting devices are also placed on other means through which local government directly raises taxation.

In contrast to many European cities, local governments in the United States can raise considerable sums through local enterprise by selling licences and franchises for the supply of utilities to their communities. They may in some cases own local gas and electricity services. In addition to these necessities, money may also be raised by awarding franchises to cable television companies. The states can, however, limit the revenue raised from these sources as effectively as they can limit property tax, since they usually establish some form of state commission to arbitrate between a city government and the local utility companies. In addition to the award of franchises some cities may charge residents for services such as refuse collection or water supply.

Grants are an important source of local government revenue and have increased as a percentage of income from 21 per cent in 1950 to 43 per cent in 1970. Before the New Deal of President Roosevelt, states received almost no aid from federal government and provided in turn little support to local governments. This system of dual federalism had been considerably eroded by the 1960s when the Great Society initiative of President Johnson transferred substantial grants-in-aid to both state and local governments. Most federal aid was in the form of categorical grants which provided money to state and local governments for specific tasks, such as urban renewal, on condition that the funds were used to provide resources to a standard specified, with some precision, by the federal government. The extensive use of categorical grants greatly increased federal interference in state and local activities and was viewed with some alarm by conservatives. The Nixon and Carter administrations began to curtail the size and, in some cases, the specificity of these grants, which by 1980 amounted to less than 10 per cent of local government revenue. President Reagan stated that he would like to return to a situation similar to the pre-1930s era of dual federalism and severely pruned federal aid and consolidated many categorical grants into block grants, which are given to the states with few strings attached. A major complaint of city mayors is that many states do not pass these grants on to the needy metropolitan areas. Since 1972 the federal government has also channelled funds to local governments with no strings attached, through a system of revenue sharing, but the funds involved are relatively small.

Grants from the states to local government form about one-third of city and county revenues and are much greater than receipts from the federal level. They are, however, usually tied to categorical demands which can seriously restrict local initiative and help ensure local conformity to state demands. States employ some form of local accounts audit to ensure their money is spent correctly. Apart from categorical grants some states provide grants to local governments on a revenue-sharing basis.

Most units of local government fund their capital expenditure through borrowing, usually secured by the issue of local authority bonds which pay to the holders a fixed rate of interest. Most states place limits on the money that can be raised and some, such as Missouri, may require any capital borrowing to be approved by citizens through a local referendum. Many larger cities and counties are also obliged to borrow money on a short-term basis to fund deficits in their revenue budgets. Several cities have compounded huge debts as a consequence of their inability to repay short-term loans. In a few dramatic cases, as in New York in 1975 and Cleveland in 1978, the cities have had to default on their salary payments and, in effect, became bankrupt when the banks refused to allow futher short-term borrowing. These events are but the tip of a huge iceberg of debts that reflect the parlous state of most city finances.

INTERNAL STRUCTURES

Although there is a surprising uniformity in the systems of local government within each of the states, there is considerable variation in the internal policy-making structures. The differences in these structures reflect struggles for control over local government as much as any desire for greater managerial efficiency.

Cities

The oldest patterns of city government mirror the presidential systems favoured by federal and state government, with a balance of power arranged between a directly elected chief executive, the mayor, and a city council that forms the legislature. The structure is found in most of the largest cities and over 50 per cent of municipal governments. In most cities where the mayor has executive powers s/he is elected by all citizens of the community, whereas the councillors are elected from ward divisions within the city. The city council debates and accepts local legislation and policy, although the mayor, like the federal President or a state Governor, can usually veto proposals from the council, which in turn will be able to override this sanction by a two-thirds majority. The mayoral systems are usually classified into strong and weak forms.

In a strong system the mayor appoints all departmental heads subject to council approval and, through the ability to initiate and veto legislation, may be the most powerful political figure in the city. A weak system allows the mayor to veto council policy but does not permit him or her to appoint all departmental officers. Many heads of departments will be directly elected and may even be responsible to separately elected boards or commissions that are only loosely connected to the full city council, although usually subject to mayoral veto. The power of the mayor in these systems may, nevertheless, be as great as in strong mayoral set-ups if the diverse executive departments are tied together by a powerful unified party. Chicago is, for example, governed by a weak system, although this structure did not hamper Mayor Daley and his Democratic Party predecessors from dominating most aspects of the city's political life.

In the first years of the twentieth century, dissatisfaction over corruption within city governments, dominated, as in Chicago, by a party machine, prompted a reform movement that led to the creation of two different forms of city government dedicated, ostensibly, to the cause of efficient government. The first of these structures, established in Galveston, Texas in 1901, is the city commission, which was superseded in the 1920s by the now more popular city-manager systems.

In commission governments the voters elect from the community at large a small number of commissioners who are responsible collectively for running the city. Each commissioner heads an individual administrative department. Although they elect one of their number to the office of mayor, this post has no further responsibilities other than chairing commission meetings and serving as a dignified head of the community. The system has been retained in only approximately 200 cities, largely because the council-managerial form of government is better able to resolve the problems of coordinating the activities of individual departments.

The council-manager system has been adopted by nearly 40 per cent of cities and has generated considerable interest among proponents of local government reform in Western Europe. In most of these cities councillors, or on occasion a smaller number of commissioners, are elected by the community at large. The execution of their decisions is placed in the hands of an appointed city manager, who is an employee of the municipality. The city manager will, however, appoint all other employees of the city, including the executive heads of each department. Unlike the strong mayor, the city manager is, in theory, not responsible for the initiation of policy and must maintain a non-partisan stance. The manager can also be removed from the post by councillors and in some towns the position is as precarious as that of a football manager of either the European or American varieties.

Counties and special districts

Over 85 per cent of counties are subject to policy decisions made by a committee, termed variously a commission, board, board of supervisors and even, in a few areas, the county judges. Although some of these bodies have up to 50 members, they are usually composed of less than ten representatives. Executive power is apportioned to a number of departmental heads who are, in many states, directly elected, although in certain areas, or for some specific functions, officers must be appointed by the state or elected from individuals whom the state deems to be properly qualified to hold the office. These individuals will include the sheriff, the prosecuting attorney, the county treasurer, auditor, the assessor of property taxes, the engineer and the coroner.

Most special districts have been established along council-manager lines. In school districts a small board, which is normally elected, determines policy within the confines allowed by the state. The board entrusts the execution of policy to an appointed officer, usually called the schools superintendent, who will be largely responsible for the appointment of staff.

PERSONNEL: RECRUITMENT AND TRAINING

Local government officers in the United States may be elected to their positions or be political appointees or professional managers. There is, therefore, a wide variation in their training and technical competence. In smaller cities operating under a weak mayoral system and in many counties, the principle of electing heads of departments will often give important technical duties to a lay person. The sheriff, city treasurer or county attorney may, for example, have had little or no training for the position. On occasion a state may demand that certain posts are occupied by individuals holding appropriate qualifications and may organise basic training for newly appointed officers to posts requiring technical skills. States will also provide their own experts to help unqualified local administrators deal with difficult problems. An elected sheriff commanding a force of two or three deputies with as little professional training in police work as the local farmers over whom they impose law and order will usually seek, or receive without solicitation, the help of the state police and lawyers in the event of a serious crime within their community.

In the first decade of this century, the best trained officer within many smaller units of local government was the city engineer, and with the rise of council-manager forms of government the professional competence of this officer often resulted in the city manager's post being filled by civil engineers. Since the 1950s, however, the post of city mananger has become increasingly recognised as a profession in its own right, requiring specialist training. Over half of the country's city managers are members of a professional body, the American City Managers' Association; this organisation strongly recommends that its members should hold a masters qualification in public administration, awarded by a university accredited with providing courses up to a standard approved by a joint council for universities offering such degrees. It is also possible to receive similar qualifications in local government finance, and many public administration courses specialise in particular subjects such as personnel management.

The largest cities and counties will employ several thousand workers and be responsible for complex bureaucracies. In cities which were controlled by a powerful party machine many jobs were allocated as a reward for political support rather than from considerations of professional competence. Few city machines now exist as complex networks of patron–client relationships although, in many large cities, the heads of departments can be either directly elected politicians or political appointees of the mayor. It is, however, unlikely that they will be called upon to exercise technical as opposed to political judgements, and their role will be to resolve the policy issues affecting their departments on the basis of technical advice given by their subordinate officials. Below the level of political appointees, large cities and counties will employ a stratum of highly qualified professional staff. In areas such as engineering, finance and the law, senior staff will usually have a degree and often appropriate postgraduate qualifications while police and fire departments will operate their own training programmes.

POLICY-MAKING

Intergovernmental relations

Since local government is essentially a creature of the state, the discretion of local leaders is only marginally compromised by federal government. The constitution does, however, place some restraints on politicians bent on discriminating between racial and religious groups within their communities. The civil rights movements of the 1960s have done much to ensure that schools are racially integrated and that black or, more recently, hispanic people are able to vote and have some chance of becoming effective political actors.

The federal government also has some impact on policy-making through grant aid programmes, although President Reagan's attempts to return to dual federalism somewhat curtailed this channel of influence. Nevertheless, there remain a number of categorical grants still conveyed directly to local government which require the recipient to follow the instructions enclosed with the funding parcel. It must be stressed, however, that even at its most generous federal aid was not forced upon local governments and they have discretion to refuse funds if they dislike the attached conditions. Few local governments refused to participate in schemes that helped improve local infrastructure at little or no cost to local taxpayers.

Federal grants were also welcomed in many cities as a means of avoiding excessive reliance on the state governments for support, given that help from this quarter for social improvements was frequently much less generous and nearly always replete with restrictions regarding its use.

The major restraints on local government come not from the federal administration but from the states. Legally, as has been shown, the states create and order their local government systems and they do so in a generally restrictive manner. Dillon's rule is strictly adhered to by most state courts, which will generally take the most narrow interpretation of the powers open to city governments. On occasion, the courts may even be more restrictive in their behaviour than the state legislatures. In Missouri, for example, the state Supreme Court insisted that all requests for borrowing by local governments should be subject to a referendum, even though the state legislators and the Governor considered that this interpretation seriously limited the capacity of local governments to fulfil their responsibilities.

State legislators show little inclination to widen the scope of city charters and have, in recent years, tended to pass increasingly detailed legislation to regulate the conduct of local services. In addition, they have become an important source of local funding by providing a large array of categorical grants and, more damagingly, eroding the ability of local governments to raise their own funds. The most publicised of these measures was Proposition 13 that appeared on the California ballot papers in 1978 asking voters to endorse measures to cut local tax revenue by approximately 25 per cent (Cohen 1984). The proposition was accepted by a considerable majority and led to immediate cuts in local services within many Californian cities. Approval of the proposition led to a rash of similar measures even within some of the more liberal states such as Massachusetts.

The restrictions imposed by states on local government appear superficially to reflect the pattern of intergovernmental relations similar, in D.E. Ashford's phrase, to 'British dogmatism' rather than 'French pragmatism' (Ashford 1982). State legislatures seem to be impervious to local interests and there does not appear to be the penetration of local interest into national decision making as exists in France. This impression, however, appears to be at variance with accepted views of policy-making at federal level, which would be expected to be replicated at state level given the similarity of government structures and attitudes at both levels.

The weak party system and balance of power between legislators and executive provide state politicians with excellent facilities for generating local support, by gaining favours for their constituencies from the state executive in return for their political support. Unlike British MPs most state legislators are, moreover, rooted within their communities and have in many cases served as local politicians before moving to higher levels of government. There is a tendency to elect to the state legislature successful local business people well entrenched in their local community (Dye 1985: 140–1).

It has been suggested that a principal cause of state restraints on local government has been the dominance of rural and suburban interests within their legislatures to the detriment of urban areas. The prosperous rural and suburban areas had no enthusiasm for diverting substantial funds to the poorer inner cities and thus creating higher levels of taxation throughout the state. This position had more substance prior to 1962, when a Supreme Court ruling (Baker vs Carr) required state legislatures to elect members serving constituencies of equal populations, and two years later (Reynolds vs Sims) prevented the upper chambers from being composed of members elected from county-based constituencies. Equalisation of representation does not, however, necessarily lead to equal power for equally sized communities. Articulate, well-educated, and above all well-funded politicians are far more likely to gain election to state legislatures than the poor and underprivileged of the inner cities. In inner cities voter turnout is generally low, and is lowest among the poorest in the population. It cannot, moreover, be assumed that all big city governments will espouse the radical demand for higher taxation to fund better services. A more substantial answer to the problems of state–local government relations requires further analysis of policy making within local governments themselves.

THE ROLE OF PARTIES AND PRESSURE GROUPS

Parties dominate the policy-making process in some United States cities and are outlawed in others. Substantial party intervention is most frequent in those older cities of the east and mid-west which were dominated in the late nineteenth century by the party that could best secure the vote of the poor majority, who were often, although not invariably, newly arrived white immigrants. Success was achieved through a party machine capable of providing work and the rudiments of social security to needy urban settlers. The machine was under the control of a small clique, frequently from the same status groups as their supporters, which was on occasion dominated by a powerful individual, the city boss. The system became a byword for corruption. Tammany Hall was the the headquarters of the New York Democratic Party at the turn of the century. The murky reputation of the city boss is not, however, wholly deserved. Although the system operated through patron–client relationships, which could dispense public largess in a highly erratic and partial fashion, in cities where the machine was likely to have a lasting future it gained wide support as the only chance given to the poor to obtain a livelihood and security in a country devoid of any other source of public welfare provision.

Few, if any, cities are now controlled by a party machine based on patron–client relationships. The decline of the system is a reflection not so much of widespread hostility to corruption but the development of federal and state social security provision and higher levels of employment. In the absence of strong patron–client ties, political parties in the United States tend to fall apart since they lack the ideological underpinning of European parties and have no need for cohesion in legislatures, given that executives in the United States are not obliged to resign if they lose the confidence of the legislature. Within many cities in the United States parties struggle for power on 'end of ideology' platforms, with each side claiming to be better managers of the municipality but rarely conflicting over more fundamental issues, such as the acceptability of high taxes and service standards as opposed to low taxes and poor service provision. The struggle to manage the political system exists not only between parties but also within them, as many select their candidates for office within local government through primary elections. In cities where one party is dominant, the primary contest will effectively become the contest to choose the city's leader and, as a contest within a party, ideological differences are not normally a feature of the campaigns.

Given the lack of discipline and the absence of the deeply rooted ideological conflict that is to be found in some European countries, city politics operates in much the same style as federal government. The mayor may, more often than not, have the support of party colleagues in the council but may not rely on their vote. Policy evolves through a process of log-rolling and trading favours, between the executive and the legislators. Behind such a process may lie the demands of interest groups. Councillors who are generally not mandated to follow a specific party programme will be open to influence from the groups with which they associate in their working and social lives or from articulate organisations able to present their cases effectively. In comparison with partisan local authorities in Europe, city government in the United States is, therefore, generally more open to group influence.

Although most party machines were geared to the interests of poorer groups in their community, they were not antipathetic to the interests of big business. The system did not, however, recommend itself to many industrialists and the middle class, since it led to high taxation and, on occasion, graft among party leaders, which became a serious source of inefficiency as well as an affront to established morality. These factors prompted, at the turn of the century, a powerfully backed municipal reform movement, which led to the adoption in many cities of commission and later council-manager forms of government and had as its basic aim the destruction of the party machine.

The reform movement advocated that elections should be non-partisan, involve primary elections and select a small number of councillors to represent the city at large. Major issues affecting city government should be subject to referendums. The execution of policy was to be the responsibility of a professional bureaucracy rather than political appointees. These measures succeeded in breaking the ability of party machines to repay local ward organisers for their support through jobs and favours. The beneficiaries of reform were groups and individuals with access to resources that enabled them to publicise themselves and their interests throughout their community. The support of the press and, later, local radio and television, along with access to sufficient money to mount a city-wide campaign, facilitated electoral success in a reformed city. These requirements are largely controlled by local business communities, and it has been argued that the reformed city governments are consequently less sensitive to the needs of the majority of citizens than cities still dominated by organised political parties (Lineberry and Fowler 1961). One of the most extreme manifestations of business influence in reformed city government has been identified by Robert Lineberry in San Antonio, Texas 'where an organisation of essentially upper-middle class people . . . the Good Government League . . . manages to elect 79 of 81 candidates it nominates over a twenty year period' (Lineberry and Sharkansky 1978: 119).

It is, however, misleading to suggest that all reformed cities are controlled by a secret confederacy of business people. Usually there will be little collusion between the middle-class business folk competing for places on the city council. It must also be emphasised that the United States is a country of small local government units which, in many cases, will be too insignificant to interest the managers of large or even medium-sized corporations. It is, moreover, possible for interest groups such as labour unions that do not represent the interests of wealthy individuals to aggregate funds to influence local elections.

It may not, however, be either party or pressure groups or gifted individual councillors that determine policy in many cities. In the absence of strong party policies and given the often amateurish ideas from elected politicians, the professional bureaucrats within cities may have a field day. In the machine-led city the bureaucrats could have little influence but, in reformed cities, where the implemention of policy is in the hands of the city manager, the bureaucracy can become a very powerful element in policy-making and this may be an increasing trend, given the importance attached to professional training required for these posts.

THE INFLUENCE OF THE ELECTORATE

The United States is the home of community studies and has generated a large accumulation of empirical research aimed at evaluating the health of democracy within cities. In the beginning the word was that cities were governed by local business élites. The Lynds' (1929) studies of Muncie, Lloyd-Warner's (1949) studies of Morris, Illinois, and Floyd Hunter's (1953) observations of Atlanta all confirmed the power of business élites in medium and large cities. This view was seriously challenged by R.A. Dahl's (1961) study of decision-making in New Haven, which argued that different élites had influence over different areas of policy-making and, therefore, that power was dispersed among a plurality of interests. The power held by each élite was, moreover, modified by popular opinion which, expressed through the ballot box, obliged political leaders to choose paths that were most acceptable to the electorate and, as a consequence, the system achieved the democratic goal of ensuring that the city council was responsive to the needs of majority opinions within the community. Dahl's model of pluralist democratic politics found many empirical supporters in studies such as Sayre and Kaufman's (1965) detailed dissection of New York City and Wildavsky's (1964) study of Oberlin, Ohio.

It is possible that some of the differing conclusions reached by community power studies reflect the wide differences in the structures of local government within the United States. It has already been observed that reformed cities appear to be less sensitive to popular pressure than those dominated by party organisations. The community debate is, however, subject to major methodological criticisms. Bacharach and Baratz (1962, 1963) pointed out that empirical studies of decision-making which concentrated on issues that are visible to the electorate did not recognise the process through which these issues were placed on the political agenda and, more important, how other subjects were excluded.

Fundamental questions affecting the interests of citizens may never be discussed through a process of 'non-decison making' in which the political agenda is manipulated by powerful interests that control the process of political socialisation. Local leaders may be responsive to pressure from the organised popular interests, but can choose whether a particular issue should be a subject of interest in the first place. The lack of strong ideological debate in cities with competing party organisations and the presence of non-partisan politics in over 60 per cent of American cities suggests that there is a very narrow range of issues placed on the political agenda of most communities within the United States. The extent to which this may be due to the suppression of sectional demands by organised élites, the manipulation of the political agenda by these groups or a convergence of public opinion freely expressed cannot be adequately answered here, but may be illuminated by an analyisis of one of the major issues facing local government within the country.

PROBLEMS AND ISSUES

Since the late nineteenth century there has been a succession of movements to reform local government. The latest burst of enthusiasm, which reached its height in the 1960s, centred on the plight of the inner cities. The dereliction that is evident within the central areas of most conurbations within the United States appears as a monument to the inadequacies of local government, although it is largely an indictment of the states that are responsible for the system.

The factors that promote inner-city decline are not exclusive to the United States, but have been ameliorated much more effectively in most Western European states. It is a consequence of the development of mass transport systems that enable middle-class and skilled workers to move to suburban communities on the fringes of the big cities, where cheap land enables them to buy their own houses and live in a more spacious environment while still being able to retain their jobs within the city. As the most important class of consumers moved out of the city centres, commercial business moved out after them, and later even the factories. Although, in many cities, a central business district remains relatively prosperous, these havens of affluence are surrounded by areas accommodating those who are too poor to live anywhere else.

The structure of local government in the United States is organised in such a way that it is almost impossible for municipal administrations to deal with the problem of inner-city decay. Conurbations are rarely under the control of a single authority. The inner-city area is usually governed by a city authority, confined within local government boundaries that have been static since the end of the nineteenth century, which presides over most of the poor within the conurbation. The wealthier suburbs adjoining the inner-city are governed by small villages that were swamped with new housing developments as the population of the conurbation grew. These suburban cities are usually prosperous and will have nothing to do with the neighbouring ailing giant from which many of their original inhabitants had fled. In order to generate the funds required to deal with the social and environmental problems created by poverty, the inner-city authorities must tax either the poor themselves or, if it remains, the central business district. If, however, the golden goose is squeezed too hard it will fly to the more cheaply taxed suburbs.

There are several partial solutions to the problems of inner-city decay. The 1960s' proponents of local government reform suggested that the many city and county governments covering a conurbation should be consolidated into a single authority, or a few tiers of authorities. Most states, however, insist that any reform of local government boundaries should follow the traditional procedure of annexation in which a municipal corporation that seeks to extend its boundaries must receive the consent of the majority of citizens in the areas to be acquired. Many referenda have taken place but few have been successful. The most effective have concerned the consolidation of city and county governments into two connected tiers of administration, as in Miami and surrounding Dade County, Florida.

Enthusiasts for the consolidation of local governments have been criticised on the grounds that there is an optimum size for efficient city government, which has been put at between 25,000 and 250,000 inhabitants (Ostrom 1972). Large metropolitan governments would, it is argued, be as inefficient as smaller units and, therefore, be of no greater help to their inhabitants. The argument does not, however, take much account of the problem of efficient government for the whole of a metropolitan area, rather than within separate isolated units. A further objection to building large metropolitan authorities is that they would destroy the local interests of smaller communities. There may indeed be much to be said in favour of this argument in relation to small towns and villages in rural areas, but it can be questioned whether dormitory suburbs of large conurbations represent either economically or socially identifiable communities. Both the arguments concerning efficiency and local interests can, moreover, be at least partially reconciled with the need for metropolitan government through the establishment of some form of tiered structures.

A further and obvious solution to inner-city problems that is practised with some success in many European states is for central governments to provide higher grants to inner-city authorities in order to compensate for their problem of raising sufficient revenue from a poor environment. This solution was accepted by the Johnson Administration and occasioned the rapid growth of categorical grants channelled directly to city governments. The programmes that were devised to use these funds were not wholly successful, but little scope was given to their liberal enthusiasts to learn from their mistakes since the succeeding Nixon Administration curtailed many of their initiatives. In contrast to the Great Society generosity of federal government, the majority of states did not enthusiastically respond to the need to channel greater resources to their inner cities, and anticipated the dual federalism of the Reagan Administration during the Carter Presidency by passing legislation such as Proposition 13 in California (Cohen 1984). Similar cuts were consequently supported by voters in other states and clearly indicated that in the late 1970s there were no votes forthcoming from the affluent rural and suburban communities to support schemes to aid the ailing inner cities.

Neither the structure of local government within the metropolitan areas of the United States nor the funds allocated to their inner-city governments are capable of resolving the problem of inner-city decay. The persistence of these structural and financial problems is a reflection of the conservatism of state governments and can be seen as one aspect of why state governments do so little despite the scope of their powers. States are, however, unlikely eagerly to espouse redistributive policies that transfer, through higher taxation, resources from wealthy smaller communities to the destitute inner cities. The alienation of the poorest sections of the population from participation in state politics produces largely conservative state legislators. These individuals respond to a highly pervasive ideology of personal freedom, which espouses the cause of local and individual independence above the interests of collective responsibility. Individuals should be free to secure a high standard of living for themselves and their descendants, and this, it is felt, can be achieved only if the individuals have the incentive to develop further what they have acquired by either enterprise or inheritance. Those who fail to generate or inherit wealth should not be bailed out by the more gifted or the more fortunate. In such circumstances, the present imbalance between local government is likely to continue. Those with ability or luck may have the luxury of being represented by a small affluent local community government, while those who are seen as failures have an administration that is neither local nor able to meet their basic needs.

BIBLIOGRAPHY

Ashford, D.E. (1982) *British Dogmatism and French Pragmatism*, London, Allen and Unwin.

Bacharach, P. and Baratz, M.S. (1962) 'Two Faces of Power', *American Political Science Review* 56, December 1962, 947–53.

Bacharach, P. and Baratz, M.S. (1963) 'Decisions and Non-Decisions', *American Political Science Review*, 57, September 1963, 632–42.

Cohen, G. (1984) 'Cutting public expenditure: Proposition 13 in California', in D. Lewis and H. Wallace (eds) *Policies into Practice*, London, Heinemann.

Dahl, R.A. (1961) *Who Governs?* New Haven, Conn., Yale University Press.

Drury, J. (1980) *The Government of Kansas* (3rd edn), Lawrence, Kansas, University of Kansas Press.

Dye, T. (1985) *Politics in States and Communities* (5th edn), Englewood Cliffs, NJ, Prentice-Hall.

Hunter, F. (1953) *Community Power Structure*, Chapel Hill, NC, University of North Carolina Press.

Lineberry, R.L. and Fowler, E.P. (1961) 'Reformism and public policy in American cities', *American Political Science Review* 61, September 1961, 701–16.

Lineberry, R.L. and Sharkansky, I. (1978) *Urban Politics and Public Policy* (3rd edn), New York, Harper and Row.

Lloyd-Warner, W. *et al.* (1949) *Democracy in Jonesville*, New York, Harper and Row.

Lorch, R.S. (1983) *State and Local Politics: The Great Entanglement*, Englewood Cliffs, NJ, Prentice-Hall.

Lynd, R.S. and Lynd, H.M. (1929) *Middletown*, New York, Harcourt, Brace and World.

Ostrom, E. (1972) 'Metropolitan reform: propositions derived from two traditions', *Social Science Quarterly* 53, December 1972, 474–93.

Sayre, W. and Kaufman, H. (1965) *Governing New York City*, New York, W.W. Norton.

Wildavsky, A. (1964) *Leadership in a Small Town*, Totowa, NJ, Bedminster Press.

Chapter 9

Canada

John Kingdom

THE PRINCIPAL INSTITUTIONS OF THE STATE

Canada today is a federal union consisting of ten provinces and two northern territories. It was created by the British North America Act passed by the British Parliament on 29 March 1867, uniting New Brunswick, Nova Scotia, and Upper and Lower Canadas (now Quebec and Ontario) as the Dominion of Canada. It has grown by subsequent increments to include Manitoba (1870), British Columbia (1871), Prince Edward Island (1873), the Yukon Territory (1898), Saskatchewan (1905), Alberta (1905) and Newfoundland (1949).

The Act of 1867 can be said, in effect, to comprise the written part of the Canadian constitution, although it has been amended in a number of ways by various institutions including the Judicial Committee of the Privy Council, the Supreme Court of Canada, and the federal and provincial governments. In addition, administrative, political, economic, social and technological developments as well as two World Wars have resulted in a number of modifications in its practical operation. The Act remains an essentially pragmatic guide to government, containing nothing of the lofty sentiment found in those formal constitutions begat through revolutionary struggle. A number of important civil rights remain protected, as in Britain, through nothing more than the Common Law.

However, the traditions and patterns of the Canadian institutions of government had been nurtured well before confederation in the constitutional development of colonial British North America. The British parliamentary tradition was well established, with assemblies operating in Nova Scotia, New Brunswick, Prince Edward Island, and both Upper and Lower Canadas, each on the basis of popular male suffrage, returning members to a lower house, which shared power with an upper house. Executives were appointed by a Governor who represented the British monarch. By the time of confederation, the powers of Governors had diminished considerably, with a corresponding increase in responsible government: executives required the confidence of assemblies. Thus, as in Britain, there existed systems of representative government which incorporated a monarchical tradition through a strong, initiating, central executive exercising powers over the budget, policy formation and policy implementation; such a tradition persists today, though with certain variations from province to province.

The British tradition is also inherited at the federal level of government located in Ottowa in Ontario, with a bicameral assembly consisting of a popularly elected House of Commons and an appointed Senate, operating in accordance with rules, procedures and relationships reflective of the Westminster system. This is true even to the extent that Bills, having passed through both chambers, require the Royal Assent before they can become law.

The doctrine of the Supremacy of Parliament applies at both federal and provincial levels; assemblies can make or repeal any law they choose within their respective jurisdictions without hindrance from any other authority including the judiciary. The original authority lies with the provincial governments, and the constitutional powers given to the federal government include powers over central banking, the criminal law, the conduct of foreign relations, defence, regulation of the economy, and administration of the postal services. In addition the federal government has taxation and spending powers which have served effectively to impose a general dominance over the state.

Within this largely British style of constitutional framework there remains special statutory provision for the cultural and linguistic traditions of French Canada, including the right of French Canadians to their own legislature. The accommodation of this sometimes passionate minority continues to present certain problems for the state and for the establishment of its national identity.

Though owing much to British traditions, Canada has, like the United States, a federal structure. It also resembles its formidable neighbour in being rather conservative in its dominant ideology. Yet in spite of these facts there has been little of the American-type suspicion of strong centralised government. Indeed, a number of contrasts can be drawn between the two countries in this respect. The relationship with the colonising power did not foment revolution. The opening of the West was, under the auspices of the highly controlled Canadian Mounted Police, an orderly process. Members of the judiciary are appointed rather than elected, government officials are permanent and do not change to reflect the political colour of the party in office, and there is no process of judicial review of federal legislation.

A further indication of this willingness to accept strong central direction is an absence of any significant populist call for local self-determination characteristic of many of the early communities in the United States. Indeed, in some cases, local government was foisted on rather unwilling communities in order to ensure their contribution to the cost of certain services. There remains a certain apolitical flavour to local government in Canada today.

STRUCTURE AND POWERS

A brief history

Canada presents an interesting case for students of local government systems. Differing contingencies in the various provinces have resulted in certain modifications of what may be termed a basic model, originating in the leading province with respect to municipal development, Ontario. Such contingencies include the cultural backgrounds of the different immigrant groups, the geographical size of each province, its population size and density, location with respect to communications, and the wishes and attitudes of the citizens themselves. Indeed, in certain cases, the desire for self-government was virtually non-existent, and provincial governments felt the need to promote the development of municipal institutions in order to secure the provision of certain services and some local funding. In other areas, however, there was an active localist tradition, much like that which occurred in Britain.

It is not possible to categorise the types of local authority in precise terms, since the provinces vary in their use of terminology. Some have established minimum populations for cities, though this may vary from province to province from a few hundred to over ten thousand. There exist similar disparities with regard to towns and villages. Generally, the largest specifications are found in Ontario and Quebec. Variations and anomalies also exist within categories so that some 'villages' have grown to be larger than towns and the existence of 'dormitory' areas surrounding towns has given to certain 'rural' areas all the characteristics of urbanity.

As in the case of Britain, what might be termed a system of local government was a creation of the nineteenth century, centrally inspired and occurring in response to a process of urbanisation. However, again like the British case, there was a history of self-rule by the communities predating the emergence of the modern system, so that it is possible to speak of both centralist and local traditions. The forms of local government that predated federation largely reflect the traditions and culture of the colonising power, though American influences cannot be ignored. However, pre-nineteenth century examples of local government are intermittent and it was not until the creation of responsible government at the senior level that province-wide inclusive local government systems emerged.

The centralist tradition, arising originally from the desire of the English monarch to rule and administer a unified state through a convenient system of subdivisions of the country, termed shires, was extended to encompass the colonies. These units were governed by justices of the peace who combined judicial and administrative functions. As in England, this was not self-government, and the positions of those in authority were open to abuse, so that local élites were able to exploit the communities they were supposed to serve in a variety of ways.

The localist tradition in England arose from the desire of local communities to regulate their affairs and provide services, on the basis of small areal units, usually parishes. The tradition of self-government grew, as towns emerged, through a quest for greater autonomy by application for a royal charter of incorporation conferring borough status. The same kind of development took place in Canada, where it was reinforced by the settlement of immigrants from New England who brought with them strong adherence to populist principles of government, and who could be induced to remain only by promises of self-government.

The localist tradition was by no means uniform in its manifestation. There are three broad forms. The establishment of the 'Ontario' model began with the movement of New England loyalists into the area along the north shore of Lake Ontario and the Niagara peninsula. Restless under a French centralist ethos, they showed a particular persistence in their localist demands. In 1791 they forced the creation of Upper Canada as a separate province, with an English system of civil law and land tenure. By fleeing the rebellious colonies, the loyalists of Upper Canada felt that they had established their fidelity to the British Crown and earned the right of self-rule. The legislative assembly of the new province passed a series of acts permitting town meetings to appoint a range of local officials, providing for the raising of funds, and giving a number of powers in relation to roads, sanitation, education, welfare, police, jails, and slaughter houses. (An important example of the developing role of local government came later, in 1861, when an Act established the right of citizens to elect trustees who would administer schools and appoint teachers.)

After the wars in North America and the Napoleonic Wars, another wave of migration from Britain created further pressure for municipal institutions. This led to the application for charters of incorporation which, though initially opposed by the central authority, were ultimately successful. Between 1832 and 1834 six towns were granted the right to locally elected councils, termed Boards of Police, which initially assumed many of the responsibilities of the justices and gradually extended their authority into other fields.

The position in Upper Canda began to resemble that in England during the same period, with incorporated, self-governing towns and cities existing alongside a traditional county system in the rural areas under the control of justices of the peace. This similarity extended to the actual quality of local administration, the towns being relatively efficient but the rural areas less so and prey to various forms of corruption. Discontent with this state of affairs was manifested in 1837 when a rebellion led the British authorities to set up an enquiry, which was to recommend greater emphasis upon municipal government as a condition of stability and efficient local administration. In 1841 the District Councils Act was passed, which gave to the rural areas a form of self-government similar to that of the towns. It created a system which was to resemble that in England after the Act of 1894, with a two-tier structure, from which certain towns and cities were excluded (to be unitary authorities). This was the system which became the model to be copied, with various modifications, throughout Canada.

Lower Canada (later Quebec) followed Upper Canada in its development. Under the French regime, which existed before British rule was established in the 1760s, there was, not suprisingly, little tradition of self-rule for local communities. However, administration by the British justices proved unpopular, so the cities of Quebec and Montreal petitioned for incorporation. Even so, unlike the Lower Canada case, there was little progress towards widespread local self-government during the first eight decades of British rule. In 1840 the colonial power itself recognised the need for some areal division of the province, and a pattern of districts was established, each of which was to be governed by an elected council which could appoint officials to implement its decisions. At a lower tier, townships and parishes of sufficient size were incorporated and given rights of representative local democracy, but with the lion's share of power remaining at the provincial level with the Governor. Subsequent Acts converted the top tiers into a county structure and effected a significant shift of functions to the lower tier. In 1855 an Act was passed which consolidated a system with many similarities to that of Upper Canada.

The Western provinces were created after confederation and accepted the Ontario model mainly because the settlers were themselves from areas where local government was well established, and they recognised the value of a range of local services in their settlements. In Manitoba, Saskatchewan, and Alberta the intention was to create Ontario-style systems, but the low density of the population rendered the division between tiers unworkable and was abandoned, to be replaced by a modified version of the two-tier system. Contingent characteristics of the area were conducive to a relatively high degree of centralisation at provincial level, so that relatively few independent corporations emerged, and much administrative authority remained at the centre to be administered through field agencies.

The quest for self-government was not always pursued with the greatest vigour. In the area ceded to Britain by France in the 1700s, which became Nova Scotia, New England settlers again brought with them populist principles through the tradition of the town meeting. However, this contrasted with the rather centralist style of public administration already in operation. In addition, the American Revolution precipitated a further wave of immigration from New York, New Jersey and Pennsylvania, bringing a different, class-based tradition which reduced the participation of ordinary citizens in favour of forms of local élitism. This centralisation was buttressed by fears among the British that populist government through town meetings would foment revolution, as had been the case in Boston. Thus, the New England traditions were submerged and Nova Scotia, along with the other maritime provinces, Prince Edward Island, New Brunswick and Newfoundland, showed a preference for centralist government with little citizen demand for participation.

The pattern of development was reinforced by the small sizes of the provinces and by the ease of access to water transportation, obviating the need for much road work, traditionally a highly important local government function. Indeed it was found that permissive legislation for the formation of municipal institutions was largely ignored, if not actively resisted, so that by the end of the 1870s it was necessary to establish local government systems on a compulsory basis and, even today, there remain rural areas in the Maritime provinces that do not have local self-government.

The central enthusiasm for local government was in part inspired by the general view, prevalent in the nineteenth century, that local government, as such, was intrinsically good, being a necessary condition for effective representative democracy at the level of the state itself. However, there was also the fact that the provincial governments were themselves perennially short of funds, and a stimulation of local institutions could produce another source of local revenues for expenditure on services.

Thus, by the end of the first decade of the twentieth century, systems of municipal government, largely based on that which had evolved in Ontario, were well established in most provinces. A major point of difference between provinces was the tier structure, with the less densely populated areas having only single tiers, known variously as cities and towns in urban areas, and as townships and parishes in the rural areas. More densely populated provinces, including Ontario, Quebec and British Columbia, had upper-tier authorities known as counties or districts. Towns and cities tended to be independent of their surrounding areas, rather like the county boroughs created in England in 1888. In British Columbia, however, rural and urban authorities were integrated fully in a tiered system. There also remained thinly populated areas with no local government at all.

The local government structures which had evolved during the nineteenth century remained largely intact until the end of the second world war. At this point it was recognised that a number of strains were being experienced. These were the result of two principal factors. In the first place was the emergence of a number of large urban conurbations, particularly in the areas of Toronto, Montreal, Winnipeg and Vancouver. This partly accounted for the second problem, which was the existence of a large number of municipalities with very small populations, acting in an uncoordinated way and with very low levels of resources. Important reforms were prompted by these factors.

The first of these reforms was during the decade beginning in 1953, with the establishment of the Metropolitan Toronto authority, covering the area surrounding Toronto and comprising thirteen municipalities. Metropolitan Toronto was the top level of government in a two-tiered system and was responsible for a range of overarching functions such as assessment, borrowing, water supply, sewage and trunk roads. In addition, it shared some functions with the lower-tiered authorities. The new system differed from the previous county system in that the upper tier enjoyed greater authority, and the constituent municipalities, though often major cities, were no longer autonomous. Initially this experiment was hailed as a marked success, and it was to exert considerable influence on developments elsewhere, particularly in the conurbations around Montreal and Winnipeg. However, in the longer term, all these developments tended to lose momentum and to regress, owing in large measure to a lack of enthusiasm from the lower-tier municipalities, which resented any loss of power, and a failure of the upper-tier governments to exert their authority to the fullest extent.

The second wave of reform took place in the 1960s. An important landmark is seen in the Province of New Brunswick when, in response to concern over different standards of municipal service, and financial inequalities between areas, a royal commission was established to consider finance and municipal taxation. The commission made a comprehensive analysis of the allocation of functions between levels of government, and recommended the transference of a number of municipal functions to the provincial level.

In Ontario the main thrust of the 1960s reform was the extension of the pattern established in Metropolitan Toronto in the 1950s. This was done with some disregard for differing circumstances. Thus, all reforms sought to impose a two-tiered system based largely on the geographical pattern set by the old counties. There had been little attempt to conduct a radical review of functions between levels of government as was done in New Brunswick. Once again it has been the case that structural reform has not proved popular.

Perhaps the most well-known structural reform of municipal government in Canada is the creation of Winnipeg Unicity. This was based on one, single-tiered authority for the whole of the metropolitan area around Winnipeg. It was established by the Provincial Government of Manitoba in 1972. Unlike the reforms carried out in other provinces, there was an underlying philosophy espousing democratic values shaping the system. The single council was unusually large, consisting of 50 members elected by wards. In addition there were community committees, each covering a number of wards, which though non-executive had certain budgetary responsibilities. These would communicate with grass-roots feeling through elected residents' advisory groups. The policy-making institutions were to incorporate a set of relationships reflecting something of a parliamentary style, with the council leader and the executive committee elected by the full council, acting rather like a cabinet. The intention behind this arrangement was to encourage the emergence of strong disciplined political parties which would provide coherent unified leadership at the political level.

However, apart from the acceptance of the single authority, the experience of Winnipeg Unicity did not prove to be an unqualified success. Strong leadership did not emerge, political parties were not able to dominate the decision-making process, councillors retained a narrow parochial approach to their roles, and the residents' advisory groups lost much of their momentum after an initial flourish. The result has been further reforms, which have reduced the size of the council and the number of community committees and curbed the powers of the mayor.

We must conclude that the structural developments in Canada since the second world war have not generally been favourable to local democracy and, even where they have, the popular response has not been enthusiastic. It could be argued that the experience here has demonstrated that the reform can only come in an evolutionary way, as a result of spontaneous behaviour and movements in political culture. We shall see later that there has been some evidence of change of this kind, manifested in the behaviour of citizens' groups and parties, in response to popular feeling.

FUNCTIONS

In a society as technologically advanced as Canada, modern forms of communication make the apportioning of functions between the federal, provincial, and local levels of government increasingly problematic. In earlier times, a system of administration by justices, or other local agents, could be explained in terms of local services. Today, however, it is feasible for both senior levels of government to provide locally delivered services efficiently. Thus, for example, field agencies of federal departments administer two important, locally delivered services: the national employment service and the family allowance system. As new functions emerge today, the tendency is to look immediately to the senior levels, with their greater expertise and stronger financial base, for administrative support. Thus there is a strongly historical element in the explanation of the functional portfolio of contemporary local government.

This portfolio can be broadly dichotomised as traditional and new. The former category consists of those functions largely acquired in the nineteenth century and reflective of the British pattern which existed contemporaneously. This pattern is composed of a wide range of functions, the need for which arises from a number of factors characteristic of the post-war period, including a dramatic process of urbanisation, changed attitudes to the role of government in society, and alterations in lifestyle resulting largely from increased utilisation of advanced technology.

Many traditional functions were essentially regulatory in character. The local authority would not so much seek to provide services; rather it would endeavour to create conditions which would be conducive to their provision by private enterprise. The kinds of areas in which regulation might take place varied from province to province: for example, in predominantly rural areas it was appropriate to control the use of guns, management of log booms, bush burning, ice cutting and the licensing of certain categories of worker. In the urban areas the more typical foci for regulation included the safety of buildings, trading hours, traffic flows, parking, and licensing restaurants and other trades. The mechanics for the creation and operation of such regulations was usually by means of by-laws, with enforcement through the courts.

Effective regulation implies the more positive functions of law enforcement, and the provision of police services has also been a major traditional responsibility. In addition, local authorities in some provinces have provided courthouses and gaols, and made provision for the maintenance of various provincially appointed officials such as magistrates and registrars.

Other traditional, yet positive functions required by the commitment to an essentially laissez-faire ideology were certain public utilities necessary to provide an infrastructure for the economy at large. Indeed, the provision and maintenance of highways has been a major reason for the drive towards local self-government in most places. Also in the category of traditional functions are inescapable special responsibilities for the relief of poverty and the provision of education, but today these are either taken over, or their administration is highly controlled, by the provincial governments. From the outset these traditional functions were under some pressure from the stresses of urbanisation, which were also experienced in Britain during the eighteenth and nineteenth centuries. Problems attendant upon these developments were compounded by dramatic population increases. In the first decade of the twentieth century some two million foreigners entered the country to settle in the urban areas. The rate of increase in the extent of urbanisation during this period exceeded that of any other western nation. Today some three-quarters of the Canadian population live in urban areas, which together cover only one per cent of the total area of the country. In spite of a building boom, housing shortages developed in all major cities, leading subsequently to a range of social problems associated with high-density urban living, and requiring migratory social policies.

Furthermore, the hasty erection of housing went in advance of sanitary provision, so that municipal systems were overloaded, with serious consequences for health, including epidemics of tuberculosis, influenza and typhoid, calling for public health measures. This led to concern for the quality of the physical environment. Initially, interest in this was confined to the design of public buildings, but the urban health hazards alerted opinion to the need for planned urban development. A public health movement grew up, which led to an expansion in the powers of building and health inspectors. Limitations were also exposed in the transport systems, creating demands for more roads, and electric power for municipal tramway systems. In addition, town planning acts were passed, based on British legislation, enabling provinces to give the appropriate statutory powers to local governments or to special planning boards which were linked to them. Latterly, Canadian towns and cities have been taking responsibility for certain aesthetic aspects of the lives of citizens, with the provision of leisure, recreational and cultural facilities.

In conclusion it can be said that functional demands have lain at the heart of the developmment of local government in Canada. This fact helps to explain why the urban areas have seen much greater development of the municipal institutions than have their rural counterparts. The growth of the urban areas increased both the demand for, and the ability to provide, a range of public utilities, social services and aesthetic facilities at the local level.

LEGAL RESTRAINTS

The legal basis of the local government systems in Canada varies from province to province. Only Ontario and New Brunswick have laid down structures and functions in single, all-embracing acts; generally these are separate acts for different categories of local unit. Quebec has one code for the counties and their constituent municipalities and another for the autonomous towns and cities. Other provinces grant general powers to their towns and cities on the basis of individual charters. Assessment legislation, relating to local taxation systems, is usually separate from other municipal legislation and there are yet further bodies of legislation associated with the administration of particular functions.

However, generally the legal framework of the local government systems in Canada owe much to the British constitutional inheritance. All authorities are bodies corporate with legal *personae* in the names of which they can enter into a variety of legal relationships. In this way they can, for example, make contracts, sue and be sued in the courts. Much municipal law is derived from decisions of English courts. In addition, because the authorities are created by provincial legislation, in which is defined the extent of all their powers, they are subject to the principle of *ultra vires*, meaning they cannot exceed these powers. In some cases the powers conferred are mandatory, so that it would be illegal not to perform them, and in others they are permissive, allowing the authority to exercise discretion.

The legal restrictions can be enforced through the courts, which may be asked by a private citizen, or other body, to consider the legality of any action or by-law. A court may decide that a by-law is *ultra vires* even if it has been approved by the provincial legislature.

FINANCE

There has been a considerable rise in municipal expenditure in Canada since the second world war. Five factors may be said to account for this: a general acceptance of a wider role for government in society, the reliance on the municipalities for the implementation of provincial social programmes, an increase in expenditure by ad hoc bodies which lie beyond the control of local government, an increase in the number of municipal services and a continuing pattern of urbanisation, creating a set of related social and economic problems. These factors have contributed to the view that local government exists in a state of continual financial crisis.

Sources of finance

Canadian local governments secure funds by three means: local taxation and charges for services provided, and grants from provincial and federal government. The relative importance of these has changed considerably during the post-war era. In 1951 over 60 per cent of funds came from local tax; fees and certain other local sources accounted for another 30 per cent and transfers from the federal and provincial governments were less than 10 per cent. However, by 1980, the transfers amounted to almost half of local government revenue, while local tax had fallen to some 30 per cent.

Local taxation

There are various forms of local taxation employed by local governments in Canada, including business tax, poll tax and personal property tax. However, by far the most important is that levied on real estate, which accounts for over 80 per cent of the taxation revenue of Canadian local government.

Initially this tax was shared by all levels of government in Canada but, as ownership of property, particularly business property, became more complex, the senior levels began to avail themselves of more sophisticated forms of taxation, leaving the property tax to the municipalities. For the most part the rate of taxation for business property and domestic housing is the same. There is a range of property which is exempt from taxation, including charitable and religous establishments, and property owned by senior levels of government.

The regulations for the collection of local taxes are laid down by each province in its Assessment Acts, which, while admitting some variations, tend to follow a common pattern. Assessment is the process of placing a value, for taxation purposes, on all liable property in the area. The value is in theory the market value, but in practice assessments do not reflect current market trends very accurately and the practical intention is to ensure just comparability between categories with overall assessment values tending to lie below real market values. Property owners have the right to appeal against their assessment. Actual payment of tax is then made on the basis of some proportion of the assessed value of the property expressed as a rate in the dollar. The level of this rate will be determined by the amount of revenue required from this source by the municipal authority. This amount is of course a function of the level of spending estimated for the forthcoming year.

The rates remain a rather unpopular tax in Canada and are criticised for being regressive, for lacking buoyancy and for being insufficient in yield. Certainly the tax bases of the provinces and federal governments are stronger, so that the financial position of the senior governments tends to increase their supremacy within the constitution. This supremacy is reinforced through the grants system.

Grants

In general local governments in Canada meet less than half of their expenditure obligations from revenue derived from their own sources. The deficit is made up by provincial and federal grants or inter-governmental transfers.

The provincial grants are usually made on a conditional basis for expenditure on certain designated services. The largest of these is that given for education, constituting well over half the total of all provincial grants to local government. Other important policy areas receiving grant aid include police, water and sewage services, roads transportation and culture and recreation. Generally speaking the size of grant is fixed by the provincial government rather than awarded on a percentage basis related to municipally determined expenditure levels. This further reduces the autonomy of the local authorities. There are also unconditional or general grants, which are given on a per capita basis. These serve an equalisation function, assisting the poorer authorities and permitting some local discretion in expenditure decisions. Such grants remain a relatively small proportion of total grant income, about 20 per cent of the whole.

The size of grants is not really determined by a rational process. Rather it is the product of bargaining between provinces and municipalities, the outcome of which reflects largely political factors. In these negotiations the municipalities endeavour to present a united front through the province-wide organisations which they form. Nevertheless, the provincial governments remain the most powerful actors in these negotiations, and the municipalities usually feel that they receive an insufficient proportion of the municipal cake. Various measures have been taken to protect grant income from political vicissitudes. In some cases the total amount of the provincial grant is linked to the yield from certain provincial taxes; in other cases, indexes are involved which link the size of the grant with the level of activity in the provincial economy.

Constitutionally the federal government has no direct relationship with the municipalities but it has been able to make certain incursions through the medium of grants. Like the provincial governments, the federal government makes payments to municipalities in lieu of rates on property owned. In the early 1980s, Ottowa announced a new programme designed to broaden the base of this form of grant by including more property categories. In addition, specific grants have been made to help combat urban problems in areas such as housing, industrial development, urban renewal and matters relating to economic infrastructure. However, at present the amount of money transferred from the federal government to the municipalities remains small and is mainly channelled through the provincial government, who jealously guard their constitutional responsibility in this respect.

Borrowing

Capital spending is largely financed from borrowing. Fears that imprudent councils might incur crippling debts for future generations lead provincial governments to urge authorities to repay loans, rather than merely service them through interest repayments; the ideal being that debt should be cleared at a point when the capital asset in question ceases its effective life. To this end municipalities have been encouraged to issue serial bonds. In addition, there are further restraints in that all proposed borrowing must be approved by the provincial governments, and in some cases there are requirements that the ratepayers be consulted. The post-war period has seen a considerable increase in municipal borrowing as local governments embarked upon programmes of modernisation and reconstruction.

INTERNAL STRUCTURE

The organisational structures of local governments in Canada reflect the twin goals of local self-determination and efficiency in the local administration of services. This produces a duality within the organisations, manifesting the classical distinction between policy and administration, formally represented in the respective positions of elected councillors and appointed officials.

Each council is headed by a leader chosen from its own membership. Leaders are titled variously, often as reeve or warden in the counties, chair or overseer in the villages and townships, and mayor in the cities and towns. The formal powers of leaders are defined by the provincial legislatures, but the legislation tends to be somewhat out of date, permitting only a very restricted role but resulting in the growth of informal power which is, in practice, much greater than that defined. The size of councils varies but the average remains small by American or British standards. Pressure for increased representation has led to some growth in size but today a council of thirty members would be among the largest, and the smallest have memberships below ten.

The majority of councils are organised on a committee basis for various practical reasons such as the division of labour and specialisation. In some counties the numbers of standing committees is fixed by law, though there tends to be no restriction in the number which may be formed on an ad hoc basis to deal with specific matters as they arise. The meetings of the councils and their committees are, by law, open to the public. The committee system is a subject of debate, with the main criticism being that it fails to produce co-ordination in policy-making and implementation across functional areas. As a result of this, most of the large cities and towns have modified their committee systems in various ways, which are examined later.

The failure to secure co-ordination is exacerbated by another feature. At the turn of the century a reform movement led to attempts to isolate certain locally administered functions from the political process. This resulted in the creation of ad hoc boards and commissions rather like those which proliferated in nineteenth-century England. These are most prevalent in Ontario, though education is administered in this way in all provinces. Usually the ad hoc bodies are appointed by the elected councils rather than elected by citizens, though the composition generally includes some councillors. This means that the boards, in addition to the problem they pose for co-ordination of municipal functions, represent impediments to local democracy in that they are, by design, less accountable for their actions than the councils. The boards do not usually have to raise their own funds and the councils have only limited control over their finances, rendering difficult the establishment and perusal of priorities for the area as a whole. Other criticisms include allegations of low efficiency, duplication, and absence of popular understanding; overriding doubt remains over the basic proposition that areas such as education, recreation and health can realistically be depoliticised in the way implied in the creation of boards.

The implementation of the policies and decisions of the councils and the boards are entrusted to full-time salaried administrators. In the former case the council bureaucracy is organised in terms of distinct departments and in the latter there is a separate organisation associated with each board. The departments fall into the traditional categories of line and staff. Council bureaucracies are of a substantial size in Canada, where the total number of municipal employees is around 250,000, which is about three-quarters of the size of the federal bureaucracy.

Several measures have been adopted to improve co-ordination in policy-making and administration. Some local governments, particularly in Ontario and Quebec, seek to provide unified political leadership through the establishment of a small executive body of elected members called a board of control, or executive committee. Initially members were directly elected, but this practice has been largely replaced by indirect election from the full council. The executive committee exercises a range of functions, including the preparation of annual estimates, awarding contracts, the appointment of senior officers and the submission of proposed by-laws to the full council. The result is a kind of cabinet system and consists typically of the leader and about four senior members of the council. In some cases, the boards are established by statute and are not responsible to the full council and, in others, they have been established by the municipalities themselves with the council itself delegating the necessary powers.

Typical problems associated with these systems include conflict between board members and other councillors, who resent the hierarchical status of council membership that is introduced; conflict between boards and senior administrators, who are unwilling to accept the subjugation of their departments to the wider view; conflicts between the boards and other committees who also wish for greater autonomy. Another problem is the tendency of some boards to become immersed in detail so that they lose sight of the overarching view they are supposed to develop. Problems also arise if there is no effective administrative leadership to complement that at the political level.

Attempts have been made to combat this lack of leadership through reforms of the administrative machinery. Foremost among these are variants of what is termed the city manager system based on the American model. This entails the appointment of a chief executive officer to whom is delegated responsibility for the administration and co-ordination of all the council's policies. Application of this model is most evident in Quebec. It has been less popular in Ontario, although the Hickey Report in 1973 endorsed the principle and it continues to be adopted throughout the country.

In other provinces, including Alberta and Saskatchewan, a similar principle is applied but with a commission rather than a single individual in the position of chief executive. The commissioners meet as a body under the leader of the council when their remit is to consider overall policy. However, the individual executive responsibilities of commissioners relate to particular, though broadly drawn, functional areas, which have jurisdictions much wider than those of traditional departments. Through this mechanism some three commissioners can be responsible for the whole range of functions of the local authority. The inclusion of the leader of the council on the commission is intended to erode the distinction between policy and administration, which has been held to vitiate the city manager system. The effectiveness of both these models remains open to debate and cities tend to develop their own variants in order to combat some of the alleged disadvantages.

We shall see later that a singular feature of Canadian politics is an absence of tightly organised political parties. This has implications for leadership and co-ordination, in that parties, particularly if they have an ideological base, can effectively provide the necessary motive force. Conversely, the absence of party domination can lead to increased reliance on the bureaucratic machinery which, because of behavioural organisational charcteristics such as departmentalism and 'imperialism', has greater tendencies towards fragmentation.

PERSONNEL

The personnel of local government in Canada can be placed within the broad dichotomy of elected members and officials. The former group, though small in size, can play a crucial role of varying importance. The latter group is vast and its members play roles of varying importance.

Councillors

Members of councils are elected directly as ordinary councillors or indirectly as aldermen. The typical local councillor in Canada may be said to have certain characteristics: s/he will be middle class, above average age, and well educated. This suggests that one might expect to find certain sections of local communities under-represented, particularly the generally underprivileged and those belonging to ethnic minorities. This is indeed the case, but since the 1960s there has been a growth in citizens' movements with a left-wing orientation seeking to redress this imbalance. With this movement comes a new type of councillor: one who is younger, less involved in commerce and business, though well educated and perhaps professionally qualified, and more committed to community action. Though remaining a minority, councillors of this kind represent a growing category, and one that is more active and vociferous than has traditionally been the case. The presence on the councils of major cities of such individuals could lead to an increased level of politicisation in Canadian local politics.

The new breed tends to place greater emphasis upon the participatory value of local government, advocating openness, and less emphasis on efficiency in matters of local administration. The role of the councillor is perceived as more of an agent of constituents than a trustee. Thus, local government in the large urban areas may be growing ever more political. This means that, increasingly, political activists are finding in the local stage a forum appropriate to the pursuit of their ambitions, such as the environment, pollution control, social and physical planning and urban transportation.

The avenue to council membership is frequently through a political party, though, as observed above, this does not mean membership of a mass national or provincial organisation. The citizens' parties which participate in local politics are at their most active during election campaigns and tend to disintegrate in the intervening periods. The absence of strong party domination means that there are viable opportunities for independent candidates.

With the exception of the leaders, councillors usually serve on a part-time basis. They are paid compensation for loss of earnings occasioned by their council obligations, and certain categories of councillors (for example, those serving on ad hoc boards, those serving in two tiers and senior councillors of large cities) receive extra remuneration. The question of increasing the allowances, or even paying salaries on a widespread basis, in order to enable councillors to operate on a full-time basis, raises formidable objections from ratepayers. The larger municipalities are able to pay quite substantial salaries to council leaders, who are thereby enabled to devote their energies on a full-time basis, making them more effective agents of policy influence. Where payment is not available, certain categories, such as non-professional lower-paid occupational groups, are effectively barred from council membership. The conditions of work for councillors leaves much to be desired. Some major cities provide members with secretarial services but there is little official support in terms of research staff, personal advisers or office space.

Officials

Although local government in Canada is labour-intensive with some 70 per cent of the expenditure used for wages and salaries, the professionalisation of the municipal bureaucracies has been a slow process and is by no means complete. Equally slow has been the development of the personnel and training function. In some rural authorities the old custom of appointing citizens on an annual basis to fulfil certain municipal functions is still practised. In others, paid officials are engaged only on a part-time basis, or are required to hold two offices simultaneously; thus, for example, the municipal clerk may also be the treasurer. In the towns and cities higher levels of professionalism exist. The local bureaucracies are organised into departmental patterns reflecting mainly the functional principle. The organisation is hierarchical in structure with city managers or commissioners at the apex.

However, even in the largest cities, personnel management as a separate function did not emerge until after the second world war and only began to develop in the 1950s with the appointment of designated personnel staff. Before this, career development was haphazard and authorities remained ill equipped in terms of specialist expertise. The first personnel officers were not trained or qualified for their profession; they were merely employees from some other section of local administration who had expressed some interest in personnel management. However, by the 1960s, personnel officers were treating their role more seriously, and seeking to acquire the skills which would enable them to identify and recruit the increasingly specialised work force which modern administration demanded. This development was considerably advanced by the unionisation of municipal staffs. Initially the unions uncovered inequities and malpractices and later they were able to render much personnel policy making a matter of collective rather than individual negotiation, often involving councillors as well as personnel managers. However, the complex nature of local government in Canada, with differing provincial laws, single and two-tier systems and urban and rural authorities with contrasting characteristics, means that collective forms of bargaining generate a host of problems.

There is some doubt about the importance placed on training officers. Municipalities appear reluctant to encourage employees to attend courses and seminars at universities and community colleges. They also show little enthusiasm for employing graduates from full-time programmes of relevance to local government. The reason given for this is that such graduates are generalists and hence unfitted for a role in a functionally specific department. The result is a continuous weakening in managerial skills at the upper levels of local bureaucracies. For the most part the personnel and training function in Canadian local government remains inchoate, poorly integrated with other management functions, and unable to stamp its authority on municipal policy.

INTERGOVERNMENTAL RELATIONS

Canada, being a federation, has two senior levels above its local government system. However, in constitutional terms, the relationship between the tiers is quite different. The municipalities are created through laws passed by their provincial legislatures, to which they remain subservient, bound by the principle of *ultra vires*. The provincial governments do not stand in the same relationship to the federal government; they are sovereign within their own constitutionally defined jurisdictions. From this it follows that there is no direct constitutional link between the federal and local governments. However, in practice a number of factors have led to a degree of federal involvement in the affairs of municipalities.

Provincial–local relations

In examining the relationships between the municipalities and the provincial governments it must be remembered from the outset that these vary from province to province. Nevertheless, it is possible to make certain generalisations. Throughout the present century provincial governments have tended to increase their level of influence in the activities of local governments. This pattern of development has been the result of three factors.

Firstly, there was the pressure around the turn of the century for improvements in the municipal institutions of certain areas, particularly in western provinces, in order to deal with the problems precipitated by sudden increases in population size. The provincial governments were actively encouraging the establishment of municipal institutions: clearly a centralist rather than a localist impetus. Secondly, the depression of the 1930s saw local government in financial stress, and provincial governments extended their powers of supervision and control of municipal financial operations. In addition, control was extended to cover the ability of local governments to pass by-laws, and the administration of a number of important functions was made subject to central review. Also the appointment and dismissal of senior officials was brought within the realm of provincial scrutiny. The extension of these financial and administrative controls was sealed in the creation of special provincial departments to deal with the municipalities and ad hoc boards. The third centralising force came from the increased financial needs of the municipalities after the second world war, resulting in an increased dependency on provincial grants. These were often provisional, requiring local governments to meet certain prescribed standards and to submit to inspection.

In addition to gaining greater powers of control and supervision, provincial governments have taken over all, or part of, the administration and financing of certain traditionally local services, including highways, liquor control, administration of justice, property assessment, education, health and welfare. Most day-to-day aspects of the provincial–local relationship take place through three forms of provincial agency. Firstly, there is the provincial department exercising control over the administration of some particular function or policy area for which it may well be providing grant aid. Secondly, there are semi-autonomous boards or commissions appointed by the provincial governments to deal with particular municipalities, often in a quasi-judicial capacity, sometimes considering appeals against the municipality and sometimes having authority in judicial matters, such as granting loan sanction for capital expenditure. Finally, in each province there is a department concerned exclusively with municipal affairs, headed by a cabinet minister. These departments conduct supervision on a continuous basis, and issue detailed guidance and regulations on the interpretation and implementation of provincial policy. In some cases they play a part in the training of municipal officers.

In their dealings with central governments the municipalities do not always act unilaterally; in each province there are associations of municipalities which seek to represent their collective interests to the central government, and which conduct negotiations and consultations on such matters as the size and distribution of the central grants.

Federal–local relations

In addition to the centralisation taking place within the provinces, recent decades have seen in Canada increasing national centralisation upon Ottawa. The provincial legislatures are not, as we have observed, constitutionally subservient to the federal legislature. However, since the 1940s, the federal government has in practical terms grown more powerful vis-à-vis the provincial governments by virtue of its stronger tax base and the use of its spending power, including the making of substantial conditional and unconditional grants to the provinces, forcing them to order their priorities in line with those of the centre. In addition, the federal government has developed areas of expertise which provincial governments felt obliged to enlist at the expense of a degree of their autonomy.

This increased domination of the federal government over the province gives it the opportunity to intervene in the affairs of the municipalities. Direct involvement at this level tends to be viewed with suspicion by provincial governments and they seek to resist and retard such incursions. However, the municipalities are well aware of the existence of the federal government, which has a ubiquitous physical presence in all areas of the country in the form of its field agencies. The federal government also provides money to local government in the form of grants made in lieu of rates and specific grants in areas such as transportation, recreation and culture, the environment and housing. In addition a number of federal policies make a direct impact upon the localities, particularly economic policies and those designed to meet a complex of urban problems.

Several factors have contributed to the growth of federal involvement at the local level. Foremost among these is the phenomenon of urbanisation, creating burdens too great for the resources of the municipalities or even the provinces. A very significant incursion of the federal government began with the Dominion Housing Act (1935) and was extended in the creation of the Central Mortgage and Housing Corporation in 1946. A second factor has been the tax bases of both local and provincial governments, neither of which has been as buoyant as that available at the federal level. Thirdly, there has been a realisation by the municipalities themselves that the federal government could be a useful source of revenue, a recognition made more important by the reticence of the provinces to provide the level of funds desired by local governments. Fourthly, there has been a growing level of awareness by the federal government of the effectiveness with which local authorities can provide certain nationally important services to the large populations living in urban areas. Finally, there are the technological advances which have rendered more feasible the involvement of the national government, in a minute way, in a range of local functions.

The probability is that federal involvement in the affairs of local government will increase, since there is little reason to expect that the capacity of the municipalities to handle their continuing and endemic urban problems will be enhanced by any other means.

POLITICAL PARTIES AND PRESSURE GROUPS

Pressure groups

The federal nature of the Canadian state means that the levels at which public decisions are made present pressure groups with a three-fold choice in the focus of their attentions. The constitutional and legal basis upon which powers and functions are allocated is not as helpful as it might first appear, owing to the blurring of the pattern through the interpenetration of the different levels of government. Thus, groups seeking locally oriented objectives may well find it prudent to petition at the provincial or federal levels of government. Nevertheless, it is possible to speak of locally oriented pressure groups in Canada.

Urbanisation has been a major factor in explaining the existence of such groups. Increases in the sizes of populations in towns and cities have tended to reduce the feeling of participation through the formal political institutions, while at the same time increasing the propensity of people to form groups on the basis of shared interests, professions or economic status. Group action in the urban areas has been evident from the first, but has been particularly noticeable since the 1960s. This increase is probably due to the wave of municipal reorganisation which resulted in the creation of larger areas, in pursuit of efficiency, but which tended to reduce the grass-roots involvement of citizens. As a result of this, policy making in cities and towns became more overtly political, and the public became more watchful of local politicians. In 1969 Pierre Trudeau was able to exploit the new feeling in his federal election campaign when he evoked positive resonances throughout the urban areas with a slogan of 'participatory democracy'.

Local pressure groups in Canada may be classified in much the same way as in other western democracies. There is a fundamental dichotomy between those seeking to advance the individual self-interest of their members and those seeking some wider good. Within these categories there are institutional groups, associational groups, non-associational groups, latent groups, etc. There are, however, some characteristics of local pressure group activity in Canada that are relatively unusual.

In the first place, as has been noted above, groups of this kind are mainly an urban phenomenon. Within the municipalities a feature of particular interest is the existence of the ad hoc boards with executive or advisory status across a wide range of functions, including education, libraries, recreation, hospitals, tourism, culture, and with differing degrees of autonomy from local government. These may be viewed as pressure groups and as such they enjoy highly favourable circumstances in terms of channels of communication to policy makers. They are able to attend meetings, produce reports, and develop informal contacts. In addition, they possess the expertise and experience which is essential to the local authority and enjoy a high degree of popular legitimacy.

We have already noted the experiment which created Winnipeg Unicity when thirteen residents' advisory groups were officially established to work in association with the council. Members of the group were to be elected by residents of areas at special open meetings in order to participate in certain aspects of decision making. However, after an initial rush of enthusiasm the effectiveness of the groups declined, chiefly because of the absence of a clear definition of their role. To some extent their quasi-official status restricted their capacity to challenge and initiate, reducing their contribution to observation and evaluation.

Below the level of quasi-official groups there is the larger category of spontaneous associations. In local government the most traditional form within this category is the ratepayers' association, representing a predictable concern about the level of local government spending. However, to a considerable extent these have been superseded by the newer-style citizens' groups of the 1960s. Such groups are relatively small and based on clearly defined geographical areas. Some of them have sought substantial changes in public policy, such as stopping the construction of trunk roads and reform of actual policy-making procedures of local government in order to secure greater openness and wider consultation. They have served to extend the notion of what citizens' groups can legitimately achieve. Nevertheless, such groups have tended to focus on single issues so that they remain short-lived, withering away once their objectives have been achieved, and failing to build up a fund of experience and expertise.

There are, however, other citizens' groups which have become better established. These are not concerned with single issues and draw members from a much wider geographical area. The concerns of such associations are much more general, often relating to the environment. They are sometimes part of larger organisations existing at the provincial, federal or even international level. However, these groups do not always enjoy high levels of popular legitimacy, and in their efforts to communicate they frequently need recourse to conspicuous but generally less effective forms of behaviour, including marches, demonstrations and strikes.

The most effective pressure groups in Canada would appear to be those associated with business interests. These may represent individual corporations, industries or collections of undertakings forming chambers of commerce. Chambers of commerce are found in all major cities and have a long tradition of municipal influence. The ideological climate of Canadian local communities seems by no means inhospitable to groups in these institutions, and with their expertise and economic strength they enjoy well established formal and informal lines of communication with decision-making centres.

Local government in Canada has been organised to place considerable stress upon efficiency, with less emphasis upon the value of local democracy. Consequently, although the political culture is recognised to be liberal democratic in character, and although appropriate freedoms of association necessary for political pluralism are guaranteed, the environment does not appear equally accommodating to all pressure groups.

Political parties

The inhospitality of the Canadian political culture towards local pressure groups extends to political parties. A number of factors can explain this. In the first place it can be argued that a model of local government based upon that operating in England at the end of the nineteenth century, when overt partisanship beyond religious difference was not marked, has persisted with greater tenacity in this century than in England itself. There is also the influence of the United States, particularly after the reform movement, when the emphasis was away from politics at the local level and towards managerialism. A third factor is the removal from the direct hands of local government of a number of important and politically sensitive areas such as education, in order to depoliticise their administration by semi-autonomous boards. It is certainly true that, whatever the reason, electors have tended to show distaste for party politics by rejecting the major national parties whenever they have presented themselves at local elections.

However, recent decades have seen some tendency towards change. In the 1960s, when pressures of urbanisation led to various municipal reforms and to some expansion of the role of local government, the national and provincial political parties began to show greater interest in contesting local elections in urban areas. However, the principal impetus for this came from the local branches of these organisations rather than from the centres, where feelings remained mixed. The outcome of the move was not impressive. National Democrats, Liberals and Progressive Conservatives all suffered differing degrees of ignominy with no marked increase in local electoral turnout.

Traditionally more acceptable to Canadian voters are the truly local parties with particularised interest in the immediate area. These groups lack many of the organisational features characteristic of the modern political party; the main reason for designating them as such is the fact that they contest elections under names such as the Civil Party, Civic Non-Partisan Association, Independent Citizens' Party or Committee of Progressive Electors. In recent decades several hundreds of them have come into existence, though their lives have often been relatively short.

Citizens' parties are quite capable of dominating local councils. The first city to be so controlled was Vancouver, where for thirty-five years after 1936, the Civic Non-Partisan Association ruled. The earliest of the citizens' parties found their model in the reform movement of the late nineteenth century. Their main goal was actually antithetic to party politics: the desire was to make the municipal institutions efficient in the managerial sense, to remove the corrupting influence of the old-style politician. These organisations were dominated by professional and business interests with very loose organisations only really evident at election times. However, the more recent examples of citizens' parties are more overtly political, with a positive ideological position, character-istically towards the left. These have a wider membership base than the traditional parties, tend to attract younger people, are larger and are more coherently organised.

There remains, however, something of an 'anti-party' ethos in Canadian local government, so that candidates with party affiliations often choose to stand as independents and, once elected, councillors often vote across party lines. This is true even in the case of the New Democratic Party, the most ideologically coherent party at all levels.

The question of local party politics in Canada remains a subject of debate. Some argue that a strong party-dominated council would provide the centralisation, co-ordination and leadership so often held to be lacking in municipal administration. In the creation of Winnipeg Unicity, a large council was established in order to encourage the participation of political parties. In an earlier version of the proposals it was suggested that the mayor should be chosen by the council rather than popularly elected. However, Canadian electors continue to show little enthusiasm for parties at local level.

THE INFLUENCE OF THE ELECTORATE

Electoral arrangements for local government in Canada are set out by the provincial legislatures and show certain variations between provinces. Until recent decades the franchise was by no means universal; with a number of qualifications required of electors, only owners or tenants of property above a certain value were eligible to vote. Even today, owners of property in one area who reside elsewhere are permitted an absentee vote. Wide property ownership can thus result in certain individuals having multiple votes. In Montreal, companies, as such, have votes based on corporate property cast by owners in addition to their personal votes.

Councillors are elected for relatively short terms of office, two or three years being a common span. Generally speaking the turnout at local elections is comparatively low. In federal and provincial elections the average turnout is some 70 per cent, whereas the figure for local elections is rarely above 50 per cent and can be as little as 25 per cent. Although councils are small in size, electoral systems in some provinces make provision for partial renewal. This means, of course, that not every election is a mayoral contest, a fact which further depresses the level of turnout.

Reasons for the low turnout can be hypothesised. There is a possibility that the pattern of boundaries within provinces does not adequately reflect the organic structure of local communities, creating some degree of alienation towards the districts. Another factor is the managerial ethos of local government in Canada, which does not view politics as appropriate in the provision of efficient services. The small sizes of the councils may also contribute, since this reduces the level of intimacy possible between councillors and electors. The absence of extended involvement by the provincial and national parties is a further relevant factor, since this reduces the amount of publicity given to local elections. There is also a history of restricted franchise and the large size of some of the areas. Finally, commentators often argue that the traditional time of the year when elections are held, the autumn when the weather is cold, is not conducive to enthusiastic voter participation. However, the most immediate reason why people do not vote is probably absence of interest in local government.

ISSUES AND TENSIONS

The pattern of local government evolution in Canada has been largely a consequence of urbanisation: firstly in the early nineteenth century, subsequently at the turn of century and again after the first world war.

Development has not been uniform throughout the country; different provinces and even different cities have sought their own solution to problems on an ad hoc basis. Another fundamental problem is finance within a federal structure. There is a tendency to weaken local government by reducing the resources available, through upward suction by both provincial and federal governments which have stronger tax bases.

At the same time there have been ubiquitous pressures for more and better services. This has fostered a predominant view of local government as a provider of services rather than as a means of personal and collective self-fulfilment through democratic participation in the government of the local community. With the exception of Winnipeg Unicity, most reforms of Canadian local government have shown a managerial thrust. It is this philosophical position that accounts for the large number of ad hoc authorities, the use of the city manager or commissioner systems and the low level of party activity.

However, it would be wrong to conclude that there is no localist sentiment in the political culture. Instances of such feeling can be found. For example, the 1971 defeat of the Alberta Social Credit Party was in some measure attributable to voter resentment about a decision at provincial level to reduce the powers of local government. In addition, there are newer, left-wing, citizens' movements serving to increase the level of politicisation of local government.

The failure to seek a more effective local democracy has its own implications for efficiency, since, as Aristotle stated, only the wearer can say where the shoe pinches. The management ethos has to some extent been eroded since the 1960s. The citizens' movements have fallen back since the early days, but it is possible that they have wrought a fundamental change at the local level, which will form a basis for the further development of local democracy. If this secures greater autonomy for local government it could lead to an increase in the functional portfolio, with a corresponding reduction in the use made of ad hoc boards. This in turn could stimulate the development of local, tightly organised, political parties, which would produce the leadership and co-ordination held to be lacking.

BIBLIOGRAPHY

Brittain, H.L. (1951) *Local Government in Canada*, Toronto, Ryerson Press.
Canadian Tax Foundation (1977) *Provincial and Municipal Finances*, Toronto, Canadian Tax Foundation.
Feldman, L.D. (ed.) (1981) *Politics and Government of Urban Canada*, Toronto, Methuen.

Hickey, P. (1973) *Decision Making Processes in Ontario's Local Governments*, Toronto, Ministry of Treasury, Economic and Intergovernmental Affairs.

Higgins, D.J.H. (1971) *Urban Canada: Its Government and Politics*, Toronto, Macmillan.

Plunkett, T.J. (1968) *Urban Canada and its Government*, Toronto, Macmillan.

Rowat, R.P. (1969) *The Canadian Municipal System*, Toronto, Mclewlland and Stewart.

Tindal, C.R. and Tindal, D.N. (1979) *Local Government in Canada*, Toronto, Ryerson McGraw-Hill.

Chapter 10

Conclusion

J.A. Chandler

Those who would seek to discover, to explain all the similarities and differences in the patterns of local government studied in this book will be disappointed. This conclusion shows that there are far more differences than similarities in these systems, and that each one is significantly and demonstrably unique. Nevertheless, within the context of their political systems, it is possible to establish some generalisations concerning the development of local governments in liberal democracies.

STRUCTURE AND COMMUNITY

The most simple structure for a local government system would be the division of a nation into one tier of similarly sized, all-purpose local government units. Such a pattern does not exist in any large liberal democracy, although it is being seriously suggested for Britain. Structures of systems vary in terms of the number of tiers, the comparative sizes of local units and the functions assigned to them. In addition, many nations have not only multi-purpose units of local government, but a number of single-purpose ad hoc local agencies.

With the exception of Britain, local government is regarded by political decision-makers in liberal democracies as an organisation representative of communal interest. The idea of community is subject to much debate but classically involves the concept of *Gemeinschaft*, developed by the German sociologist Tönnies, denoting the relationships between people living within a defined area who know about one another as individuals and share common interests and loyalty to their locality.

In pre-industrial societies, local government was based on a sense of community. Small towns and villages were relatively isolated self-governing organisations, often controlled by a dominant landowner or small commercial oligarchy. Their boundaries emerged as a consequence of land settlement rather than from a nationally planned system of administration. Their legal status was, in most cases, simply ratified by central governments when they established a national rule of law in the late middle ages. These structures, such as the commune in France, parish in England or township in the eastern United States, formed the foundation of local government systems before the advent of mass communications. Outside this pattern, a few communities, often centres of commerce or government, had grown into substantial towns and cities before the formation of nation states and, in consequence, often held greater powers of self-government as chartered towns. Some of these centres in Germany formed independent city states.

Although pre-industrial states were content to leave administration in the hands of communal governments, they were not eager to allow these units to act independently of central control or to assign to them all the functions of the state. Thus, most western nations superimposed above the communal level an additional tier of government that was, in many cases, a creation of the state and was used to serve the interests of central government, even when based on traditional structures. In France, these structures were created as the departments by Napoleon Bonaparte, while in England they emerged much earlier through the adoption of the Anglo-Saxon county or shire structure. The principal role of these units was the supervision of the communal governments and the securing of repression of dissent against the state.

As industrialisation transformed the economies of what are now western liberal democracies, the organic lower-tier structures were subject to pressures for change, in order to accommodate the more onerous administrative tasks needed to serve a larger and more mobile population within a capitalist economy. In most states reformist-minded politicians have argued that small communities cannot efficiently serve the needs of their citizens, especially where expensive and complex services such as social security or education are involved.

Local government systems evolved along different paths, as a consequence of the extent of central enthusiasm or local resistance to demands for modernisation, into larger units that could provide economies of scale in service provision. Some systems have retained community units of government. Local government in these countries is divided into numerous lower-tier units which differ greatly in size, so that a few enfold large urban populations while most encompass populations of less than a thousand individuals. In these small communes most inhabitants know and recognise fellow members of their community. These small-scale units are still well established in France and Italy, which retain small communes that fiercely defend their integrity. In the United States, cities, that in reality are no more than villages, have successfully resisted efforts to incorporate them into larger political units. Local government in these countries still encapsulates a sense of communal *Gemeinschaft* and is resistant to root-and-branch reforms to local boundaries, despite demographic change and major developments in communication.

In contrast to the communal pattern are local government systems which have undergone what is euphemistically termed 'modernisation'. In these states there are only a few hundred lower-tier units of local government which are generally large and relatively uniform in terms of population. Britain has progressed furthest along this road as successive reforms of local government structure have, since the nineteenth century, bypassed the communal tier of parish government. The operative local structures are the districts and counties that encompass large areas with populations of upwards of 25,000.

The other states in this study range between the extremes of the communal model and the 'modernised' administrative structure. West Germany has undertaken some regrouping of communal units, but still retains small traditionally developed units of government for rural areas. Sweden has, however, subjected local government to major reforms that have created much larger structures, although the municipalities are not so large that they exclude any ideas of community. Ireland is a nation which has a system of arrested modernisation. Pulled by British dominance, it developed early in the twentieth century a modernised structure yet still maintained strong, rurally based communities. The system therefore retains, as part of its generally unloved inheritance from Britain, relatively large units most akin in population size to those of Sweden but nowhere near as large as the populations of English local government structures that developed in the 1960s and 1970s long after Irish independence.

FUNCTIONS

Although structures of local government systems vary widely, there are several functions that appear to be universally assigned to at least one level of the local government systems of each country. These activities are responsibility for refuse collection and disposal, promotion of recreation ranging from the arts and sport to parks and children's playgrounds, maintenance of, at least, minor roads, and the provision of personal social services such as care of the elderly and children under threat. It is, however, not always possible for smaller community local government to take up these services nor are they always demanded by their electors. In the

United States or France, many smaller local government units choose not to exercise their powers directly over some of their permissible functions. In addition to these commonly held services, there are many other major administrative tasks that are assigned to local government in some nations but not in others. Education, for example, is managed by central government in Ireland, France and Italy, whereas health care is centrally, rather than locally, controlled in Britain, Canada, France and Ireland.

There are a number of theories concerning the allocation of functions to local authorities but, as Dunleavy (1984) points out, no one theory seems wholly satisfactory. In the early 1980s, centre stage in Britain was held by the dual-state hypothesis, a complex and fashionable neo-Marxist explanation of functional allocation. Its foremost exponent, Peter Saunders (1981), built on several earlier theories to maintain that the role of cities within the state is to reproduce labour: that is, to provide the services necessary to furnish manufacturers with the healthy and sufficiently educated workforce that they require to supply labour for the processes of capitalist accumulation. Local authorities, therefore, tend to be responsible for tasks such as social services, education, housing and recreation. This pattern of functional distribution is also maintained from a very different ideological perspective by public choice theory. Its exponents argue that in democracies individuals will choose to consume and enjoy goods and services privately rather than publicly, if they have the means to do so. Thus, public provision tends to be for essential activities that are too expensive to be provided by most poor or average income families. Public bodies provide health care, public transport or personal social services to those who cannot buy these services through their own private means. Thus, local authorities will be a mode of providing public services to the less affluent.

Some local government systems appear to fit the implications of the dual-state and public choice hypotheses better than others. In Britain, in particular, local government under the Thatcher governments was increasingly forced into the role of administering social service schemes, to provide safety net relief to the poor under strict guidelines managed by the centre. In addition to this role, local authorities may award contracts to private companies to administer recreational and housing facilities.

This arrangement has not, however, always been the role of local authorities. In the late nineteenth century, British cities were more involved in administering and profiting from productive processes, such as gas and electricity production, than in providing unprofitable social services or facilitating private provision of communal profitable services. Locally based productive services are still retained in many liberal democracies, especially in larger urban units. In the United States many city governments can regulate the private gas and electricity suppliers or, in some cases, such as in San Antonio, Texas, the city itself supplies power through municipal enterprise. Some German city councils have been able to develop highly acclaimed integrated systems of refuse disposal and incineration linked to power generation.

In fairness to the dual-state hypothesis it may, however, be argued that these activities were developed in the late nineteenth century, when cities were more economically self-sufficient and subject to control by local manufacturers who were interested in the supply of cheap raw materials and energy to their local businesses. The city of this pre-multinational company era could act as if it were an economically integrated state. As manufacturing became an enterprise managed at a national rather than local level, the interest of capitalists in using the local authority to aid production came to an end; major industrialists and bankers defended their interests by putting pressure for aiding capitalist growth at national level.

Notwithstanding a tendency to allocate consumer functions to the local level, there will also be pressures to allocate functions in relation to size and economies of scale. The extent to which a state has 'modernised' its local government structure or retained a communal basis will have an important bearing on the capacity of the system to undertake certain activities. Large-scale expensive services or systems of production cannot be operated by small communal authorities. Tasks such as power generation, education or health care cannot be undertaken by small village communities. If France or Italy is to retain communal local government, it cannot allocate complex and expensive functions to this level of government.

There is, clearly, a major discrepancy in the functions of large cities in the United States or Germany and those of their small communal units of local government. Small townships or *Gemeinden* are only able to provide a few recreational and cleansing functions and must rely on higher tiers of government to manage more expensive and complex functions. Education, in particular, can be managed at local authority level in Britain but, owing to the scale of this undertaking, it is a state function in France, a federal function in Germany and subject to ad hoc school boards in the USA.

It may, however, be suggested that where local government has not been 'modernised' local authorities will be able to undertake productive functions if the units are of sufficient size to make it practicable to tackle such tasks. In the modernised systems of centrally created large units, there is a much greater tendency to impose on local authorities functional arrangements in line with public choice or neo-Marxist theory whereby, despite a capacity in terms of size, in order to manage productive enterprise the local authorities are forced into the role of managers of last-resort social services.

THE POLICY PROCESS

Local government, within each of the countries studied, claims to have a democratic structure that ensures that local decision-makers are accountable to their local citizens. Following the theories of pluralism as developed by R.A. Dahl, it is to be expected that the élites who are elected to positions of power within an authority must be responsive to public opinion within their communities if they are to retain office.

The decision-making structures in each of the countries are generally based on some modification of a parliamentary model, with an elected council approving policies decided by an executive composed of members who are either directly elected or drawn from the ranks of local councillors. The major exceptions to this pattern are the commission system and the presidential 'strong mayor' systems in some cities of the United States.

In Europe, local government, in all but the smallest communities, is party government, so the local parliamentary system of most cities is controlled by a majority party or a coalition of parties. The dominant party selects a leader, who normally becomes the most important decision-maker and spokesperson for the local authority, while other senior party members will chair important specialised committees. Decisions are, therefore, usually made by party group meetings, which gather in closed semi-secret enclaves before formal meetings of the local council. Party dominance has, however, been outlawed in some cities in North America and is much less established in small communal councils in Europe.

In all but the smallest units of the eight systems studied, there is a tendency to establish a local bureaucracy under the control of a senior officer, variously entitled the chief executive or city manager. The head of the bureacracy is, in most countries, an appointee of the locally elected politicians, but in the second-tier structures of the Napoleonic systems of France and Italy and also in Ireland the post is subject to central government appointment, although, in practice, informal central–local political links may diminish the practical authority of such a centrally selected chief executive.

A crucial question that has dominated analysis of policy making within local authorities is the extent to which they are fully democratic and allow their citizens to participate in the decision-making process. On the one side, élite theorists argue that local governments are controlled by small coteries, by self-selecting political party leaders often allied to local business people, by senior bureaucrats, or by a combination of all three. Opposing this pessimistic view of local democracy, pluralist theory suggests that the élites, who appear to make the final authoritative decisions for a local council, are obliged to heed the demands of those groups which represent majority opinions in the community, if they are to retain power.

It would be tendentious in an introductory work of this form to suggest that local governments in liberal democracies were either élitist or pluralist in their decision making. Although it can be affirmed that all systems have the apparatus for pluralist democracy, the extent to which this is practised differs, not simply from nation to nation, but between local governments within each state. For example, while a city such as Bordeaux appears to be dominated by an entrenched political party, which has been subject to the leadership of one individual for over thirty years, in other French cities, such as Grenoble, elections are open and keenly contested between political parties and even factions within each party.

The extent to which individual citizens may have an opportunity to participate extensively in local decision making will be, in part, a reflection of the size of an authority. The government of a small community, which may, as in France or the United States, enfold less than a thousand voters, may often be open to influence from many of its citizens. In the government of New York or Paris, a much smaller percentage of politically interested voters can affect policy making within the city. However, a small community government is never likely to be able to affect the quality of life of its members as substantially as can a relatively powerful city administration.

It may, however, be argued that the question of the effectiveness of local democracy within a community may be largely irrelevant if central government does not provide any significant power to local councils. In Britain, for example, however open and participatory the local government system, the dominance of central government over local actions is such that locally determined ideas will not be enacted if they offend central government. Indeed, under the Local Government Act of 1986, local councils even lost their right to voice political views on behalf of their citizens. The key to local democracy lies not only in local structure and practice of government but in the relationship of localities to the centre.

CENTRAL – LOCAL RELATIONS

The relationship between central and local government is crucial in determining the nature of any local government system. Since, in all the countries studied, local governments are sanctioned by legislation emanating from a superior unit of government, their structure, functions and, in most cases, even their policy-making processes are a reflection of this relationship.

Superficially, legal and financial arrangements appear to give almost total dominance to central government. In the eight political systems that have been analysed in this study, local government is either a creation of the centre or a traditional structure allowed continued existence by central legislative fiat. All the systems are based on legal arrangements that give to a higher unit of government, either the national parliament or a state parliament, the right to determine the structure and funding of local government and hence the ability to determine the rules of the bargaining game. There is, in the United States or Germany, for a few cities, some slight legal protection through home-rule charters that permit a local authority to undertake any action that is not expressly permitted by law. Legislation in these states can, nevertheless, curtail local initiative that is not to the liking of central governments.

Legal controls are, however, powerful but unrefined means of control. Within a democracy, major legislation to change the behaviour of local governments takes time to develop and must also compete with many other proposals awaiting debating and committee time in the legislature. Central tutelage requires other, more immediate controls, obtained in all countries by some form of delegated legislation and powers of inspection. Control over localities can be greatly enhanced through financial means. Within liberal democracies there is considerable variation in funding arrangements, although most systems ensure that local authorities must either rely on central government for much of their income or receive permission from the centre to raise funds above a nationally determined limit.

Formal legal and funding arrangements are not, however, the only factors influencing the inter-governmental relationships. The centre can deploy an impressive array of controls but may, in practice, be politically incapable of using these powers because of fears of local pressures that may damage the national government. In some liberal democracies there is clearly a strongly developed sense of local patriotism which promotes popular support for local decision making. Central government may, as a result, face powerful local grass-roots dissent if it curtails local autonomy.

This attitude is difficult to measure, but in some nations, such as France and Italy, there have always been strong local loyalties. In the United States, through local referenda, communities have shown a highly resistant attitude to incorporation into large units. Changes in the structure of communal government would create a storm of local grass-roots protest that might keep predatory central administrators at bay.

Local patriotism as a grass-roots ethos is unlikely to be sufficient to stave off centralisation, if this interest is not shared within central government through close integration of central and local policy makers. In recent years several studies have pointed out the extent to which the interconnection between local and national politicians plays a part in determining the freedom allowed to local government. This relationship has been unravelled most clearly in France (Ashford 1981), where key local politicians are highly influential in central government, enabling favoured localities to gain considerable autonomy from central pressures. In France, most members of the government and deputies to the Assembly are also mayors of communes. Similar relationships exist in Christian Democrat controlled localities of Italy. In these countries, local government has powerful friends at court, who ensure that the localities retain considerable autonomy from the centre by manipulating from that source legal controls over localities. In West Germany and Sweden some measure of local autonomy is also obtained through the influence of local politicians on the national policy making within powerful political parties.

If the political system has not developed a close integration between central and local policy makers, there will be little to prevent subordination of local government to central authority. In contrast to France and Italy, local government in Britain is distinctively bereft of local representation in Parliament. Rather than combining local and national political roles, an MP, who has gained election as a councillor, soon drops his local offices. This tendency, which developed in the late nineteenth century, has ensured that local authorities in Britain have few friends in the central courts of Parliament and Government. This absence of support has permitted the centre to reform the structure and functions of local government, with a frequency and thoroughness that would not be tolerated in any of the other regimes studied in this work. These reforms have further fuelled the capacity of the centre to dominate, since, through the creation of large anonymous local authorities, there is little potential for generating widespread grass-roots community support in defence of these largely artificial creations.

It can, nevertheless, be argued that, despite these sources of support, local government retains some discretion, since it performs a valuable role in taking from the centre many complex managerial tasks of fitting the nationally determined policy frameworks to local circumstances. Without local governments taking on these roles, the centre would be overloaded with tasks. This is, however, a factor that at best assuages the extent of central direction and substitutes for an agency relationship between centre and locality that of stewardship (Chandler 1988). Local government in Britain is given discretion to undertake a wide variety of administrative tasks which are too detailed and numerous for the centre to manage but which are, nevertheless, allocated by the centre and are frequently subject to change or intereference in their detailed implementation by the Government in Whitehall.

THE HISTORICAL PERSPECTIVE

In a comparative context it is impossible to draw exact similarities in respect of central–local relations between the regimes we have studied. Each is, of course, unique. It is, however, possible to suggest that each system finds a balance between two major conflicting pressures, the interest of central government to control the periphery and thus keep the nation as an integrated whole, and the demands of the periphery, often strongly articulated at the centre, to maintain local freedom. At one extreme, as typified by Britain, the centralising tendency is dominant and local interest kept in check. France exhibits the other side of the balance, in which local politicians have sufficient power to manipulate the centre to serve the needs of their communities. Between these poles it is possible to range other systems. Italy and West Germany tend to resemble France, while Ireland and Sweden conform more to British centralism. The United States and Canada exhibit a rather hybrid format, with considerable devolution to the states which, while rarely approaching the central controls exerted in Britain, do not allow much practical discretion to their subordinate units.

The reasons for the differing forms of central–local relationships must be found in the processes of nation building within each particular state. It may be suggested rather sweepingly that a crucial factor in this development is the extent to which the current systems of central government either were built through changes imposed from above by a national élite or were the consequence of local, peripheral revolt and revolution or consolidation of small independent states into a nation.

In Britain the cabinet–parliamentary structure was a product of compromise forged in the sixteenth and seventeenth centuries between the monarchy, a small coterie of wealthy landowners who formed a closely connected cohesive élite and powerful commercial and industrial interests.

In the eighteenth century the Whig oligarchy controlled local government through appointing themselves as Lord Lieutenants and Justices of the Peace. With the introduction of the industrial and commercial bourgeoisie into the oligarchy in the early nineteenth century, the cities in which these new liberal entrants to the oligarchy made their fortunes gained considerable power and independence as manufacturers tried to ensure that local authority action gave their municipality commercial advantages over their rivals in other cities. However, as major local industries developed within a national rather than a local arena, the leaders of the bourgeoisie lost their interest in city politics and transferred their political activity to the national arena.

In contrast, in France, the Revolution of 1789 was, as Barrington Moore (1966) argues, forged by an uneasy alliance of provincial peasantry and the middle class determined to break the central power of Paris. The bourgeoisie operating at a national level were too weak to dominate on their own the leaders of the many rural communities that had participated in the revolution. The post-revolutionary governments, therefore, were obliged to respect local interest and, indeed, became at times a forum where these local interests reconciled their differences. Industrial growth in France was, moreover, more hesitant and provincially based than in Britain, and thus generated less pressure towards central controls over the economy that eschewed any local participation.

Most other regimes studied in this work have built up the nation more along French lines. Italy was forged through a process of peripheral rebellion against foreign control, which required an alliance between peasantry and local-based bourgeoisie. Germany was similarly created through agreements between many separately independent agrarian and industrial states. Even though these nations have experienced radical political reconstruction in this century, their political élites retain a sense of regionalism and provincialism. Indeed, given that unification of these states posed serious threats to the peace of Europe, the victorious allied powers in 1945 did much to foster this sense of provincialism in post-war reconstruction. The United States and Canada are not dissimilar to Italy and West Germany in that both were formed from a merging of once separate independent states and communities.

Ireland and Sweden are closer to the British centralist model. Ireland directly experienced British centralist rule, although, as a predominantly rural nation, it has not been subject to as great a pressure to consolidate local government units for the sake of commercial efficiency. Sweden experienced a centralised monarchy, which was obliged, from the eighteenth century, to make concessions to the interests of large landowners and the peasantry. This process created a much greater sense of national unity than in any of the other regimes studied in this work save Britain, although an extensive and influential estate of small independent farmers will have tended to help retain a greater concern for communal autonomy.

FINAL WORDS

In 1981 the Council of Europe drafted a Charter on Local Government that was primarily concerned to protect

> the existence of local authorities endowed with democratically con-
> stituted decision making bodies and possessing a wide degree of
> autonomy with regard to their responsibilities, the ways and means by
> which these responsibilities are exercised and the resources required for
> their fulfilment.

Local authorities should also be organised so as to ensure that their responsibilities be 'exercised . . . by those authorities which are closest to the citizen'.

The Charter is endorsed by thirteen West European nations and, were they not divided by the Atlantic, could be endorsed by the governments of the USA and Canada. The Charter emphasises the values of local government as an essential element within a flourishing pluralist liberal democracy. Local authorities can ensure that decisions affecting day-to-day lives of individuals are made within small communities in order to allow maximum participation of members of a community in the decisions that affect primarily that community. The part played by local government as a foundation for liberty has, indeed, been long recognised in North America through the work of de Tocqueville and is current in European thought through Rousseau's ideas about the city state.

One major European state has not, however, signed the European Charter on Local Government: the United Kingdom. The British system of local government must be seen as the odd man out in this study. It is far from local, being based on large units which cannot encapsulate any notion of a community in which individuals who know one another can jointly participate in local decision-making. It is, moreover, a highly centralised system, which permits the national government to exert day-to-day control over local actions if it so desires, and forces localities to undertake administrative tasks as a steward of the centre and not as an independent fount of communal interest.

Britain's failure to endorse the Charter suggests a rejection by the British government of the values of community government that are shared by other states of Europe. Given the values of local government for partici- pative democracy, it is important that British citizens are more aware of the nature of local government in other liberal democracies and become aware that their system has serious shortcomings that require revision.

BIBLIOGRAPHY

Ashford, D.E. (1981) *British Dogmatism and French Pragmatism*, London, Allen and Unwin.

Chandler, J.A. (1988) *Public Policy for Local Government*, London, Croom Helm.

Dunleavy, P. (1984) 'The limits of local government', in M. Boddy and C. Fudge (eds), *Local Socialism*, London, Macmillan.

Moore, B. (1966) *The Social Origins of Dictatorship and Democracy*, London, Penguin.

Saunders, P. (1981) *Social Theory and the Urban Question*, London, Hutchinson.

Index